*Inchon to Wonsan*

# INCHON TO WONSAN

*From the Deck of a Destroyer in the Korean War*

James Edwin Alexander

Naval Institute Press
*Annapolis, Maryland*

Library of Congress Cataloging-in-Publication Data
Alexander, James Edwin, 1930–
    Inchon to Wonsan : from the deck of a destroyer in the
Korean War / James Edwin Alexander.
            p.        cm.
    Includes bibliographical references and index.
    ISBN 1-55750-022-3 (alk. paper)
    1. Korean War, 1950–1953—Personal narratives, American.
2. Korean War, 1950–1953—Naval operations, American.
3. Alexander, James Edwin,   1930–  . I. Title.
    DS921.6.A52      1996
    951.904'2—dc20                          96-17785

Printed in the United States of America
on acid-free paper ∞

03 02 01 00 99 98 97 96     9 8 7 6 5 4 3 2

First printing

*All photographs are from the U.S. Naval Institute photo collection
unless indicated otherwise.*

*Frontispiece:* The minesweeper *YMS-516* suffered heavy losses
when it was blown up by a magnetic mine at Wonsan, Korea,
October 1950.

To Ann Lacy

# Contents

# Maps

# Preface

A U.S. Navy destroyer is fast, maneuverable, and loaded with weapons. Pound for pound, it is probably the best all-around fighting ship ever built.

Known as the "workhorse of the fleet," the destroyer has a well-balanced design, capable of carrying out a wide range of missions while bearing weapons that give it capabilities approaching those of much larger ships.

For example, if the fleet commander needs a ship to shoot up hundreds of miles of coastline, the destroyer can do that. If he needs a ship to perform an antisubmarine mission, the destroyer can do that. If he needs a ship to go against an air threat, the destroyer has a robust capability there too. It can provide gunfire support for ground troops ashore. It can carry out a strike against surface ships much larger than itself.

Submarine hunter, antiaircraft ship, surface fighter, shore bombardment ship, radar picket patrol, search and rescue, or blockade duty, the navy destroyer has been called upon to do them all—and it has done them well.

"Of all the tools the navy will employ to control the seas in any future war," Fleet Adm. Chester Nimitz remarked, "the destroyer will be sure to be there. Its appearance may be altered and it may even be called by another name, but no type—not even the carrier or the submarine—has such an assured place in future navies."

# Introduction

The United States has fought nine major wars, four in the twentieth century. Clay Blair, in *The Forgotten War*, has pointed out that of these conflicts, the war in Korea, 1950–53, ranks among the most important, yet is the least remembered. To the several generations born since it was fought, the "Korean War" is little more than a phrase in history books.

Recently I found myself engaged in a conversation with a former artillery officer when the subject of the navy's role in the Korean War came up. Startled, he asked, "The navy? What did it do? The navy didn't do anything in the Korean War, did it?"

Having spent eleven months in the combat zone aboard a U.S. Navy destroyer, during which time we dodged bullets, encountered mines, rescued pilots, and nearly triggered World War III, I took his comment as a rejection of all the sacrifice and effort put forth by navy men and women. It was a slap in the face to the thousands of reservists who had already fought in one war and now found their lives, their families, and their careers disrupted by being called back to fight yet another.

The Korean War was a long and traumatic experience for the nearly 1 million sailors who served in the more than 350 ships—97 of them destroyers—that saw action during the three long, brutal years of that war. Casualties were heavy, too, with 5 ships sunk and 89 damaged. Seven Congressional Medals of Honor were awarded to navy men for heroism in battle.

Of the hundreds of books written about the Korean War, I can count on one hand the number of serious works describing the navy's part in that conflict. For that reason, if for no other, I believe our story deserves to be told.

The navy's role may not have been as glamorous as that of the air force shooting down planes over "MiG Alley," nor as deadly as the marines fighting their way out of the Chosin Reservoir, and consequently it did not get written about as much. But damn it, we were there! We endured our share of hardships. A lot of good sailors got killed. We made an important, if not decisive, contribution to the prosecution of the war.

This is a story of not any one ship. It is the story of many. And of their crews. The USS *John J. Borland* (DD-855) is a composite of several destroyers that fought in Korea. The stories are true. They are taken from the author's recollections, supported by deck logs, war diaries, and action reports of various ships. Secondary sources are noted.

Because a writer needs to write from a particular point of view, I have used my own ship and its crew as the platform from which to tell this story. Occasionally, where a person's reputation is at stake, a character has been disguised or an event rearranged to better fit the purpose of the narrative.

In so doing, I have sought to accomplish two goals. One is to describe the progress of the war as we experienced it from the sea. The second is to capture the flow and the feel of what it was like to serve aboard one of the navy's destroyers during that period in our nation's history.

To further the goal of authenticity, I have quoted each day from a ship's war diary. I am not aware of any other writer who has used this technique. It has posed certain difficulties, principally that it tends to interrupt the flow of continuous narration. On the other hand, it has imposed a discipline that has forced me to deal with the war on a day-by-day basis as it was actually lived on the deck of a ship rather than by some broad, sweeping political paintbrush of the historian.

This book is a close study of the first year of the war, covering the period July 1, 1950, to about July 1, 1951, when the battle lines became static. The highlights of the final two years are summarized in the last chapter. Though the navy was extremely busy during the last two years, the political aspects of the armistice negotiations moved to center stage, and combat operations in this phase had little or no bearing on the final outcome of the war.

I acknowledge my personal debt of gratitude to Capt. Marion H. Buaas, commanding officer of the USS *John A. Bole*, Capt. Marshall Thompson, commanding officer of the USS *Walke*, and John Meyers, whose father died aboard the *Walke*. I'm indebted to shipmates Joe Doresky, Ray Franks, Claude Gray, Don Hanley, Pete Hoffman, Jerry Jerome, Jay Passarelli, Sam Stock, and Al Weber who helped enrich my memory and corroborate certain facts. Also, I extend my thanks to the staff of the Naval Historical Center for putting up with my persistent, and sometimes insistent, requests for documents.

In reflecting back on the Korean War, I am struck by how often the events of history repeat themselves. It is ironic that nearly half a century later our great nation should find itself engaged in yet another confrontation with the leaders of North Korea at a time when our armed forces are suffering a post–cold war meltdown painfully similar to that which preceded the Korean War. Indeed, the words of Adm. Chester Nimitz are as relevant today as they were then, namely, that we have done to ourselves "what no enemy could do, and that is to reduce the navy to almost impotency."

*Inchon to Wonsan*

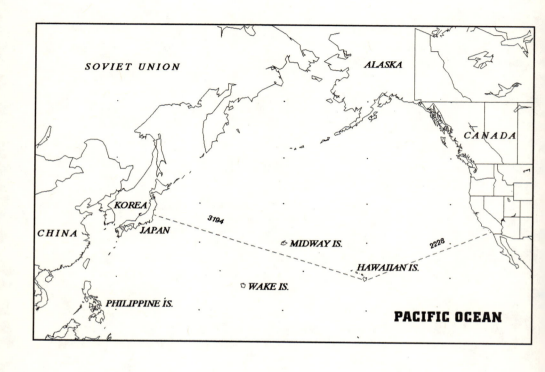

**CALLED TO COMBAT**

*July 21–25, 1950*

---

**Ship's Log: Friday 21 July 1950**   At 0242 hours the USS JOHN J. BORLAND (DD-855), a unit of DesDiv 71 and Task Unit 52.2.1 entered an action area as promulgated by Naval Operations. Position 150E, 17-45N, en route from Midway Island to Sasebo, Japan. Task Unit 52.2.1 is a movement unit of Cruiser-Destroyer Force, Pacific Fleet, and is composed of USS HELENA (CA-75), USS THEODORE E. CHANDLER (DD-717), USS CHEVALIER (DD-805), USS HAMNER (DD-718), USS WILTSIE (DD-716), plus the USS JOHN J. BORLAND (DD-855).

---

At 4:45 A.M., the crew of the USS *John J. Borland* (DD-855) was rudely jarred to wakefulness by a loud Boing! Boing! Boing! reverberating throughout the steel hull of the vessel, followed by the shrill squeal of the bos'n's pipe. "General quarters! General quarters! All hands man your battle stations! All hands man your battle stations!"

Like everyone else, I scrambled out of my bunk, hurriedly pulled on my trousers, shoes, and shirt, and made a mad dash up the ladder toward my battle station in the main battery gun director. The sky and sea outside were still dark, with only a faint glimmer of light creeping up on the eastern horizon.

Four men besides myself comprised the crew of the main battery gun director. Ensign Robert C. "Bob" White, a boyishly good-looking, fun-loving, popular young man from Allendale, Illinois, was the control officer. The others were Stan Houk, trainer; Floyd Manders, pointer; and Robert Kinsey, optical rangefinder operator. I operated the fire control radar.

I answered to two names: "Rusty" for the color of my hair, or "Gamble" for my last name. Seldom did anyone call me by my given name, Edwin.

As soon as all stations had checked in, the captain's voice crackled over the ship's loudspeaker: "This is the captain speaking. At zero-two-four-two hours this morning, we entered the war zone. Every day from now on, so long as we remain within the war zone, we will be having dawn alerts like this. The most dangerous time for surprise attacks from enemy submarines or aircraft is the hour before sunrise.

I do not enjoy it any more than you do, but this is something that we all will get used to. It will become a way of life."

He continued, "This morning, it took us twelve minutes before all stations reported in. That is unacceptable! I will not be satisfied until we can all reach our battle stations within five minutes." He paused for a moment. "Gentlemen," he said gravely, "if this had been a submarine attack, the *Borland* would be dead in the water by now. I expect you to do better. Carry on."

---

**Ship's Log: Saturday 22 July 1950**   Steaming in company with DesDiv 111 and USS HELENA (CA-75). Conducting training en route. Fired antiaircraft burst practice, expended 12 rounds of 5" AAC, 144 rounds of 40MM projectiles.

---

Steaming westward across the great expanse of the empty Pacific, I couldn't help reflecting on the series of events that had led to this situation. For me, it had begun barely three weeks earlier when the navy began a hurry-up mobilization of ships for service in Korea.

I was an electronic technician first class (ET1) on the USS *Dixie* (AD-14). The *Dixie* was a destroyer tender stationed in San Diego, California. It was a kind of "mother ship" to the destroyers assigned to our care. We provided them with technical service, logistical support, and repair facilities beyond the capabilities of their own crews to perform.

It was considered a cushy job. We stayed in port most of the time. Crewmen joked about dragging us off the "coffee grounds" every few months so we could keep our sea pay. Aboard the *Dixie* we thought of ourselves as the "elite of the fleet."

Electronics was a new specialty. Those of us early graduates from the forty-eight-week school were put on a "fast track." I was only twenty years old, and I guarantee you, no one was more puffed up with self-importance and pride than I was.

I was hoping for an appointment to the faculty of the Navy Electronics School at Treasure Island, California. Instead, I got orders to report aboard the *Borland*.

Lt. Eugene Rice, my division officer explained, "I know you're disappointed, Gamble, but there are a couple of things you need to know. First, the North Koreans invaded South Korea last week and President Truman has authorized use of force to repel the invasion. You're aware of that?"

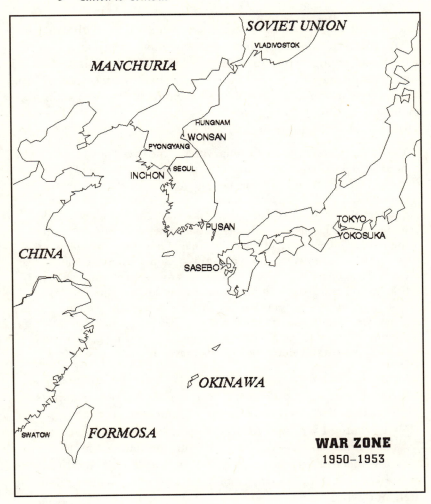

"Yes, sir."

"Well, the *Borland* is being ordered to depart for Korea as part of the first contingent of ships sent to fill the breach. She's due to leave in just a few days."

"I see, sir." A thought flashed through my mind: "What will I tell Anna?" Anna Remick was the sister of a shipmate, Carl Remick, who introduced us a month earlier when she came to visit her brother. She was a tall, blonde, eighteen-year-old Czech girl from Texas soon to begin her sophomore year at Texas Woman's University in Denton. In facial features and hair style she reminded me a lot of the actress Lauren Bacall. We had agreed to correspond with each other.

Rice's voice droned on. "Second, we were caught with our pants down. The peacetime navy has been woefully undermanned—often with barely enough crew to take ships out of port. In fact, Admiral Nimitz complained to Congress that the postwar meltdown has 'done what no enemy could do, and that is to reduce the navy to almost impotency.'"

His complaint continued:

That lack of foresight is catching up with us. The navy has such an urgent need for ships to go to Korea that it is mobilizing every vessel for which it can muster a crew. Severe budgetary ceilings have greatly decimated the navy. We had only eighty-six combatant units in Pacific Fleet, three-quarters of which were based here on the West Coast. But even those numbers were deceptive, inasmuch as personnel shortages kept many of these ships in port much of the time. We find it impossible to fill out the personnel complement rate-for-rate. This personnel shortage made it necessary for yeomen strikers to qualify as radarmen overnight; cooks and bakers suddenly became 40-mm gunners; and stewards qualified as repairmen and ammunition passers. In order to meet this national emergency, we are calling untrained reserves into uniform and will be sending them straight out to sea. Consequently, men like you are going to find yourselves facing a helluva job training these guys how to be sailors.

I mumbled an acknowledgment.

Rice concluded. "The *Borland* is just coming out of the shipyard at San Francisco. You'll report aboard her tomorrow."

That evening I wrote to Anna: "It looks like I won't be coming to Texas any time soon. As you can see from the return address on this letter, I've been transferred to a new ship. We're expected to set sail for the Far East within a couple of days. I hope you will think of me often, and write."

---

**Ship's Log: Sunday 23 July 1950**  Conducting training en route. At 1300 hours fired antiaircraft burst practice, expended 12 rounds of 5" AAC, 144 rounds of 40MM projectiles. 1745 Arrived Yokosuka, Japan, for refueling.

---

The USS *John J. Borland* was a destroyer of the *Sumner* class, hull number DD-855. She was 376 feet long and displaced 2,200 tons. She was equipped with an impressive array of firepower—six 5-inch, 38-caliber dual-purpose guns in dual mounts, sixteen 40-mm antiaircraft guns in four quad mounts, two "hedgehog" batteries firing twenty contact-fused charges each, and five 21-inch torpedo tubes. A full crew complement was 350. With a top speed of thirty-five knots, the *Sumner*-class ships were faster than any destroyers previously built, but because of their top-heavy superstructure they were apt to roll badly in stormy seas.

Named after Lt. Comdr. John J. Borland, commanding officer of a ship lost near Rabaul, Solomon Islands, February 16, 1943—coincidentally, my thirteenth birthday—the *Borland* was commissioned March 3, 1945. She saw action in the Pacific during the closing days of World War II.

I reported aboard the *Borland* on the afternoon of the Fourth of July. She was tied up at Berth 51 in the San Francisco Naval Shipyard. Despite this being a national holiday, the ship was a bustle of activity.

Lt. Frank Howland was the operations officer. I found him in CIC (combat information center). This was located forward, one deck up in the superstructure, and dominated by a huge plotting table in the center, a number of radar screens around the periphery, plus a jumble of loudspeakers and telephone handsets dangling from the overhead and protruding out from side bulkheads. Forward and to the right of the plotting table was a large, edge-lighted plexiglass screen big enough for a man to stand behind and plot the movement of airplanes.

Howland was a big, rugged redheaded fellow who carried himself with an air of self-assurance. My initial impression of him was of someone who was serious and steady, and would be totally "unflappable" in a crisis. He was the driving force in putting the *Borland*'s combat information team together.

Lieutenant Howland briefed me on what my duties would be. We had four other technicians: Charles Sellers, ET2, and Solon Gray, John Sorcek, and Kenneth Beggs—all ET3s. Soon, he said, we should be getting a couple of reservists.

Ensign Jack MaCamont, a brand-new ensign out of the Naval Academy, was the electronics officer—the man under whom I'd be working. Ruggedly handsome, MaCamont was square-jawed, muscular, quiet-spoken, and intense.

He had pretty much remained silent until now:

> One of the things I pushed the guys real hard to do in the shipyard was to establish a really first-rate spare parts inventory and control system. You see, if a piece of equipment breaks down while we're overseas, we can't be waiting six weeks for the replacement part to come in from the States.

We need to have it then; we need to know that we do have it; and we need to know where it is located. We can't waste time searching through innumerable boxes and bins to find something we aren't even sure is there. So, I hope you'll give this a high priority.

I assured him I would do my best.

The *Borland's* captain walked through. Comdr. Marion H. Buaas was a solidly built man of thirty-five, above-average height, with sandy hair and a rounded, somewhat freckled face. He sported several rows of decorations on his uniform, topmost being a set of pilot's wings. Howland later explained that Buaas was a former blimp pilot who had transferred back into the surface navy. Buaas had an impressive war record aboard cruisers and destroyers during World War II.

The briefing ended with Howland saying we'd be getting underway the next day for Korea without the benefit of a full shakedown cruise.

---

**Ship's Log: Monday 24 July 1950**  0711 Underway from Yokosuka en route Sasebo, Japan. Continued training exercises. 1105 Fired AA practice at towed sleeve target. Expended 188 rounds of 40MM projectiles.

---

On July 6 the *Borland* rendezvoused at sea off San Diego with the cruisers *Helena* and *Toledo,* the four destroyers of DesDiv 111 *(Chandler, Chevalier, Hamner,* and *Wiltsie),* and four fleet oilers *(Cimarron, Cacapon, Caliente,* and *Platte).* Together, we formed the first unit dispatched from the West Coast to the new Asian conflict. As tiny as our flotilla was, our arrival would nearly double the number of fighting ships in Asian waters.

Our group reached Pearl Harbor on the eleventh and left again on the thirteenth. The slower oilers were left behind to plod along at their own pace while the cruisers and destroyers forged ahead at maximum speed.

The four-thousand-mile expanse of ocean from Pearl to Japan posed problems of fuel consumption for the destroyers. We could get there a day earlier by steaming at twenty-four knots but it would require refueling en route. Unfortunately, the facilities at Midway Island had been deactivated the previous May as a part of the military meltdown. Therefore, the navy improvised. Two chief petty officers who had previously served at Midway were rounded up and embarked in the *Chandler*. Upon arrival the chiefs activated the fueling system and replenished two of the destroyers while *Helena* refueled the others.

Throughout the journey westward, our days and nights were filled with exercises to check out guns, equipment, and men. Believe me, we needed the work.

---

**Ship's Log: Tuesday 25 July 1950**  0928 Arrived Sasebo, Japan. 1032 Moored starboard side USS MADDOX (DD-731) at Buoy #20. 2344 Underway en route to operating area with Task Force 77.

---

Our first mail since leaving Pearl reached the ship shortly before noon. Sam Stock was our mailman, a job that on a day like today made him enormously popular. A smiling, fun-loving radarman third class who exuded the unmistakable aura of his native Texas, Sam stood a little over six feet tall, weighed 175 pounds, had sandy hair and chipmunklike cheeks, and always bore a cheerful and unpretentious expression.

Stock grew up in Corpus Christi, where as a high school student he and two buddies formed a company that installed metal hurricane blinds. Since I was from Iowa, where we had tornadoes but no hurricanes, I had to take his word for it that hurricane shutters were a big business in Corpus Christi. He also said he drove around town in a battered old panel truck with an eye-catching sign boldly emblazoned on its side: SAM THE BLIND MAN.

I could imagine people doing a double take when they saw that improbable sign passing by. Sam impressed me as the type of person who would do well in life. He said that after he got out of the navy he wanted to go to college and study to become a history teacher.

Being the mailman was a volunteer activity, a job over and above Stock's regular duties as a radarman. It contributed greatly to the ship's welfare and morale.

"How did you get to be the ship's mailman?" I asked one day, assuming the job would more naturally fall to one of the storekeepers.

"It gives me something worthwhile to do with my time," he explained. "You see, in port, there isn't a helluva lot for a radar operator to do, and I get bored just sitting around drinking coffee and shooting the bull."

He handed one letter to me. It might be another hour or two before the rest of my mail caught up with me, but for now I had this one treasure in my hands to ease the longing in my heart.

Dear Rusty: More than 300 Texas Marines, a call-up of reservists, had a baptism of tears on Sunday as they boarded the train in Fort Worth bound for war. Their departure brought the Korean War directly to our doorstep. Neighbors, in-laws, parents, wives, children dressed in their Sunday best, all were there to say goodbye.

Goodbye! The saddest word in the English language. Sad even if it means an absence of only a short while. Almost unbearably sad for mothers and fathers when the absence will be long, may even outlast the life of someone left at home. Sad for wives who face the loneliness of rearing children with no man around the house.   Anna

# 2    BIRDDOG STATION YOKE

*July 26–August 2, 1950*

---

**Ship's Log: Wednesday 26 July 1950**   0350 Arrived in operating area off west coast of Korea. From 0625 until 2017 HMS TRIUMPH and USS VALLEY FORGE (CV-45) launched and received aircraft making strikes, close support for ground troops ashore.

---

The strike force consisted of the British light carrier *Triumph* and the American fast carrier *Valley Forge*. These two ships made something of an odd couple, owing to the fact that the *Triumph's* maximum launch speed of twenty-three knots was ten knots slower than that of the *Valley Forge*. The two navies flew different types of aircraft.

Throughout the day and into the night the carriers launched and received planes in close air support of UN troops ashore, some 150 miles distant.

Most of us were too young to have been in World War II. None of us really expected to engage in any ship-to-ship duels like the great sea battles of that war. Nevertheless, many of us were as nervous as a virgin in a motel, not knowing what to expect. Combat was something we trained for, drilled for, and planned for; but it was something we all dreaded.

In a nutshell, "close air support" can be described simply as the use of an airplane in behalf of and near to a soldier on the ground. It was a team effort that required the use of a trained party on the ground, called a "spotter" or "controller," to select the targets and call in the air strikes—which may be from fifty to two hundred yards away.

Unfortunately, at this stage of the war ground-to-air coordination was not all that it should have been. Many early missions went awry as the strike aircraft, unable to reach army controllers on the prescribed radio frequencies, resorted to attacks on secondary targets. Frustrated by the inability of the strike groups to reach controllers ashore, Vice Adm. A. D. Struble, Commander Seventh Fleet, proposed the deployment of a Seventh Fleet tactical control party (TacRon). His proposal was vetoed by the air force.

A thousand miles southward in the Formosa Strait another crisis was emerging that could seriously sap the UN's ability to wage warfare in Korea. Military intelligence reported massive troop buildups along the South China coast and the assemblage of five hundred to fifteen hundred sea-going junks in river estuaries. Gen. Chu Teh, commander in chief of the Red Chinese army, declared, "We are determined to conquer Nationalist Formosa and oppose United Nations aggression." Certainly, if an invasion of Formosa were contemplated, this would be the time to launch it, inasmuch as the UN's meager fleet was tied up in Korea.

To deal with this crisis, the cruiser *Helena* and the four destroyers of DesDiv 111 *(Chandler, Chevalier, Hamner,* and *Wiltsie)* were ordered to proceed to Formosa at flank speed. This was a pitifully small force to fend off a large-scale invasion, especially one embarked in a fleet of nearly unsinkable junks.

We were at the end of a six-thousand-mile pipeline, and resources were spread thin. Very thin!

---

**Ship's Log: Thursday 27 July 1950**   Steaming as before. This vessel has plane guard for launching antisubmarine patrol aircraft.

---

The *Borland*'s duties were two-fold. First, with other destroyers, we formed a protective screen around the carriers to defend them from submarine and air attack.

Second, we served as "plane guard." During carrier launch and recovery operations we took up a station a thousand yards astern of the carrier to fish out any pilot unfortunate enough to land in the drink.

To launch and retrieve aircraft was risky, dangerous work. It was a dance between men and machines in constant motion. The carriers turned into the wind and cranked up to maximum speed in order to reduce the plane's relative speed with reference to the landing deck. The mathematics were simple. A navy plane normally landed at about 135 miles an hour; by steaming away from the plane at, say, 20 knots, the carrier reduced the relative speed to 115 mph; and if they were headed into a 20-knot wind, the relative speed was now cut to 95 miles. Comparatively speaking, 95 mph offered a higher probability of a safe landing than did 135.

"I'll bet old Captain Buaas is in his glory now," remarked Stuart "Shorty" Hall as he came down from the bridge.

"Why is that?" I asked.

"He's a former naval aviator, you know, and I'll bet he wishes he was in one of those warbirds taking off from the carrier."

Shorty was chief quartermaster. He and I hit it off right from the beginning, though at first glance we might have seemed to be an unlikely pair—a kind of "Mutt and Jeff" combination. I was six-two and 190 pounds; Shorty was a foot shorter and probably didn't weigh more than 105 pounds soaking wet. Nevertheless, he was a fountain of wisdom about the sea, and I was an avid learner.

Knowledge of the sea came naturally to Shorty. His family ran a fishing fleet out of Sitka, Alaska, and he joined the navy at sixteen, serving in the Aleutians during World War II. Shorty had a brother who was also in the navy, an officer, whom he always referred to as "my black sheep brother." Despite his apparent disdain for officers—any officer—Shorty had a lot of respect for Commander Buaas's seamanship.

Pilots returning from morning strikes reported that air controllers on the ground had more planes than they could handle and radio channels were overcrowded. As a result, instead of mounting controlled attacks, the planes broke off and pursued "targets of opportunity" to dispose of ammunition. Admiral Struble again emphasized the need for proper communications with commanders in the field.

The USS *Toledo* (CA-133) got the honor of becoming the first heavy cruiser to bring her 8-inch guns to bear upon the invading army. She was supported in this effort by the destroyers of DesDiv 91 *(Collett, De Haven, Mansfield,* and *Swenson).* They fired on troop concentrations, supplies, and revetments around Yongdok by day, and illuminated the battle line with starshells by night.

Then the six-thousand-mile pipeline reared its ugly head. Ammunition in the Far East was still so scarce that the *Toledo* was instructed to conserve her use of ammunition in order to make it last at least ten days.

---

**Ship's Log: Friday 28 July 1950**   0750 Proceeding to birddog station Yoke. 0925–2055 Exercised crew at general quarters. 2124 Rejoined Task Force 77 on station #4 in 10-ship concentric circular screen.

---

In the navy's lexicon, "birddog" is defined as radar picket patrol. This was an invention born of necessity late in World War II in an effort to counter the threats of the Japanese kamikaze attacks. Existing radar was unable to detect low-flying, "over the horizon" formations of planes until they were almost upon our fleet. In response, certain destroyers were designated as radar picket to extend the horizon of the fleet's radar coverage. These picket destroyers were placed about fifty miles away from the fleet's center to give early warning of low flyers.

Early in the kamikaze experience, Japanese pilots tended to ignore the lonely picket destroyers in favor of juicier targets like carriers and cruisers. But when they figured out what the picket destroyers were really doing out there, they exacted a heavy toll.

Our birddog station was sixty miles north of the main task force. We steamed a slow triangular pattern of twelve miles per leg around an imaginary point in the ocean designated as Point Yoke. We also controlled two combat air patrol (CAP) planes that circled continuously overhead, available to investigate or intercept any unidentified bogies.

Two events occurred to remind us that we were now in a war. The first involved a VHF radio transmission from a *Triumph* pilot who was going down in flames. He had the double misfortune of being shot down over enemy lines and then being picked up by a helicopter that also went down from lack of fuel. Happily for all concerned, both pilots made contact with friendly forces.

The second event occurred about midafternoon when the radar screen picked up a plane that was showing no IFF (identification friend or foe) and therefore was presumed hostile. Air controllers vectored a *Triumph* CAP fighter pilot out to investigate the radar contact. He somewhat absentmindedly closed on a U.S. Air Force B-29—the plane that showed no IFF—only to find himself shot down west of Anma Do in the Yellow Sea. He, too, was lucky; he was picked up by a destroyer.

---

**Ship's Log: Saturday 29 July 1950**   0600 Departed from formation on course 040T, speed 25 knots, to proceed to birddog station Yoke. 0735 Exercised crew at general quarters until 1855. 2000 Rejoined Task Force 77.

---

The pride and joy of the *Borland* was its SPS-6 radar, the newest and most powerful air search radar available to the fleet. The SPS-6 was designed to provide maximum antiaircraft warfare (AAW) capability. In navy lingo, that meant detecting aircraft at the maximum possible range, determining their speed and direction, and directing fighter planes to intercept them if necessary. We regularly were able to track aircraft out to a range of three hundred miles—depending on the plane's altitude, its radar cross section, and the prevailing weather conditions.

Of course, we couldn't keep the radar and other electronic equipment running without good technicians. One of the best was Charles Sellers, ET2. Sellers was a slightly built, boyish-faced, likable chap from Chipley, Florida, where his father ran a newspaper. His one fault was that he was an inveterate gambler. If ever we needed him—and didn't know where he was holed up—we only had to look as far as the nearest poker game.

John Sorcek, ET3, was a skinny, pinched-face, hawk-nosed, blond-haired Czech from Chicago who looked and acted a lot like Huntz Hall of Dead End Kids fame. Indeed, we sometimes thought Sortek might have watched too many Dead End Kids movies, because he was continually telling us incredible tales of his boyhood with gangs on Chicago's northside. We seldom knew when to believe him and when not.

Solon Goodrich "Soley" Gray III, a graceful, darkly handsome, six-footer from Grand Junction, Colorado, was the son of a C-47 pilot who flew the hazardous Burma Hump during World War II. Gray was a multitalented individual who could do almost anything he set his mind to, including sing, dance, and play almost any musical instrument he picked up. His goal was to become a radio-television announcer after the war.

The fourth member of our team was Kenneth Beggs, ET3, from Tyler, Texas. Unlike the stereotypical Texan, Beggs was quiet, unassuming, and blessed with a low-key sense of humor. He seldom spoke unless spoken to, and then with slow deliberation. No one could remember hearing him use a curse word—a rarity in a navy where the use of coarse language is elevated to an art form.

In fact, about the strongest words I ever heard him utter occurred one day when he had spent two hours repairing a radar unit, only to see it go up in smoke again as soon as he lit it off. Beggs drew himself up to full height, placed his hands on his hips, glared menacingly at the offending unit, and then exclaimed, "Why, that gol-darned thing!"

---

**Ship's Log: Sunday 30 July 1950** Proceeding independently to birddog patrol station Yoke in Yellow Sea off west coast of Korea.

---

During the night, the *Valley Forge* and eight destroyers retired from the area and set a course for Okinawa for replenishment. The Happy Valley had no choice: she was down to a little less than a one-day supply of aviation fuel and was perilously low on aircraft ammunition. As yet, not enough of these vital commodities had reached Japan to supply the needs of one U.S. carrier—much less a whole fleet. Nor had the ammunition ship *Mount Katmai* yet arrived in Far Eastern waters.

The *Borland* remained to provide birddog patrol for a Commonwealth cruiser-destroyer force. The Brits did not take lightly the value of early-warning radar. On July 2, the British frigate *Black Swan* earned the dubious distinction of being the first UN ship to come under attack by enemy aircraft. Two fighters, thought to be Russian-built Stormoviks, came in on the *Black Swan* from over land and out of the haze, inflicted minor structural damage, and escaped without being hit.

---

**Ship's Log: Monday 31 July 1950**   Independent patrol at birddog station Yoke off west coast of Korea.

---

From the viewpoint of protecting a fleet of aircraft carriers, the Yellow Sea was fraught with special dangers. It is a large, shallow body of water that occupies the area between the land mass of northern China and the Korean peninsula. It gets its name from the great quantities of yellowish-brown mud that washes down from the great rivers of China, giving the water a muddy color.

The defense problem was potentially larger than the size of the North Korean Navy would indicate. Our operating area was only one hundred miles from Chinese Communist airfields on the Shantung Peninsula and less than two hundred miles from the Soviet air garrison at Port Arthur.

Nor could one discount the submarine threat. A Soviet submarine fleet known to exceed eighty in number was operating out of Vladivostok—only forty-five miles from the border on the other side of North Korea. So long as Soviet intentions remained unclear, the U.S. fleet could ill afford to take chances.

---

**Ship's Log: Tuesday 1 August 1950**   Birddog station Yoke. 1600 USS FLETCHER (DD-445) came alongside to port to transfer mail.

---

Dear Anna: The realities of this war impressed themselves upon me this day when, steaming some 70 miles offshore, we passed through water containing many floating bodies tied together in bundles and with their hands lashed behind their backs.

When the lookouts first spotted the gruesome mass, they thought they were seeing bundles of floating logs, possibly washed down one of the rivers by flooding in the aftermath of Typhoon Grace. Little did they dream that upon closer inspection the "logs" would turn out to be human bodies. Clearly, these were products of a mass execution.

We were told that this was a common Communist technique. They would tie bodies together and float them down a river to serve as a warning to others who might be tempted to resist authority.

I didn't want to look, but I forced myself to. I wanted it clearly etched in my mind the reason why it was so important that we come to the defense of South Korea. We counted hundreds of bodies. God knows how many more people were executed whose corpses didn't drift out this far. Further, I would hazard a guess that any crew member viewing this scene quickly lost whatever bit of naivete he might have had about why the U.S. viewed its involvement in this struggle as a moral obligation.

---

**Ship's Log: Wednesday 2 August 1950**   0902 Relieved on station by HMAS BATAAN and set course for Sasebo, Japan, for replenishment.

---

The threatened Communist invasion of Formosa never materialized. Either the Chinese were playing cat-and-mouse games with us, or our intelligence reports were wrong. But keeping a heavy cruiser and four destroyers in the Formosa area had the effect of tying up a lot of firepower that could better be used in Korea, so Admiral Struble formed a new task group composed of the light antiaircraft cruiser *Juneau* and two destroyers, the *Maddox* and the *S. N. Moore,* plus the oiler *Cimarron,* to patrol the strait. The *Helena* group then headed north again to Korean waters to do what they came here to do.

Dear Rusty: The *Dallas Morning News* reported that leftist "peace" marchers clashed with police yesterday in New York. An estimated 3,000 marchers formed ranks and tried to disrupt the going-home traffic of thousands of workers at the height of the rush hour. "We want peace! Stop the war!" they cried.

It seems ironic that the very freedoms you are striving to protect should become the vehicle to protest your efforts at preserving those freedoms. With men facing death on the battlefield in freedom's defense, these marches serve only to cheapen your sacrifice and sully your heroism.   Anna

# 3 ENFORCING A BLOCKADE

*August 3–25, 1950*

**Ship's Log: Thursday 3 August 1950**   1420 Underway from Sasebo, Japan, for east coast of Korea. 2310 rendezvous with Task Group 96.5 off Yongdok. Other ships include USS TOLEDO (CA-133), USS DE HAVEN (DD-727), and USS LYMAN K. SWENSON (DD-729).

During the time we were steaming northward, a "peace-making" conference of sorts was taking place in Tokyo between air force and navy brass. The occasion for this conference was a series of raids on July 18 and 19 by Skyraiders and Corsairs from the *Valley Forge*, which destroyed the oil refineries at Wonsan. The results were spectacular. Large fires poured out so much smoke, photographic damage assessment was difficult. Smoke, rising to five thousand feet, was visible many miles at sea. Ten days later air force B-29s made another raid, after which the Far East Air Force Command (FEAF) claimed full credit for total destruction of the refinery. FEAF said, "reconnaissance photographs [showed] that only a small portion . . . had been damaged by previous small air strikes." Apart from the question of who hit what, that statement did not sit well with the navy.

However, this was hardly a meeting of equals. Arrayed on the navy's side were one captain, two commanders, and two lieutenant commanders. They were greatly outranked by four air force generals and a colonel. The outcome of this meeting of unequals was a plan that coordination of all attacks south of the 38th parallel was to lie with the air force, and navy attacks on bomber targets north of that line required advance clearance from the air force.[1] That inevitably meant the operations of carrier aircraft would fall largely under the control of the air force's Joint Operations Control (JOC).

Unfortunately, the air force control mechanisms were so inadequate to the task and the JOC so inappropriate to Korea, that the system was doomed to work poorly if at all.

Admiral Struble was reported to be furious at not having been consulted regarding this agreement. He saw it as a wasteful employment of his very considerable air strength.

**Ship's Log: Friday 4 August 1950**    0600 Relieved USS DE HAVEN (DD-727) on station at Yongdok. 0628 Expended 118 rounds of 5″ AAC shells on targets called by U.S. Army. 1120 rescued U.S. Air Force P-51 pilot after he had bailed out of plane following engine damage after strafing inland targets. 2025 night bombardment mission for U.S. Army, expended 20 rounds 5″ AAC in vicinity of Yongdok.

Streaks of yellow light were breaking through the early morning mist to expose the scraggly silhouette of South Korea. The land appeared deceptively peaceful. Pristine green, forested mountains came right down to the sea, virtually untouched by signs of human habitation. Behind that seemingly serene facade, however, a deadly battle was raging.

We moved in to four thousand yards offshore to replace the USS *De Haven* on the firing line. For most of us, this was our induction into the brotherhood of combat veterans. Somehow, it had always seemed to me that if you see an individual, be he army, navy, air force, or marine, and if he has been in combat, he's different.

"Mr. White, do you think they'll be shooting at us?" asked Bob Kinsey, peering anxiously through the powerful lenses of his rangefinder, searching for signs of enemy activity.

"I doubt it, I doubt it. The fighting is all inland," he assured us. "The army is trying to anchor this end of the perimeter and hold it against a concerted North Korean effort to close in on Pusan. Basically, our job will be to provide artillery support for the troops ashore. We probably won't even see an enemy."

Realization is seldom as great as anticipation. I had always imagined shooting at an enemy who would be shooting back. It came as somewhat of a letdown when the *Borland* fired her first shots of the war at an enemy we could not see. It all seemed so very, very sanitary.

Nevertheless, we figured we must have done a good job from the gratifying compliments received from army ground personnel. Our shellfire had dispersed an enemy troop concentration and started several large fires at the site. Even as smoke from the fires began to clear, spotters witnessed Korean firefighters already at work trying to put out the flames; so they had us repeat the process.

\*    \*    \*

"Paddycake, Paddycake, this is Ganymede, over." That was our radio voice call. Ganymede was the task force commander.

"Ganymede, this is Paddycake, over."

"Request you break off firing. Repeat, break off firing. Air force pilot in water five miles south of your position, bearing one-nine-zero. Proceed immediately to effect rescue. Do you copy?"

"Roger. Confirm one-nine-zero, distance five miles, pilot in water. Will advise when on station. Out."

Immediately, we set course for the designated location and cranked up the speed to twenty-five knots. Almost as soon as we got in the area the lookouts spotted the pilot right where we had been told he would be, bobbing around in the ocean in a yellow rubber life raft, unharmed. He had bailed out of his plane after being shot up on a strafing run.

"The funny thing about it," I wrote to Anna, "is that this Air Force flyboy was not aware the ships off Yongdok were friendly. I guess that says something about the quality of our inter-service communication—but I'm not sure what."

---

**Ship's Log: Saturday 5 August 1950**  On patrol Yongdok. 0700 Completed night hourly harassing fire of targets designated by U.S. Army. Expended 135 rounds of 5″ AAC and 3 rounds illuminating. 0718 On station seaward of USS TOLEDO (CA-133) as she conducted bombardment.

---

The air force produced its first Medal of Honor winner that day. Maj. Louis Sebille led a three-plane flight of P-51s into the Hamchang area at the northwestern terminus of the Naktong line, about fifty miles west of our position off Yongdok.

"Elsewhere Easy Flight Leader," barked the JOC at Taegu, "check in with Mosquito controller vicinity of Hamchang." (Mosquito was an aircraft used for air spotting purposes.) When Elsewhere Easy Flight roared into the area, the Mosquito was orbiting at two thousand feet over a camouflaged truck that he had picked for attack by the fighter bombers.

Sebille, followed by his two fellow aviators, went down for a look at the situation and spotted, in addition to the troops, horse-drawn artillery, some of which was hung up on a sandbar in the middle of the river—sitting ducks.

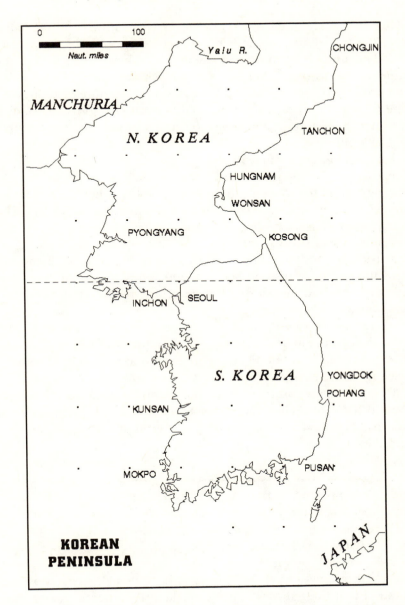

The first order of business was a bombing run on the sandbar. Sebille made his first pass, lined up his target, and pressed the release lever. Only one bomb dropped from his P-51, so Sebille flipped over and came back for another try—and then another, but he couldn't get the release mechanism to work.

It was quickly evident that the P-51s were drawing ground fire from the troops around the vehicles. Sebille completed his run and pulled up ahead of his wingman, Lieutenant Johnson. When Johnson came up and banked into line behind Sebille, he didn't like what he saw. Sebille's plane had been hit and it was either afire or losing engine coolant. Frantically Johnson tried to get the major on the radio, but the conversation channel was so clogged he couldn't get through until the third try.

Sebille told him in clipped tones, "They hit me."

It was but five minutes flying time to safety, or at worst a crash landing behind friendly lines. Johnson was jolted when he heard the calm voice of the squadron commander tell him, "I can't make it back. I'm going to go down there and get the sonofabitch!"

The words were no sooner out of Sebille's mouth than he made a tight turn to the right and went into a thirty-degree dive, diving toward the ground at a speed between 300 and 350 miles an hour. He never wavered off the course he had set for himself—straight for the camouflaged truck.

As Sebille drew into point-blank range, he opened up with his six .50-caliber guns and flew squarely into the truck with all guns blazing. He still had one 500-pound bomb on board and a number of rockets when he "hit the target."

The other pilots watched with horror and fascination as Sebille dove to his doom. First, there was a tremendous explosion, then a huge ball of fire careened crazily along the ground for several hundred yards.[2]

---

**Ship's Log: Sunday 6 August 1950**   On patrol sweep to north coast of Korea. 1400 Expended 60 rounds of 5" AAC shells at railroad junctions vicinity of Yangyang. 1700 Expended 32 rounds at railroad junctions, area Samchok.

---

"How in the hell are they getting supplied?" That was the question that bugged MacArthur's headquarters staff in Tokyo. The North Korean Army, 140,000-strong, required vast quantities of ammunition, personnel, and supplies. The use of the sea was denied them; they were not bringing it in by air; and that amount of material could not all be hand-carried. That left only rail and truck routes as the likely transports.

The proposed solution was to expand the blockade beyond its original concept of denying the enemy use of the seas to that of interdicting rail and truck traffic along the coast. Accordingly, the *Borland* was now detached from the *Toledo* group and sent to patrol independently a sixty-mile stretch of coast from Samchok to Yangyang where the railroad ran close to the sea.

Much to my chagrin, I learned that operating the optical range-finder required a special skill and was a lot harder than it appeared to be. We had completed our initial firing mission at Samchok but were still hanging around the area in search of targets of opportunity. I persuaded Bob Kinsey to let me take a crack at the rangefinder. Mr. White gave his OK, saying it was important for each man to know how to operate the others' positions.

The procedure called for me to adjust the range-setting knob until I got a stereoscopic image of the intended target in my viewer, then press a button on top of the knob to send the setting down to the fire control computer. But getting a true stereoscopic image, for me, proved to be an elusive task. My first shot landed in the water a good 150 yards short of the beach. We cranked in a range correction, but my second attempt didn't fare much better. After the third splash, the captain got on the phone wanting to know what in the hell was going on up there. Mr. White gave some sort of obfuscation, and I beat a retreat back to my radar position, a chastened man.

Task Force 77 was enhanced by the arrival of the USS *Philippine Sea* (CV-47), now entering action for the first time.

Carrier pilots were still reporting difficulty in establishing contact with air force controllers. Disgusted with these kinds of control problems, which he considered inexcusable, Rear Adm. J. M. Hoskins in the *Valley Forge* sent four pilots to JOC at Taegu for liaison purposes and to help in the direction of naval aircraft. This sharing of the burden led to measurable improvement, but periods of overload still persisted.

---

**Ship's Log: Monday 7 August 1950**   On patrol off Yongdok area. 1000 Received U.S. Army artillery liaison officer via highline from USS TOLEDO (CA-133), proceeded to Ko Ko Do harbor (off Yongdok), sent boat ashore and exchanged artillery liaison officer and U.S. Army radio operator. Returned to patrol area and transferred new U.S. Army personnel to the USS TOLEDO via highline. 1400

Proceeded as directed to Pohang harbor where debarked via ship's boat U.S. Air Force pilot previously rescued.

---

We were a player in a near-tragic drama that pointed up an ever-present hazard of war. A four-plane flight of air force aircraft arrived over our area, showing no IFF, and presumed to be hostile. Immediately, we went to battle stations and soon had a radar "lock" on the planes. We held off firing until the last possible moment. It was fortunate that we did, for our CAP finally made visual contact with the planes and identified them as friendly. Whether through pilot error or equipment failure, those four pilots came within a gnat's eyebrow of being shot down by friendly fire.

I was glad we didn't have to live with the nightmare of having shot down one of our own.

The heavy cruiser *Helena* and the destroyers *Chandler, Chevalier, Hamner,* and *Wiltsie* now entered action, having returned from their wild goose chase to Formosa. They began shooting up the town of Tanchon, which at latitude 40°28', was the farthest north of any raid made thus far by UN forces. Tanchon offered tempting rail and highway bridge targets, a marshaling yard, and some minor industrial facilities. The force shot up boxcars in the yard and the town power plants and inflicted a satisfactory 75 percent damage on the railroad bridge.

Dear Anna: The *Borland*, which yesterday had been acting like the "BB-855" in shooting up the Korean coast, now became the "APA-855" (personnel transport) for a day, shuttling people from shore-to-ship, ship-to-ship, and ship-to-shore again. In perhaps one of our most unusual experiences thus far, we found ourselves transferring personnel onto one side of a heavy cruiser while at the same time she was firing 8-inch salvos at enemy positions from the other.

Of course, no one ever suggested that life aboard a destroyer would be dull. In fact, constant variety is one reason why destroyermen tend to be so attracted to this kind of duty, not withstanding the inconveniences and hardships involved in serving on one of these vessels. In our case, we are continually being shifted from one type of mission to another—one day on bombardment, the next on blockade, and a third day as personnel transport. Never a dull moment.   Rusty

**Ship's Log: Tuesday 8 August 1950**   On patrol off Yongdok area. 2000 Directed by U.S. Army Forces ashore to fire 36 rounds 5" AAC hourly at 9 targets designated as interdiction points north of Yongdok.

Communication problems still dogged carrier pilots' efforts to provide close ground support. On the basis of information reported back from the four *Valley Forge* liaison pilots sent to Taegu, Admiral Hoskins identified the problems as the "understandable" ignorance of carrier capabilities at Fifth Air Force headquarters and the inadequate communications setup there. He urged Admiral Struble, commander of Seventh Fleet, to tell ComNavFE (Adm. Turner Joy) "the whole story" and suggest the use of naval air support to improve communications.

**Ship's Log: Wednesday 9 August 1950**   On fire support mission in Yongdok area. Screening USS TOLEDO to seaward.

Admiral Struble did attempt to tell "the whole story" in a lengthy message to Adm. Turner Joy in Tokyo. Unfortunately, not much came of it. In a rather tepid reply, Struble was merely instructed to furnish air controllers as requested by JOC, and the Fifth Air Force was invited to state any needs for personnel and communications assistance it might have. Predictably, neither JOC nor the air force felt they had any needs they couldn't meet themselves.

Dear Anna: One of the little absurdities of war occurred when we went out to investigate an unidentified sampan. The boat turned out to contain sixteen fleeing South Korean men, one of whom claimed to be an American citizen.   Rusty

**Ship's Log: Thursday 10 August 1950**   On patrol off Yongdok area, east coast of Korea. 0902 This ship was released (with USS COLLETT (DD-730)) from formation and set course for Sasebo, Japan, for replenishment.

Despite massive efforts to mobilize the navy's supply arm, the fleet was still suffering the consequences of the disastrous decisions of 1948–49 to shut down everything west of Pearl Harbor. At any given time, probably a third of our ships were away from the firing line en route to or from Japan for replenishment. The more the demands for firepower intensified, the longer that six-thousand-mile pipeline from the United States seemed to be.

Not only that, we were unnecessarily handicapped in our ability to maximize the tremendous capability of naval air. Historically, naval aviation had been more sympathetic to close support than had the air force. Navy tradition was reflected in pilot training and doctrine, in tendencies in aircraft design that permitted heavier loads and more time on station, and in techniques of accurate dive bombing derived from a generation of training for attack on maneuvering ships. It was absurd to leave running the show in the control of air force personnel who had little knowledge, experience, or sympathy with conducting this kind of warfare.

Dear Rusty: More and more the papers are filled with stories of local boys killed in the war. This morning they reported two men killed and four injured in a fire aboard the cruiser *Manchester.* I pray you're not in any danger, my love.   Anna

---

**Ship's Log: Friday 11 August 1950**   0413 Underway from Sasebo, Japan. 1314 Rendezvoused with Task Element 96.51 off Yongdok. 1949 Assigned hourly harassing fire on targets selected by U.S. Army ashore.

---

After a quick turnaround at Sasebo, the *Borland* hurried back to the firing line. Every ship was needed. The situation at Kosong was becoming critical. The North Korean advance was gaining momentum, and heavier demands were being placed on gunfire support ships.

The *Helena* lobbed a few 8-inch shells into the town of Yongdok, which flushed an estimated hundred vehicles seen heading westward out of town at high speed. Overhead, a flight of Corsairs from the *Badoeng Strait* reported seeing trucks retreating down the narrow mountainous road so fast that some missed the turns and rolled down the embankment.

Our curtain of gunfire was not enough to stem the tide of battle, however. Even though the *Helena* destroyed four enemy tanks, troops of the North Korean 5th Division still managed to fight their way into the town.

---

**Ship's Log: Saturday 12 August 1950**  0800 Completed night harassing fire, expended 240 rounds of 5" AAC. 0845 On call from U.S. Army, commenced firing on enemy cavalry unit one mile south of Ko Ko Do. 0900 Relieved of fire mission by two U.S. Air Force attack planes. 1510 Detached from duty and proceeded to Sasebo, Japan.

---

New vessels were arriving from the States almost every day. Yet the military situation in Korea was still so precarious that every bit of available sea and air power was needed on the firing line. Reports of Soviet shipping activity at the port of Wonsan stirred up renewed efforts to block the coast. The *Helena* and the destroyers of DesDiv 111 were sent north to interdict any attempts to resupply the North Korean war effort by sea.

The destroyer *Collett* was given an independent assignment to proceed into Yosu Gulf on Korea's southern tip to conduct a bombardment of rail and transportation facilities. She carried out her mission with great success.

On the night of the thirteenth, the fast transport *Horace A. Bass* (APD-124), recently arrived from San Diego, carried out a series of coastal raids north of the 38th parallel. She had embarked a group of UDT (underwater demolition team) and marine reconnaissance personnel. The raiding party's efforts resulted in the destruction of three railroad tunnels and two bridges.

Once again, the lack of a mobile replenishment group at sea made it necessary for the *Borland* to make a flying trip to Sasebo for replenishment. It seemed as if we were spending as much time shuttling back and forth as we spent on station—not a very efficient way to fight a war.

We were in port such a short time that the only person to get liberty—if one could call it that—was Claude Gray, gunner's mate second class. He got permission to go over to the base to have a wisdom tooth pulled. On the way back he stopped by the canteen for a couple of drinks.

---

**Ship's Log: Monday 14 August 1950**  1517 Rendezvoused with Task Element 96.51 off east coast of North Korea. Other ships include: USS HELENA (CA-75), USS CHANDLER (DD-717) and USS

WILTSIE (DD-716). 1947 directed to proceed to Pohang, Korea, speed 25 knots.

---

"This is the craziest, most mixed-up naval blockade I've ever seen," exclaimed Floyd Manders in what was, for him, an uncharacteristic outburst. We were at Sinchang, a railroad town about 120 miles north of the 38th parallel, awaiting our assignment of targets.

"What do you mean?" I asked.

"Well, I always thought the purpose of a blockade was to deny the enemy the use of the sea for trade, communication, and supplies. Hell's bells, here in Korea we have ships at sea chasing trains and trucks on land. It all seems so screwy."

Indeed, much importance was attached to interdicting the east coast railroad, which continued to be a major North Korean route of supply to its troops in the south. We'd tear up the tracks by day, and the North Koreans would repair them by night.

Before we could receive our gunfire assignment, word came of deteriorating conditions at Pohang in the south, coupled with rumors of an enemy landing at Kuryongpo. The entire battle group was ordered to break off shooting and set a course for Pohang.

---

**Ship's Log: Tuesday–Wednesday 15–16 August 1950**   0020
Steaming as unit of Task Element 96.51 with USS HELENA (CA-75), USS CHANDLER (DD-717), and USS WILTSIE (DD-716). 1047 On gunfire support station, Chongha, Korea.

---

The situation was critical at Chongha. ROK forces were surrounded, isolated, and in danger of annihilation by the advance of North Korean troops ten miles north of Pohang. Tank-led troops from North Korea's 5th division fought their way into the outskirts of town.

Our immediate task was to throw up a curtain of gunfire that would enable the ROKs to hold their little perimeter until shipping could be assembled for an evacuation. To accomplish this, we effectively concentrated gunfire on the coastal road to prevent the enemy's further advance.

A related problem arose when ROK vehicles, cut off from their own sources of supply, were running out of motor fuel. To remedy this situation, a destroyer was dispatched from Pusan with a load of gasoline that was then shuttled to shore in barrels by whaleboat.

In addition to cruiser and destroyer gunfire, naval air also weighed in. At 2:45 P.M. a flight of fifteen planes from the *Philippine Sea* bombed and strafed North Korean troop concentrations, and between 12:30 and 5:30 the *Valley Forge* flew twelve Skyraider and eleven Corsair sorties into the Pohang area.

Fearful that rescue shipping might not reach Chongha in time, Rear Adm. C. C. Hartman on the *Helena* prepared a contingency plan. As a worst-case scenario, he planned to evacuate the ROK troops on rafts towed by whaleboats and to transfer them to naval vessels offshore. Fortunately, such heroic measures were not necessary.

Comdr. M. J. Luosey, U.S. liaison officer for the ROK Navy at Pusan, saved the day. He managed to rustle up four LSTs, one manned by Koreans and three by Japanese. These reached the evacuation area just as darkness was falling. The destroyer *Wiltsie* led them onto the beach with the aid of jeep headlights ashore. Throughout the night, as embarkation proceeded, the gunfire ships maintained a schedule of harassing fire, and at 4:15 A.M. the LSTs cleared the beach.

This proved to be one of the least-publicized but most successful evacuations of the war. All 327 officers and 5,480 troops of the ROK Third Division were evacuated, plus 23 members of the Korean Military Advisory Group (KMAG), and 1,200 civilian refugees, along with some 100 vehicles. All was accomplished without loss of personnel or equipment.

---

**Ship's Log: Thursday 17 August 1950**   0710 Proceeding independently to join Task Element 96.52 with USS TOLEDO (CA-133). At 1922 fired 32 rounds of 5″ AAC at industrial buildings and smokestack adjoining.

---

Enforcing the blockade was not without its difficulties. Only a meager number of ships were available to cover over five hundred miles of coastline, and these had to divide their time between shore bombardment, coastal blockade, and screening the carriers.

During daylight hours, we cruised as screen for the USS *Toledo*, in company with the *Mansfield, Collett,* and *Swenson,* along a forty-mile stretch of coast from Songjin south to Iwon where the railroad runs close to the sea. Targets were plentiful, and the 297 rounds of 8-inch HC expended by the *Toledo* against three railroad bridges and several hundred freight cars were considered to have been a profitable investment of resources.

At night we cruised independently to patrol assigned sections of coastline. Our task was to intercept shipping and cut off North Korean attempts to supply their forces by sea.

---

**Ship's Log: Friday 18 August 1950**  0200–0400 Fired 12 rounds 5″ AAC and 4 rounds 5″ starshells at vehicular traffic along coast road. 0830 Transferred mail to USS WILTSIE and passengers to USS DE HAVEN.

---

Dear Anna: The "6,000-mile pipeline" from the U.S. got just a tiny bit shorter today with the arrival of the USS *Mount Katmai.* She is the first ammunition ship to reach Far Eastern waters. With her on station it will be possible to rearm the carriers at sea without the necessity of their returning to Sasebo or Okinawa for supplies, and this, in turn, will permit the warships more time on the firing line.

---

**Ship's Log: Saturday 19 August 1950**  On patrol off Pohang area, east coast of Korea, in company with the USS TOLEDO (CA-133), USS DE HAVEN (DD-727), and USS MANSFIELD (DD-728). 2020 Expended 6 rounds of 5″ AAC and 69 rounds of 40 mm ammunition on vehicle targets on coast road.

---

With the sea cut off as a route of supply and with rail lines being made inoperable by aircraft strikes during daylight, the North Koreans turned to their only other alternative to resupply themselves. They moved at night. Aerial photographs revealed camouflaged bypass railroad tracks around ruined bridges, crude log caissons placed in streambeds, and tunnels that showed smoke from trains that were hiding in them, waiting for nightfall. Infrared photography revealed trucks running at night.

The navy's answer to those nightly excursions was the use of starshells to illuminate a section of coastal road where trucks were thought to be moving. The starshell was a magnesium flare that detonated in the air and floated down on a tiny parachute; these flares put out a tremendous amount of light that lasted more than a minute— plenty long enough to get a fix on a convoy of moving vehicles. A few rounds of 5-inch AAC common or 40-mm projectiles usually sufficed to destroy the target.

The destroyer *Swenson* (DD-729) put 102 rounds into iron works, harbor installations, railroad yards, and radio stations at Chongjin with devastating effect. By the time she concluded her evening's work of destruction, flames from the burning facilities were visible for eighteen miles seaward.

---

**Ship's Log: Sunday–Monday 20–21 August 1950** Effected rendezvous with USS SWENSON (DD-729) at "Point Arthur." Bombarded waterfront docks, railroads, and industrial area of Songjin at range 14,000 yards. Expended 168 rounds of 5" AAC, 4 white phosphorus, and 8 starshells. Much smoke observed.

---

The 5-inch, 38-caliber (5"/38) guns comprised our main offense weapon. We carried six of them housed in three twin mounts. Curious about their workings, I queried my friend Claude Gray, gunner's mate second class.

Back home, meaning Rome, Georgia, Gray had worked for Coca Cola, the town's largest industry, before joining the navy in World War II. With eight years under his belt, he was every inch a gunner. At five-eleven and a trim 165 pounds, he had wavy brown hair with a red tint to it and sported a fox-red beard that he started growing the day we landed in Japan.

Gray explained that the 5-inch, 38-caliber guns were labeled "dual-purpose" because they were capable of firing on both aircraft and surface targets. Projectiles measured five inches in diameter and weighed a hefty fifty-four pounds. "Where does the term 'caliber' come from?" I asked, having in mind the caliber of a pistol or rifle.

"When you're talking about big guns," he said, "'caliber' refers to the length of the barrel. A 5-inch, 38-caliber gun has a barrel that is 38 times longer than the bore, which in this case comes out to be a length of 15.8 feet. Similarly, a 16-inch, 50-caliber battleship gun would have a barrel measuring 66 feet."

I also learned that each 5"/38 was capable of firing fifteen rounds per minute at a maximum range of 17,300 yards, or nearly ten miles.

"Incidentally," he said, "the longer the barrel, the longer the range. A battleship's 16-incher can lay one out there twenty-five miles."

Each twin 5"/38 took a crew of twenty-seven to operate—nine in the mount and eighteen in the magazines and handling rooms.

---

**Ship's Log: Tuesday 22 August 1950**   On patrol in vicinity of "Point Arthur" off the northeast coast of Korea.

---

The first attacks by enemy aircraft in over a month posed a new threat. Two enemy aircraft surprised and damaged two vessels in the Yellow Sea. One plane damaged the British destroyer *Comus,* and the other hit an ROK vessel.

The surprise attack produced a call for air cover from the escort carriers, which otherwise spent most of their effort in close support of army forces on the perimeter. It also resulted in a directive for gun crews to step up their antiaircraft target practice.

---

**Ship's Log: Wednesday–Thursday 23–24 August 1950**   Commenced firing pierheads, railroads, and Mitsubishi Iron Works near Chongjin and Tanchon. Expended 497 rounds 5" AAC. Observed fire 10 miles distant.

---

Despite the limitations of darkness and the absence of air or ground spotting, we were developing some effective techniques for night bombardment. Our favorite method was to pick out a prominent rock that we could lock onto with the fire control radar. Using that as the benchmark for range and bearing, the gunners would crank in the appropriate adjustments so as to bracket the designated target areas.

When we were finally able to leave our battle stations after a shoot, the acrid smell of burnt gunpowder was everywhere and empty shell cases were scattered all about. Whenever possible, we saved the cases and stacked them like cordwood for return to the supply depot the next time we took on more ammunition.

The day also brought reports of seven engagements with enemy coastal shipping—all by units of the ROK Navy. The best work of the day was done by the *YMS-514,* which in three separate engagements in less than three hours sank three enemy vessels and damaged eight.

---

**Ship's Log: Friday 25 August 1950**   Directed to destroy railroad cars located south of Songjin. Expended 66 rounds 5″ AAC and 30 rounds 5″ common.

---

Dear Anna: One thing you have to give the North Koreans credit for is their industriousness and tenacity. We can blast the hell out of some place one day, only to come back a few days later and find the damage largely repaired. Such was the case today at a place named Tanchon, which the cruiser *Toledo* leveled barely two weeks ago. By the time we arrived this morning, hardly a sign remained of the previous devastation.

# 4   SWINGING AT SASEBO

*August 26–31, 1950*

---

**Ship's Log: Saturday 26 August 1950**   In company with USS COLLETT (DD-730) proceeding to Sasebo, Japan. 1800 Arrived Sasebo.

---

Dear Anna:  At long last, liberty in Japan!

Sasebo is located on the westernmost main island of Japan. By tradition, the area is known as the birthplace of Japanese culture. Because of its proximity to China and Korea, the island of Kyushu served as the natural gateway to these culturally sophisticated neighbors.

Some of the older sailors experienced strongly ambivalent feelings about setting foot on a land that they had been fighting against barely five years before. Some harbor bitter feelings of personal injury or loss—perhaps of a friend or shipmate. Chief Willoughby, for example, remembers the devastation of cities like Tokyo and Yokohama where, as far as the eye could see, the only structures left standing were the chimneys of factories that had been consumed by firebombs.

Before turning us loose on the town, we had to exchange our American currency for military *scrip*. Scrip is paper certificates redeemable only by the issuing agency, namely, the U.S. Occupation Command. It is illegal for military personnel to carry, exchange, or spend U.S. dollars. Not only would the currency be confiscated, but the offender would be punished.

The reason, so I am told, is economic. General MacArthur, the military governor of Japan, is trying to rebuild this war-ravaged nation's economy. Integral to that plan is keeping the Japanese currency pegged at 360 yen to the dollar. Therefore, if Japan's economy were flooded with U.S. hard currency—as surely would happen with the influx of military payroll spending—then the yen would be driven down in value and unbalance the fragile economic recovery.

As far as I'm concerned, it doesn't make a tinker's dam whether we get scrip or real money. A dollar is a dollar is a dollar. The certificates spend just the same. I suppose that if I were willing to take the chance, I could smuggle some American dollars ashore and exchange them on the black market for more yen than the official rate. But that's not my style.  Rusty

---

**Ship's Log: Sunday 27 August 1950**    Moored as before. Ready for sea.

---

Chief Fred Pierce and I drew shore patrol duty. Shore patrol (SP) was the navy's counterpart to the army's military police (MP). The big difference was that MPs were generally full-time, trained professionals, whereas the shore patrol were ordinary petty officers who received that duty on a rotating basis. Our only badge was an arm band and our only weapon a nightstick.

Pierce was a big good-natured guy who had a great personality. He was pretty damn good looking, too. Pierce wore several medals from World War II, during which he served on a destroyer. He never talked much about those experiences. I also knew very little about his family life because he didn't talk much about that either.

Pierce and I were assigned a tame beat. About the only potential trouble spot was the China Nights restaurant and club. This was a large, two-story establishment that had several party rooms on each floor. It was jam-packed with sailors from several different ships. Each ship's crew seemed to have its own party room. Since there was quite a bit of rivalry among them, our main worry was that some drunken sailor might pick a fight with someone from a rival ship, in which case and we might end up with an old-fashioned donnybrook on our hands.

Liberty was up at 9:30 P.M. A half-hour ahead of time we began banging on doors and urging the guys to drink up and head back toward fleet landing.

One young sailor on the dock was sobbing almost uncontrollably. Two of his buddies tried to console him. Over and over he wailed, "What will my mother think of me?"

I asked what was going on. His buddy explained, "Oh, he got drunk for the first time tonight, and he got screwed for the first time tonight."

With that, the kid let out another heart-wrenching wail, "Oh . . . what will I tell my mother? I'll never be able to face my mother again!"

The poor lad couldn't have been more than seventeen.

---

**Ship's Log: Monday 28 August 1950**   Moored buoy 8, Sasebo, Japan.

---

Shorty Hall and I went ashore for a little serious drinking. Ensconced on both sides of the gangway as we departed were two corpsmen, dutifully handing out "pro-kits" (condoms) to each man as he passed. They warned that the VD rate in Sasebo ran as high as 80 percent.

It was about a mile into town. The most popular mode of transportation was the pedicab. We wrongly called it a rickshaw. The pedicab was a three-wheeled, hooded vehicle with a driver up front who pedaled it like a bicycle; it had room for two passengers sitting abreast. Technically, a rickshaw was a foot-drawn cart, but the distinction was lost on us. A ride into town cost one hundred yen per passenger, about thirty cents American money.

There were also a few taxicabs clamoring for business, but riding a rickshaw was a lot more fun. The Japanese automobiles were tiny, funny-looking, smoke-belching things bearing the strange name *Toyota*. To us the name was appropriate, for they indeed seemed like toy cars.

The area of town where we headed was called the "X" area. This section had been bombed out during World War II and only recently rebuilt. Both sides of the street were lined with souvenir shops and nightclubs, a tinsel town catering to the Yankee dollar. The whole scene, with its garish, lighted signs, music spilling forth from the bars, and people reveling in the street, called forth images in my mind of an old-time western boomtown or perhaps San Francisco's Barbary Coast of the 1890s. Each of the bars had an American cabaret name, and it all seemed so out of place here—not at all like I had imagined Japan to be.

Shorty and I made our way to a club called the Blue Moon, which we were told was the favorite watering hole for tin-can sailors. As joints go, this was probably the classiest one on the strip. It had a stage, a live combo that played everything from jazz to country, and a girl singer who didn't appear to be more than twelve or fourteen but, boy, could she belt out a song.

Shorty Hall was a drinking man. Drinking, for him, was serious business. "I'd rather have a bottle in front of me than a frontal lobotomy," he was fond of saying. The only "war stories" he ever told were drinking stories. The only people that mattered in life were his drinking buddies. He bragged that his idea of a perfect liberty would be for him and a drinking buddy to take a taxi to the farthest edge of town, get out, and then drink their way back to the ship, hoisting one in each bar along the way.

The bar Shorty and I went to, like all joints that catered to servicemen, was well supplied with B-girls—known locally as *pan-pan* girls. They were sexily dressed "hostesses" whose job it was to provide the sailors with female comfort and entice them to buy drinks. These girls were well schooled in the art of making a man feel like a man, and many sailors found their charming entreaties hard to resist.

One B-girl tried to work her charms on Shorty. No dice. Time and again he tried to shoo her off. "Go 'way, woman," he said gruffly.

She was persistent, practically smothering him with her body. Again, he suggested politely that her continued presence was not welcome at the table. But the more he resisted, the more she persisted.

Finally, he took his false teeth out of his mouth and dunked them into her glass, saying sweetly, "You don't mind if I rinse off my teeth, do you?"

She let out a scream and got the hell out of there. After that Shorty was able to pursue the business of serious drinking without further interruption.

---

**Ship's Log: Tuesday 29 August 1950** Moored buoy 8, Sasebo, Japan.

---

A surprise was in store for the men who bunked in the after crews quarters. When they got up and went to the head, they found above one of the urinals a ten-penny nail welded to the bulkhead about chin-high. Underneath were printed the words, In Case of Pain, Bite Down.

The point was not lost on anyone who had ever contracted gonorrhea (the clap). Pissing *was* painful.

Our ship's "doctor," Chief Hospitalman Hugh "Doc" Combest, didn't have much of a sense of humor when it came to things like VD—probably because he'd treated too many cases during his career. As he was walking past a group of guys standing in chow line, one of the machinists called out to him, "Hey, Doc, that must have been a pretty good piece of ass I got the other night. I'm still coming!" Though the other guys laughed, "Doc" Combest did not; he just glared daggers and said nothing that would dignify the gross attempt at humor.

---

**Ship's Log: Wednesday 30 August 1950**   Moored buoy 8, Sasebo, Japan.

---

"Gamble, you're wanted in the captain's cabin." I wondered what I had done wrong.

Commander Buaas looked up from his desk. "Put your uniform on," he said curtly. "We're going ashore."

"Aye, aye, sir," I replied, still wondering what the deal was.

We rode in his captain's gig over to the dock. Captain Buaas explained, "We're going out to the air force base to pick up a couple of AN/ARC-7 aircraft radio transceivers that are tuned to air force frequencies. The navy's been having a lot of problems communicating with air force jets because of the incompatibility of equipment."

During the half-hour or so ride to the air base, I learned more about our skipper's war record. It turned out to be impressive.

Upon graduating from the Naval Academy in 1938, he shipped aboard the cruiser USS *Houston*, flagship of Adm. Thomas C. Hart, commander of the Asiatic Fleet, headquartered at Manila Bay. A week before Pearl Harbor, he became executive officer of the USS *Isabel*, reserve flagship for Admiral Hart, and was present at Cavite on December 10, 1941, when the Japanese bombed that base to extinction. Soon after, his former ship, the *Houston*, was sunk at the Battle of Sunda Strait, near Java. Buaas returned to the States in 1943 for pilot training in lighter-than-air craft (blimps). He said he chose flight school after he'd been denied command of the USS *Heron*, a seaplane tender, owing to a rule that only a naval aviator could command an aviation-type ship. After a year as executive officer of a blimp squadron, he went back to the destroyer fleet as executive officer of the USS *Harry S. Hubbard* (DD-748) at the Battle of Okinawa. Later, he commanded the destroyer *Mayrant* (DD-402) at the 1946 Bikini atom bomb tests, then spent three years at Stanford University as associate professor of naval science in the ROTC program. Buaas took command of the *Borland* July 15, 1949.

---

**Ship's Log: Thursday 31 August 1950**   0200 Underway from, Sasebo, Japan, for patrol duty off Pohang, east coast of Korea. Other units included are USS DE HAVEN (DD-727), USS COLLETT (DD-730), USS MANSFIELD (DD-728), USS LYMAN K. SWENSON (DD-729). 1600 Joined USS HELENA (CA-75), USS DOYLE (DMS-34).

---

Dear Rusty: You should see me now—I'm in the midst of going through all the debris on top of my desk and I have folders all over the floor. Looks like a disaster has hit. In all this I must stop to write a few thoughts because you keep tumbling through my mind. Tonight it seems clear to me—as at other times of deep thinking—that we are able to share our deepest thoughts and feelings with each other. I feel free to say anything to you and disclose myself to you in a way that I feel good about. It's such a good feeling. And for that to happen, there has to be a basic confidence in one's self and the other person. With us, it seemed to be there from the very beginning with no effort on our part. You are a magnificent person, and I am proud to know you. Love, Anna

*September 1–11, 1950*

---

**Ship's Log: Friday 1 September 1950**   On patrol off Pohang area, east coast of Korea. 2000 Relieved USS DE HAVEN as fire mission ship. 2039 Directed by U.S. Army Force ashore to fire on selected shore targets.

---

The UN forces had been driven into a small semicircle scarcely fifty miles in diameter, which came to be known as "the Perimeter." It was located at the southern tip of Korea and centered around the port city of Pusan.

Late on the night of August 31, the enemy launched his greatest effort to date. With the UN forces already bottled up inside the fifty-mile-wide perimeter, the North Koreans now committed great forces along the entire front. It was a final, massive effort to push the UN forces into the sea. For them, victory seemed in sight.

At 8:10 A.M. Task Force 77 received an emergency message from the UN Command: Major enemy attack launched across Naktong River from Tuksongdong south to coast. All available effort for close support required southern sector immediately. Situation critical. Request armed recco from beach north to Tuksongdong to depth of ten miles west of bomb line.

Pohang was a minor port city about fifty miles up the coast from Pusan. The heavy cruisers *Helena* and *Toledo* and the destroyer *De Haven* moved in close to shore where they provided "call fire" as requested by U.S. Army forces ashore. The remaining destroyers patrolled to seaward to guard against possible submarine attack.

Task Force 77, consisting of the carriers *Valley Forge* and *Philippine Sea*, the cruiser *Worcester*, and Destroyer Squadron 3, had been 275 miles to the northwest in the Yellow Sea. Their response was immediate. As soon as the call for help was received, strike missions were recalled. Rear Adm. E. C. Ewen, carrier division commander, turned his force to the southeast and built up speed to twenty-seven knots, landing planes as they went.

Simultaneously, the two small escort carriers, the USS *Badoeng Strait* (CVE-116) and USS *Sicily* (CVE-118) were heading northward from Sasebo, Japan, with all the speed these "baby flattops" could muster—barely twenty knots. As soon as they reached the operating area, they turned into the wind and launched marine pilots to provide close support for the marine brigade at Naktong.

At 6:00 P.M., another emergency call from the operations center requested all available effort against continuing enemy pressure on the front. The carriers responded with a series of extremely hazardous night launches and landings.

One of the lingering problems stemmed from different ideas the navy and marines, on the one hand, and the air force, on the other, had regarding close air support. Airplanes and infantry functioned as a team in which navy and marine aircraft quickly and effectively delivered their ordnance on close-in targets. A certain number of aircraft constantly orbited the battlefield, ready to strike, and the ground commander could use their services when and where he saw fit.

The air force system developed against a different backdrop, primarily the European war. It was anathema to air force pilots that foot soldiers should exercise command over airplanes, or that airplanes should be viewed as a vehicle for supplementing or increasing the firepower of ground forces.

When the Korean War broke out, the navy-marine system was available and ready, whereas the air force system of tactical support was not. Unfortunately, the air force system was the one adopted in Korea.

---

**Ship's Log: Saturday 2 September 1950**  Fire support off Pohang area, east coast of Korea. 0819 Proceeded at maximum speed into Pohang Harbor to assist pilot of F4U which made crash landing. 1300 Rendezvoused with USS BADOENG STRAIT (CVE-116) for transfer of pilot.

---

Dear Anna: Without question, one of the prettiest war birds ever built is the Grumman F4U Corsair. It's a gull-wing, propeller-driven plane that came on line late in World War II and immediately became popular among both Navy and Marine pilots fighting in the Pacific. The Corsair proved to be an extremely effective weapon against the famed Japanese Zero. Here in Korea, they're used mainly by Marine pilots for close support of ground troops.

Today we fished a Marine pilot out of the water who crash-landed his plane after being shot up by enemy territory. His name was Cap-

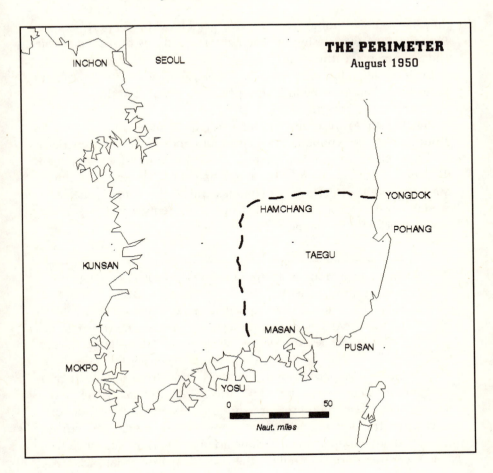

THE PERIMETER
August 1950

INCHON    SEOUL

YONGDOK

HAMCHANG

POHANG

KUNSAN    TAEGU

MASAN    PUSAN

MOKPO    YOSU

0    50

*Naut. miles*

tain A. E. Phillips. When we returned him to the carrier, they transferred back to us his weight in ice cream as an exchange. It's only on
occasions like this that we get ice cream on a tin can.    Rusty

---

**Ship's Log: Sunday 3 September 1950**   Speed reduced to 7
knots by high wind and very heavy seas. Marine squadron unable
to launch aircraft.

---

The North Koreans struck at first light at Yongsan in a heavy
attack, penetrating the marines' first line of defense. The marines
counterattacked with artillery, tanks, and automatic weapons. But

they had to do without marine air overhead for close support because Typhoon Jane was closing in. The fighter squadrons of *Badoeng Strait* and *Sicily* were weathered in.

Even the large fleet carriers of Task Force 77, the *Philippine Sea* and *Valley Forge,* had to suspend flight operations. They used this opportunity to refuel and rearm.

The Eighth Army called for help. Air force bases in Japan were grounded by the typhoon. Once again all hands on the carriers doubled to their flight stations. Despite the bad weather, they launched their first strike at 3:47 P.M. The pilots had considerable success near Masan where they destroyed two tanks and fifteen field pieces, damaged two other tanks, and strafed troops. The enemy was disorganized by the shock of this unexpected engagement.

---

**Ship's Log: Monday 4 September 1950**   0200 Proceeding independently to relieve USS HERBERT J. THOMAS (DDR-833) for radar picket duty at TOMCAT station in the Yellow Sea. At 1329 USS THOMAS reported radar contact on an unidentified aircraft. At 1343 intruder destroyed by aircraft from USS VALLEY FORGE.

---

Skies were partly cloudy, wind six knots from the south, and sea conditions choppy in the aftermath of Typhoon Jane. The North Koreans were keeping up the pressure on the perimeter. A radio dispatch from the destroyer *De Haven* reported that she and the cruiser *Toledo* had broken up a tank attack near Pohang with rapid 5-inch fire.

We were sent north to relieve the USS *Thomas* on radar picket patrol. Shortly after noon, activity in our sector suddenly picked up. It came from an unexpected quarter.

The *Thomas* reported, "Bogie at 315 degrees, range 60,000 yards, altitude 12,000, speed 180, closing on heading 160. No IFF."

"Please confirm, no IFF?" answered *Valley Forge.*

"That is affirmative, no IFF."

The *Thomas*'s skipper, Comdr. S. L. Ward Jr. looked at his VJ radar repeater then stepped over to the quartermaster's desk to examine the navigation chart. The unidentified aircraft was closing from the direction of the Russian base at Port Arthur. He reported this to the *Valley Forge.* Combat air patrol, consisting of two F4U Corsairs circling overhead at ten thousand feet, were vectored toward the target.

As the two fighters closed on the target, the radar blip separated into two parts. One part retreated in the direction from whence it came; the other continued on its original track. Apparently, two planes had been flying in such close formation that they showed up on the screen as only a single blip. The second plane continued on a course toward the task force, seemingly oblivious of our presence. That was his first mistake.

Then the intruder made another mistake, a fatal one. He opened fire on his pursuers. This was reported to base, and permission was granted to return fire.

Tracking the action from the *Borland,* we were able to sight the explosion and column of smoke in the sky, followed by a second explosion on the surface. The *Thomas* recovered the body of a Russian aviator. For a full hour, the medics tried artificial respiration but brought no sign of life.

We stayed in the area another hour picking up debris from the downed aircraft for later analysis by military intelligence. Emotions were still running high at 5:30 P.M. when the body of the dead Russian aviator, now zipped in a gray canvas body bag, was transferred via highline, together with his plane markings, to the *Valley Forge.*

---

**Ship's Log: Tuesday 5 September 1950**   Operating in the Yellow Sea as a screening unit of Task Force 77 conducting air strikes against various targets.

---

Hard fighting was still going on within the perimeter. Brig. Gen. E. A. Edward Craig, the marine brigade commander, evinced his concern in another emergency dispatch in which he reported the "situation intense." He requested eight carrier planes be on station throughout the day.

Fortunately, the fighting on the third seemed to have broken the back of the enemy's advance. The North Korean 9th Division, though fresh from garrison duty, was deficient in training and unable to stand up to the staunch marine defenders. They broke and ran, allowing large numbers to be cut down by artillery and marine air. By evening the marines were securely dug in on the hill.

---

**Ship's Log: Wednesday 6 September 1950**   Relieved TOLEDO on firing line at Pohang. 2125 Commenced firing harassment on targets designated by U.S. Army ashore.

---

Much of the difficulty with air controllers now seemed to have been solved. The solution? Joint Operations Control, which had been the bottleneck, finally agreed to allow the navy to supply air controllers for the battlefront. For its part, the air force agreed to waive the requirement of checking all planes through JOC.

These new procedures had an immediate effect. Despite deteriorating weather conditions, the carriers sent in 127 sorties, 99 of which received positive direction. The troubles of the other 28 were attributable to ground fog over the target area.

At Yongsan, the marine brigade was coming under great pressure. Two Communist divisions were now across the river and had advanced about four miles eastward along the Yongsan road. The weather was very bad. Air-support was somewhat problematical. Marine pilots had to break off by midafternoon because the seas became too rough for pilots to take off and land on the badly bouncing baby flattops.

---

**Ship's Log: Thursday 7 September 1950**   On fire support mission off Pohang, Korea. Expended 240 rounds of 5" AAC.

---

Dear Rusty:  President Truman, who seems to suffer from a severe case of hoof-in-mouth disease, really stuck his foot in it yesterday when he charged that the Marine Corps has "a propaganda machine that is almost equal to Stalin's." His comment came in a letter to a Senator who had requested the President to name a Marine to the Joint Chiefs of Staff along with the Army, Navy, and Air Force. Truman wrote, in part: "I read with a lot of interest your letter in support of the Marine Corps. For your information, the Marine Corps is the Navy's police force, and as long as I am President that is the way it will remain. They have a propaganda machine that is almost equal to Stalin's. The Chief of Naval Operations is the chief of staff of the Navy, of which the Marines are a part. Sincerely yours, Harry S. Truman."

As you can imagine, the President's unpresidential comment touched off a firestorm of protest from Marine veteran groups and senators. Love, Anna

**Ship's Log: Friday 8 September 1950**   1050 Underway for carrier operating area off west coast of Korea. 1740 Joined Task Group 96.8. 1910 Rescued Capt. L. D. Lennox, USMC, when his F4U aircraft crashed off port beam.

Our two baby flattops, *Badoeng Strait* and *Sicily,* at 535 feet and a top speed of 20 knots, were 335 feet shorter and 13 knots slower than the fast fleet carriers *Valley Forge* and *Philippine Sea.* Those differences in speed and length made the margin of pilot error that much slimmer—particularly when trying to bring a "sick chick" in for an emergency landing.

Marine captain L. D. Lennox hit the water, quickly vacated his cockpit, inflated his Mae West, and paddled away from his doomed airplane. He was in the water just seven minutes when our guys fished him out. Two swimmers went over the side to render assistance and help him climb up the rope ladder onto the ship's main deck. Except for being cold, wet, and suffering a bang on the forehead, he was okay. The medics wrapped him in blankets and took him up to the captain's cabin to await transfer back to his own ship.

Later, we transferred Lennox over to the *Badoeng Strait* in a bos'n's chair and received back our traditional payment of thirty gallons of ice cream.

**Ship's Log: Saturday 9 September 1950**   Marine Air Groups in USS BADOENG STRAIT and USS SICILY making air strikes in Kunsan area of Korea. Fired AA practice at towed sleeve target. Expended 188 rounds 40MM.

Dear Anna: Ever since two incidents where enemy aircraft penetrated our perimeter, the fleet has been ordered to step up its air defense training. Today, between flight operations, one of the carriers sent a plane aloft to tow a target sleeve past the destroyers so we could get in a little 40-mm target practice. The cloth sleeve, roughly the length and diameter of a small plane's fuselage, was towed behind the plane at the end of a long cable. The target passed down our port side at a speed of 200 knots, distance 1,500 yards, altitude 500 feet. I am happy to report that the accuracy of our 40-mm crews is improving with each practice session.

---

**Ship's Log: Sunday 10 September 1950**   1210 Proceeded northward with BADOENG STRAIT to launch Marine air strikes at Wolmi
Do, Inchon Harbor.

---

In one of those tragicomic events that is so characteristic of
war, we had the living hell scared out of us that day. It started when
military planners decided to neutralize fortified Wolmi Do, which lay
in the middle of Inchon Harbor. Because its heavily forested terrain
masked numerous gun emplacements, napalm was ordered to burn
off the cover. Marine pilots of the *Badoeng Strait* were assigned the job.
Launch was scheduled for 3:30 P.M.

On the *Borland* we picked up a radio transmission between the *Badoeng Strait* and a flight of planes coming in from an air base somewhere in Japan. What we thought we heard is not what they thought
they said.

"Knee High, Knee High, this is VA-42, do you copy?"

"VA-42, Knee High. Copy affirmative. Over."

"Knee High, VA-42 position 120 miles south-by-southeast of your
location. ETA ten-fifty-five. Over."

"Roger, VA-42. Copy your ETA ten-fifty-five. Out."

Translated into plain English, that meant a squadron of planes was
coming in from the south, 120 miles away, and their estimated time of
arrival was 10:55. This message was followed a few seconds later by
another transmission:

"VA-42, Knee High?"

"Go ahead, Knee High."

"Are you carrying the napalm?"

"Roger. We've got the napalm."

*A-bomb* is what we thought we heard. Our hair stood on end. The
rumor spread like wildfire throughout the ship.

General MacArthur had been widely quoted as saying he wanted to
"nuke" the Commies. So, it wouldn't have been a big surprise to learn
he was now going to drop the bomb.

Rumors tend to take a life of their own. This one was particularly
hard to kill. In fact, the rumor didn't die until we got reports that a total of ninety-six thousand pounds of flaming napalm was dropped
that afternoon with the resultant destruction of over 90 percent of the
natural cover on the western half of the island.

*   *   *

Over on the east coast, the *Brush* (DD-745) and *Thomas* (DDR-833) got into a gun duel with eight PC-type North Korean patrol craft. One was set afire; direct hits were obtained on four; and three nested together were cut adrift. No American ships were hit.

---

**Ship's Log: Monday 11 September 1950** En route with USS BADOENG STRAIT and USS HENDERSON to Sasebo, Japan, to replenish fuel, ammunition, and stores.

---

Hardly had we settled down from the excitement of one event when another event of even greater magnitude loomed on the horizon. Reliable rumors hinted that we were getting ready to take part in the first full-scale amphibious landing since World War II. These rumors said the landing would take place at Inchon.

# 6   IN TO INCHON

*September 12–22, 1950*

---

**Ship's Log: Tuesday 12 September 1950** 0446 En route from Sasebo, Japan, to Inchon, Korea. Other units included are USS TOLEDO (CA-133), HMS KENYA, HMS JAMAICA, USS MANSFIELD (DD-728), USS DE HAVEN (DD-727), USS SWENSON (DD-729), USS COLLETT (DD-730), USS GURKE (DD-783), USS HENDERSON (DD-785).

---

General MacArthur conceived the idea for a decisive counterstroke that would cut off the enemy advance and force them to withdraw. It would be a brilliant but risky amphibious landing directed at the Inchon-Seoul region, the strategic solar plexus of Korea.

The venture was designated Operation Chromite. D-day was set for September 15, 1950.

Beginning at D-day minus 10, a series of diversionary moves was made to mislead the Communists. On the east coast, the cruiser *Helena* and destroyers *Brush* and *Maddox* shot up shipping and trenches below Yongdok. At Pusan, marines were given a not-so-secret lecture on the hydrography of Kunsan, a port city about halfway up the west coast, knowing full well that word would filter back to the North Koreans. Kunsan was a credible place to establish a beachhead.

The USS *Badoeng Strait,* the British carrier HMS *Triumph,* and four destroyers were a key part of this feint. Sortie after sortie of U.S. Marine and British planes devastated railroad bridges, rolling stock, and electrical transformer stations. A British cruiser and two British destroyers moved in close to shore to begin bombardment of potential landing sites.

Operation Chromite placed a particularly heavy load on the navy. Total strength amounted to some 230 ships of all shapes and sizes. Except for a few gunnery ships held back to support the perimeter, it included all combatant units available in the Far East. Just to carry the troops to battle would require more than 120 amphibious vessels, while the rest of the ships were involved in gunfire, air support, screening, minesweeping, and a myriad of other duties.

Most remarkable was the speed with which preparations were carried out. From the time the final operational orders were issued on September 2, the largest fleet since World War II was assembled. Yet despite the pressures under which the operation was carried out, there were few mistakes.

---

**Ship's Log: Wednesday 13 September 1950**  0916 Formed column led by USS MANSFIELD and proceeded up Flying Fish Channel toward Inchon, Korea. 1145 Sighted 12 mines abeam to port 1,000 yards. Destroyed mines with small arms. 1300 Commenced firing on targets, primarily gun emplacements. 1415 Received counter battery fire from Wolmi Do. Returned fire. Received no damage. A total of 25 splashes were observed in the immediate vicinity of which five were close aboard. Expended 170 rounds of 5" AAC, 6 rounds of 5" common, and 320 rounds of 40MM projectiles.

---

Inchon was the port city for Seoul, capital of South Korea. An amphibious landing there would be fraught with difficulty. For one thing, the approach to the city was through a narrow and tortuous channel that restricted the movement of shipping for the last thirty-four miles of the approach. For another, the harbor was cursed with extraordinarily high tides, rising and falling as much as twenty-eight

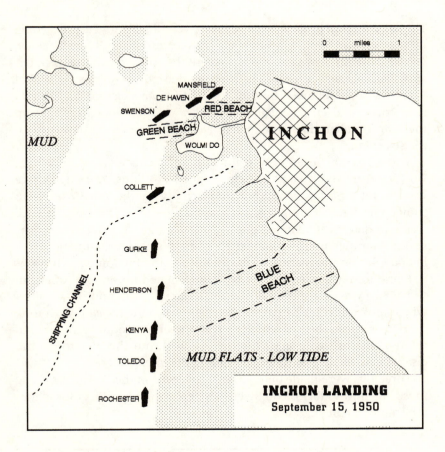

feet twice daily. Only at high tide could a landing be negotiated; at low tide the area was nothing but mud flats.

Only two beaches were suitable for landing—Blue Beach on the southern edge of the city and Red Beach four miles away on the western shore. Piers and seawalls lined the beaches, and their assault would require scaling ladders.

An island called Wolmi Do presided over the inner harbor and split the two landing beaches. Connected by a causeway to the mainland, it sat there like a cork in a bottle. The island was heavily fortified and would have to be neutralized before an amphibious landing could successfully take place. That job fell to the U.S. Marines.

The operation would have to be carried out in full daylight, thereby eliminating the possibility of surprise.

          *   *   *

The softening-up process began with six veteran destroyers proceeding up the narrow channel in single file—the *Mansfield, De Haven, Swenson, Collett, Gurke,* and *Henderson.* These were the so-called sitting duck destroyers, intended to draw fire from hidden gun positions on Wolmi Do. They were followed by the U.S. cruisers *Rochester* and *Toledo* and two British cruisers, the *Jamaica* and *Kenya.* The *Borland* brought up the rear. Combat air patrol circled overhead. The weather was clear, the sea calm.

The *Gurke* anchored only eight hundred yards away from Wolmi Do, the other destroyers in their assigned positions. Although there was boat traffic in the harbor and activity in the city, Wolmi Do showed no signs of life. Lookouts scanned the island in fearful silence trying to detect the telltale signs of concealed gun emplacements. For several minutes nothing happened, then destroyers commenced deliberate fire on the island's fortifications and the Inchon waterfront.

Some minutes later, enemy batteries opened up on the American ships. Fire was concentrated on the *Swenson, Collett,* and *Gurke,* all of which took direct hits. Heaviest damage was to the *Collett,* which took four 75-mm hits, one of which pierced the engineroom and fractured a low-pressure steam line. Another plowed into the plot room and disabled the ship's computer, wounding five men.

Three hits were made on the *Gurke,* and one on the *Swenson.* Among those killed was LTJG David Swenson, nephew of the officer for whom the ship was named.

---

**Ship's Log: Thursday 14 September 1950**   0830 Hove to in company with Task Group 90.6 paying tribute to LTJG Swenson, USN, killed aboard USS SWENSON (DD-729). 1256 Commenced firing on targets in Inchon area. Expended 156 rounds of 5″ AAC and 950 rounds of 40MM.

---

Bombardment of Wolmi Do resumed. From ten in the morning until four in the afternoon six destroyers pulverized the island with shellfire, expending some seventeen hundred rounds of 5-inch ammunition. This time, not a shot was heard in retaliation from the island's defenses. The gunfire appeared to have done the job. Shrouded in smoke, it was now ready for capture by the marines.

For their gallantry, all six ships received the Navy Unit Commendation and the Korean Presidential Unit Citation. We earned our second battle star.

The USS *Missouri* (BB-63) arrived in Korean waters late in the evening of September 14 after dodging several typhoons, having made a full-speed run from the East Coast of the United States. Adm. A. E. Smith, commander of Task Force 95, wrote, "When I was informed that the *Missouri* would join Task Force 95, I planned to use her, the *Helena*, and several destroyers as a diversionary effort on the east coast, on the same day as the initial marine landings on the west coast at Inchon."[1]

The Mighty Mo, as she was affectionately known, celebrated her arrival by firing fifty rounds of 16-inch fire at a bridge near Samchok, using a helicopter spot. The results were excellent.

---

**Ship's Log: Friday 15 September 1950** 0135 USS SOUTHER-LAND joined column to replace USS COLLETT damaged during action on 13 September. 0540 Commenced firing pre-arranged fire on Inchon area. 0635 First landing wave arrived on Wolmi Do. 0647 Second landing wave arrived on beach. 0651 Third landing wave arrived on beach. 1823 assigned call fire mission various targets. Expended 598 rounds 5" AAC, 1281 rounds 40MM projectiles.

---

Shortly after midnight, the attack force started up the channel, navigating by radar. Again, destroyers led the way, followed by an LSD, three tank-loaded LSUs, and the fast transports *Bass*, *Diachenko*, and *Wantuck*. Cruisers brought up the rear, now joined by the command ship *Mount McKinley*.

North of Wolmi Do, *Mansfield*, *Swenson*, and *De Haven* concentrated their preinvasion bombardment on the northern shore of Inchon. The *Collett*, *Gurke*, and *Henderson* bombarded the southern shore of Inchon. Cruisers concentrated on the two landing beaches. Marine aircraft bombed, strafed, and rocketed the landing area. Fifteen minutes before landing time, three rocket ships, each with a thousand 5-inch spin-stabilized rockets, let go.

At 6:28 A.M. the bombardment group ceased fire to permit the landing parties to hit the beaches. The first troops moved ashore at 6:33 in a scene of smoke, dust, and devastation. They met negligible resistance.

The ships and planes continued to provide fire support throughout the day as additional troops and supplies were put ashore. By day's end the basic objective was accomplished. Casualties were relatively light—222 killed or wounded—a modest price for such an important objective.

Most of the marines who landed at Inchon were reservists like my friend Hershall Burns. Seventeen years old, he had been called up, organized, and shipped into action in less than three months. Had the enemy been more strongly garrisoned, such a shoestring operation could have been costly in terms of U.S. lives and material.

The Communists seem to have followed Mao Tse-tung's famous dictum:

Enemy advances, we retreat.
Enemy halts, we harass.
Enemy tires, we attack.
Enemy retreats, we pursue.

---

**Ship's Log: Saturday 16 September 1950**  1338 Commenced firing as directed by shore fire control party. 2020 Commenced night illumination at direction of shore fire control party.

---

D-day plus 1. As troops moved inland, they began to encounter stiffer resistance. Although North Koreans seemed willing to abandon Inchon, their resistance was hardening around Kimpo Airfield and the approaches to Seoul. This created an increasing need for air and artillery support.

The process went like this: We took directions from a shore fire control party (SFCP), also known as an artillery spotter or forward observer. The SFCP would call in certain map coordinates, which our guys would crank into the ship's computer. Then we'd let go a single salvo, known as a "ranging round." Based on where that salvo hit, the SFCP would call in corrections, say, "Up 150, right 100." Then we'd loose another salvo. More corrections if needed. As soon as we had zeroed in on the objective, he'd call for rapid fire. The effect of 5-inch rapid fire was devastating.

Against tanks, artillery positions, rolling stock, and similar objects we fired mostly antiaircraft common (AAC). The projectiles weighed fifty-four pounds each and carried a timed fuse mechanism set automatically from commands sent by the ship's main computer. Occasionally, the ground controller might call for a starshell to light the target area.

The destroyer *Southerland* was slightly damaged by counterbattery fire.

---

**Ship's Log: Sunday 17 September 1950**   0600 Completed firing night illumination having expended 50 rounds of 5" starshells. 0604 Exercised general quarters due to "Flash Red–Control Yellow." 0656 Commenced firing as directed by shore fire control party on enemy troops. 2216 Replenished ammunition from USS NEWELL (AKL-14) having received 672 rounds of 5" AAC.

---

In a surprise dawn attack, two Russian-built Yak aircraft attacked the U.S. cruiser *Rochester* and the British cruiser *Jamaica*. One 100-pound bomb bounced off the *Rochester*'s aircraft crane and failed to explode, and seven others were near misses. On board the *Jamaica*, one man was killed by strafing. One of the Yaks was shot down by the British cruiser. The other managed to get away.

On land, the North Koreans reacted vigorously with strong counterattacks. Destroyers and cruisers continued to provide artillery support for the marine troops pushing eastward along the Seoul highway. By nightfall, the 5th Marines occupied the high ground east of Kimpo field and had pushed troops out onto the landing area itself.

Meanwhile, the 1st Marines, pushing eastward against stubborn opposition, gained possession of a commanding hill overlooking Sosa, the halfway mark between Inchon and Seoul. They received significant help from carrier aircraft and naval guns.

---

**Ship's Log: Monday 18 September 1950**   Replenished from HMS WAVE KNIGHT. Assigned call fire duty.

---

During the night, we refueled from the HMS *Wave Knight*, a British oiler that was manned by a Chinese crew. This was our first experience in being resupplied from a British ship. It bordered on being a comedy of errors. First off, the color coding on their fuel lines was different from that on American oilers; it took us a while to figure out which hose went to which fitting.

Second, the Brits weren't as keen on keeping records as we were. The fun started when our "Oil King," F. J. "Skip" Rauscher, tried to get a report on how much fuel we'd taken aboard. They didn't seem to know.

After much haggling back and forth, Lieutenant Stubblefield, our engineering officer, took matters into his own hands. He came up to CIC to call over to the British tanker on the radio telephone. Instead of stiff military protocol, he received a casual reply.

"Oh, I don't know, mate. Wadayou make of it?"

Stubblefield wasn't used to this lackadaisical approach. He tried again, "I need a report on how much fuel we took. Surely, you have a record of it. I need a number to write in my report."

"Write down whatever number you want," the Brit shot back.

"Let me speak to your supply officer," Stubblefield demanded.

"I *am* the supply officer, Mate."

"Then why can't you give me a report?" Stubblefield doggedly insisted.

Exasperated by now, the Brit lectured the American. "Mate, the way I look at it, we're out here to supply the fleet with fuel. We're doing our job, and you've got your bloody fuel. What difference does it make whether you took 50,000 pounds or 150,000 pounds? It all comes out of the same bloody tanks and goes to fight the same bloody war, doesn't it? Now if you need to write down a number just to satisfy some twit behind a desk somewhere, then you jolly well write down whatever number you want. But don't bother me with your silly accounting problems."

---

**Ship's Log: Tuesday 19 September 1950**   1615 This ship escorting USS MISSOURI up Flying Fish Channel to assigned anchorage. 2010 Conducting sonar sweep.

---

By now, the advancing troops had outranged the destroyers' guns. While the cruisers with their longer-range 8-inch guns continued supporting the fighting around Sosa, we shifted our gunfire to support troops engaged in mopping up on the Kimpo peninsula, north of Inchon.

Meanwhile, a tricky rescue operation was taking place over on the east coast of Korea. Ten miles north of Pohang, a troop-laden ROK LST had run aground, broached, and couldn't be refloated. It became necessary to send in another LST to evacuate the troops. The sea was rough. In the midst of the evacuation, the enemy directed heavy mortar and machine-gun fire at the operation.

The USS *Brush* (DD-745) moved in to a thousand yards off the beach to provide fire support. For nearly two hours *Brush* laid down a heavy barrage of 40-mm and 5-inch gunfire while loading operations were completed. More than one hundred wounded were aboard the rescue vessel, but because of the roughness of the sea it was impossible to render medical assistance.

---

**Ship's Log: Wednesday 20 September 1950** Anchored in Inchon Ko, Korea, in company with USS MISSOURI.

---

The battleship *Missouri* moved up the main channel as far as possible to a berth where her big 16-inch guns could interdict the Seoul-Wonsan road, some twenty-eight miles away. However, the battle front was moving so fast that the *Missouri*'s efforts were largely unneeded. The Mighty Mo was able to get off only eleven shots before the advancing troops had outranged even her big guns.

Despite close air support by planes from the *Sicily* and *Badoeng Strait*, the advance on Seoul itself was stiffening and becoming costly. By nightfall, though, the 5th Marines had reached within a mile and a half of the capital city and were occupying the ridges that guarded its western border.

At this point, a dispute arose between marine major general O. P. Smith and army major general E. A. "Ned" Almond, MacArthur's lackey. Almond told Smith that he strongly desired to deliver Seoul into MacArthur's hands on September 25, which would be exactly three months after the date of the North Korean invasion. He insisted that the marines should adhere to that timetable. Smith, on the other hand, was less interested in symbolism than he was in getting the job done right. He said he did not desire to put his troops on a timetable dictated by public relations. The capture of Seoul was likely to be bloody, house-to-house, street-by-street fighting, and his troops were already exhausted from constant fighting since Inchon. Smith wanted to move west around Seoul, then strike from the north—a move that would cut off reinforcements from North Korea.

Almond was not persuaded. He bluntly told Smith if the marines did not move decisively within twenty-four hours, he would turn the

Seoul capture over to the army's 7th Division. Smith was furious at the threat, most of all that Almond thought good marines had to be goaded into fighting. Against his professional judgment, Smith launched a frontal assault that practically demolished the South Korean capital. Had he been allowed to attack from the north such destruction would have been unlikely—all for the sake of stroking MacArthur's insatiable ego.

---

**Ship's Log: Thursday 21 September 1950**    Anchored Inchon, Korea, in air defense station.

---

Dear Anna: By now you will have read about our surprise landing at Inchon. It appears as if MacArthur's bold gamble has paid off handsomely. The North Korean army, having come so close to triumph, now finds itself facing irredeemable disaster. With their main forces concentrated 140 miles to the southeast and already suffering from serious supply problems, the invaders now find their supply spigot turned off. The U.N. occupation of Inchon and Seoul has brought a halt to the Reds' southern campaign and they are now forced to pull back all available resources to the defense of their homeland. Hope this brings me home soon.    Love, Rusty

---

**Ship's Log: Friday 22 September 1950**    Anchored in Flying Fish Channel, Inchon, Korea.

---

No targets remained within gunnery range. Most gunnery ships had departed Inchon and were busily engaged elsewhere. Remaining naval strength was concentrated on protecting the movement of troops and supplies into Inchon, supplying logistic support of the fleet, and providing air defense for escort carriers offshore. Air operations continued at a high pitch.

Meanwhile, buoyed by the success at Inchon, MacArthur's fertile mind was already cooking up another scheme. This scheme was so bold that he felt confident enough to tell his aides it would end all organized resistance by Thanksgiving and "get the troops home by Christmas."

*September 24–October 9, 1950*

---

**Ship's Log: Sunday 24 September 1950**   0710 Alongside USS HELENA (CA-75) to transfer mail and passengers. 1034 Commenced screening USS WORCESTER to seaward while she gave fire support for friendly ground forces in vicinity of Chongha, South Korea. 1700 Sighted two drifting mines; destroyed by 30 Cal M-1 rifle fire.

---

A mine is a fearsome thing. Not only that, it's ugly to look at. Packing five hundred pounds of TNT, a mine can blow a twenty-foot hole in the hull of a destroyer.

As early as July 1950, the North Koreans had begun a massive minelaying campaign designed to threaten UN control of the sea. Unbeknownst to U.S. intelligence sources, shipments of mines were rolling southward down the east coast railway from Vladivostok. Soviet technicians were conducting mine schools for their North Korean friends at Wonsan, on the east coast, and at Chinnampo, on the west.

Only later was it learned that the Soviet naval personnel who had been assigned to North Korea had achieved considerable success not only in teaching mine warfare to the North Koreans but in assembling magnetic mines, planning the minefields, and supervising their planting. Barges towed by motorized sampans were used for minelayers. Local labor was used to load the barges and to roll the mines off the stern.

The nasty thing about mines is that they're so damned hard to detect. Too often, your first indication of their presence is a crippling explosion.

There was no way of knowing how many thousands of mines had been laid—or of which types. Additional minesweepers would be long in arriving. Yet the battle had to go on. For the moment, the most we could do was increase our vigilance and hope for the best.

---

**Ship's Log: Monday 25 September 1950**   0023 Left formation for patrol duty along eastern coast of Korea. 0305 Fired at vehicles with lights moving on shore. 0600 Boarding party investigated small fishing boat dead in water. 1137 En route to Chong Jon, Korea, to investigate four freighters anchored there. 1322 Fired on boxcars on shore.

---

Although fighting remained intensive in the dark and twisted streets of Seoul and showed no sign of slackening off, General Almond issued a statement to the press stating that Seoul had been liberated. MacArthur followed with his own statement: "Three months to the day after the North Koreans launched their surprise attack . . . the combat troops of X Corps recaptured the capital city of Seoul."[1]

That was news to the marines fighting in Seoul. For despite Mac-Arthur's presumptuous claim, the fighting there would continue for another three days.

Dear Anna: We spend much of our time chasing down and passing out warning leaflets to fishing boats. In what seems to me to be one of the crueler aspects of the war, the UN has decided to extend its blockade of the North Korean coast to include fishing boats offshore. Since fish is one of the main staples of their diet, this ban could seriously impact their food supply. I guess the idea is to starve them into submission.   As ever, Rusty

---

**Ship's Log: Tuesday 26 September 1950**   Steaming on blockade patrol in company with USS BRUSH (DD-745) and USS MADDOX (DD-731). 1219 BRUSH received external explosion underwater port side frame 72, presumed to be drifting mine. 1335 Maneuvered alongside BRUSH to render assistance and rescue survivors.

---

At 11:00 A.M. the *Brush* moved in close to shore at Tanchon to investigate some boxcars on a railroad siding. These turned out to be the same boxcars that we had shot up the day before. The *Brush* then proceeded on down the coast in a southwesterly direction.

At 12:19 the *Brush* was rocked by a tremendous explosion on her port side about a third of the distance back from the bow. The force of the explosion broke the ship's keel, disabled her steering control, and blew out all electrical power on the bridge. Smoke and fumes were so intense in the pilot house that all personnel were forced to leave that area. Steering control was restored in secondary conn, located in the aft part of the ship. The captain commenced pumping fuel and water to correct a rapidly developing port list that could have capsized the vessel. Preliminary estimates indicated thirteen men missing and thirty-three injured as a result of the explosion. A plane from Patrol Squadron 6 reported sighting three men in the water; the plane dropped two life rafts and reported that one man was seen boarding a life raft.

The blast occurred slightly forward of midships about ten feet below the waterline on the port side, undoubtedly caused by an anchored mine. It left a hole some forty-five feet long and twenty-four feet high that extended vertically from the waterline to the keel. Number one fireroom and eighteen other compartments were flooded.

The *Maddox* came alongside at 2:00 P.M. to transfer the medical officer and plasma. After it was determined that the *Brush* was no longer sinking, the *Maddox* left to try to recover survivors. An hour later *Maddox* rescued one survivor who had swam to nearby Keito Island. The search continued throughout the night. No other survivors were seen.

In the final tally, casualties were eleven dead, thirty-two injured, and three missing.

---

**Ship's Log: Wednesday 27 September 1950** Continued search for men reported overboard. 1040 USS THOMAS reported another man had been found in good condition aboard life raft near the scene. 1246 Provided escort for USS BRUSH; speed reduced to 4 knots because of increased flooding.

---

Controversy arose almost immediately. There were several unanswered questions about the *Brush*'s actions following her mining: (1) Why didn't ComDesDiv 92 report *Brush*'s troubles to any superior until 1:40 P.M.? Fifty valuable minutes were lost there. (2) After the explosion, why didn't *Brush* determine whether any men had fallen overboard? The only sightings were by patrol planes. (3) Why didn't ComDesDiv 92 undertake direct aid to water survivors until early evening? More timely action might have rescued all three men sighted by the patrol planes, not just one.

Investigators concluded that *Brush*'s attitude toward recovering water survivors had only two possible explanations. Either she did not know that any men had gone overboard, or she considered herself to be in such imminent danger of sinking that saving the ship took priority over saving the crew.

**Ship's Log: Thursday 28 September 1950**  Providing escort for USS BRUSH en route to Sasebo, Japan, speed 4 knots. 1310 Passed Futagami Shima light abeam to port, distance 7 miles. 1330 Changed course to rejoin Task Group off east coast of Korea.

By now, the fighting in Seoul had slackened enough for General MacArthur to plan a triumphal return to that city. Ever the showman, he insisted on nothing less than a full-scale motorcade from Kimpo Airfield. The only problem was there were no bridges over the Han River, which he would have to cross to get into the city. A helicopter would not do, said his aides. Instructions were short and unambiguous: if no bridge exists, build one!

Accordingly, it fell to the marines—still mopping up around the city—to build a bridge for MacArthur. And they had only twenty-four hours to do it. Pontoons, rafts, and bridging materials were scrounged from all over the area, and by midnight MacArthur had his bridge.

The Korean *YMS-509* was mined off Yongdok, with twenty-six killed or missing and five wounded.

**Ship's Log: Friday 29 September 1950**  0600 Left formation for blockade and interdiction gunfire. 1731 Received request for 20 rounds at enemy troops attempting to cross river.

MacArthur, as anticipated, made a triumphal return to Seoul, accompanied by an adoring press. Even though the vaunted motorcade only consisted of one Chevrolet sedan, four staff cars, and a couple dozen jeeps filled with reporters, the press didn't seem to mind. They gloried in the photo opportunities presented by the general as he handed the now-destroyed city over to Pres. Syngman Rhee at the shattered and fire-blackened National Capitol building. "Mr. President," he said, "my officers and I will now resume our military duties and leave you and your government to the discharge of the civil responsibility."

Syngman Rhee, for his part, shook MacArthur's hand, tearfully saying, "We admire you. We love you as the savior of our race."

Notably absent from the ceremony were the marine troops who had done the bulk of the fighting. Except for the presence of General

Smith and two of his subordinates, Generals Craig and Puller, the marine troops were directed to keep out of sight. Not even the honor guard included any marines; it consisted entirely of spit-and-polish army MPs flown up from Tokyo for the occasion. Understandably, the marines felt slighted.

---

**Ship's Log: Saturday 30 September 1950**   1220 Urgent dispatch directed MANSFIELD and this ship to proceed at best speed possible to Latitude 38-45N, Longitude 128-15E to assist B-26 aircraft reported down at that point. 1547 Explosion portside forward on MANSFIELD; bow of MANSFIELD severed and sinking.

---

Four days after the *Brush*'s encounter, it was the *Mansfield*'s turn to hit a mine. As she approached Chosen Do to search for a downed B-26 aircraft, radio contact was established with a search-and-rescue (SAR) plane that was already on the scene:

Mansfield, SAR1: We are not quite sure of our position in reference to vicinity of downed bird. We are about one mile north of the point. Is that correct? Over.
SAR1, Mansfield: That is correct.
Mansfield, SAR1: Have you had any luck locating downed bird?
SAR1, Mansfield: Negative.

A second plane was now on the scene, a B-17 with a rescue boat.

Mansfield, SAR2: Plane is reported to have exploded upon contact with sea.
SAR2, Mansfield: Roger. What is your position?
Mansfield, SAR2: I am bearing 285, 5 miles from you. Do you have me in sight?
SAR2, Mansfield: Affirmative. Can you make another pass over the wreckage? It has been reported approximately 500 yards east of Toi Do.
Mansfield, SAR1: I am going down to 500 feet and have a look at the coast near the point. Is that correct?
SAR1, Mansfield: That is correct. Will you look in the point also?

The sound of machine-gun fire could be clearly heard on the ship.

Mansfield, SAR2: They were throwing some lead in there. Pretty good sign of wreckage there.
SAR1, Mansfield: Request approximate location.

Mansfield, SAR1: Halfway between the point and the point due south on the peninsula.

SAR2, Mansfield: We are almost directly over the wreckage now.

Mansfield, SAR 2: Submerged reef, southern and northeastern entrance to bay. Also possible submerged mines at entrance to smaller bay. The wreckage is 500 yards east of the island with the solitary tree on top.

The *Mansfield* had stopped engines at 3:35 P.M., and at 3:36 both engines were backed to bring the ship's way off at the point twenty-two yards from the reported wreckage in twelve fathoms of water. Some objects were now visible in the cove near the beach—a raft of logs about three thousand yards to port, some net buoys about three thousand yards ahead. At 3:39 a sonar contact was identified as a shoal called Chu Rai. No sign of the suspected wreckage was seen by the many lookouts and officers on the bridge of the *Mansfield*. Neither was anything seen in the water near the ship. The main lookout, recently stationed in the eyes of the ship with rifle and binoculars, reported nothing.

SAR2, Mansfield: Can you positively identify debris in water as wreckage of plane?

Mansfield, SAR2: Negative. Objects appear to be box and life preserver.

SAR2, Mansfield: Making another pass to see if I can spot wreckage visually.

Suddenly, a high-order explosion was seen and heard under the bow of the ship. A geyser of water rose up on the port side to the height of the gun director.

SAR2, Mansfield: We have hit a mine! Damage unknown.

Mansfield, SAR2: Roger, we will stand by to give you assistance.

Although many of the crew were temporarily stunned by the detonation, the commanding officer backed both engines full. The ship was steered while backing through the same water she had entered. The engineering officer promptly left his station at the repair control and rushed forward to begin damage control and rescue injured personnel.

The bow was clearly observed to be sinking as soon as the explosion subsided. The damage control party's first efforts were to remove the wounded and shocked, and then to determine the extent of the damage. The party penetrated the smoke and debris forward on the main deck and found that the first platform deck was still above water but badly holed in the chief's quarters. Shoring was immediately begun on all decks.

The *Mansfield* immediately backed clear of the area to the vicinity of the *Swenson,* a distance of about four miles. The engines were stopped and an account made of the casualties and damage. An all-hands muster on abandon ship stations confirmed the preliminary count: twenty-eight injured but none missing or dead. The fact that not a man was dead or missing was considered a miracle.

About 9:00 P.M., nine of the most seriously wounded were transferred to the *Helena* for further surgical treatment.

At 10:45, the *Mansfield* got underway for Sasebo with the *Samuel N. Moore* acting as escort. She would be outfitted with a temporary bow and proceed across the vast Pacific for permanent repairs.

---

**Ship's Log: Sunday 1 October 1950**   1935 Commenced firing diversionary mission while USS PERCH carried out commando operations.

---

In a stern warning against U.S. ambitions in Korea, Communist China's premier, Chou En-lai, observed that his government would not tolerate the crossing of the 38th parallel and "would not stand aside" if American troops crossed the 38th parallel. In a Peking radio broadcast, he said that his nation would not "supinely tolerate seeing their neighbors being savagely invaded by imperialists." The broadcast, which was monitored in Tokyo, contained a thinly veiled threat that the Chinese people were "deeply interested" in the progress of events in Korea.

MacArthur dismissed Premier Chou's admonition as empty talk. But other Western observers did not take it so lightly. They felt that China had great anxieties about Western intentions and would not tolerate seeing her neighbor fall, fearing that Allied occupation of all of Korea would inevitably lead to MacArthur's further predations across the border into Manchuria.

The USS *Magpie* (AMS-418), recently arrived from Guam, hit a mine, blew up, and sank with the loss of twenty-one of a crew of thirty-three. The loss of the *Magpie,* combined with heavy damage and personnel casualties to four other ships—all from enemy mines—made this an extremely costly week for UN naval forces.

---

**Ship's Log: Monday 2 October 1950** In company with MAD-
DOX, THOMAS, and PERCH in Task Unit 96.9.7. 1245 Burial services held by Royal Marines on PERCH.

---

Dear Anna: I witnessed my first burial at sea today. Burial at sea is sad
because it is so casual, brutal, beautiful, and final. When we're near a
port, the dead man is put in the refrigerator room until his body can
be transferred to the proper authorities. At sea, loving hands prepare
him for burial. Canvas from the boatswain's locker is cut and sewn
shut at the bottom. Two 5-inch shells weighing 54 pounds each are
put inside the canvas to make the body sink. The boatswain, or someone he appoints, sews the body into the canvas. The canvas bag is
then placed on the side of the ship at the fantail. A prayer is said, taps
are blown, and a gun salute fired. The board on which the man rested
is tilted until the body goes feet first into the sea, leaving only the covering flag. Many tears fell as the deceased started the long fall to the
bottomless deep on a ride that lasts forever, a most final and solemn
act. Keep me ever in your prayers. Rusty[2]

---

**Ship's Log: Tuesday 3 October 1950** 0200 Rendezvoused with
USS WORCESTER (CA-144). 0633 Detached to patrol area between
40-0N and 40-51N.

---

Chou En-lai was reported by the Indian ambassador at Peking
as stating that if non-Korean troops crossed the 38th parallel the Chinese would enter the war. He voiced no objection to South Koreans
crossing the parallel; however, if foreign troops—the Americans, Aus-
tralians, or British—crossed over and entered North Korean territory,
then he said that China would enter the war on the side of North Korea.

This thunder out of China fell on deaf ears in MacArthur's headquarters. Considering it a bluff, MacArthur reiterated his goal of uni-
fying all of Korea by force of arms and ensuring its stability by territo-
rial occupation.

**Ship's Log: Thursday 5 October 1950**  Steaming with USS MADDOX (DD-731), USS DE HAVEN (DD-727), USS THOMAS (DDR-833), and USS WORCESTER (CA-144). 1315 Relieved USS SWENSON (DD-729) on fire support station.

Dear Rusty: I guess President Truman is not the only person given to making reckless statements. It's an infectious disease. Today the Air Force suspended one of its top generals for offering to attack Russia's atom bomb centers. Major General Orvil A. Anderson, commandant of the Air War College, made a speech in Montgomery, Alabama, in which he said, "Give me the order to do it and I can break up Russia's five A-bomb plants in a week. And when I went up to Christ, I think I could explain to him that I had saved civilization."

This talk about atom bombs scares me; I hope this so-called "police action" in Korea doesn't end up getting us into a worldwide nuclear war.  Anna

**Ship's Log: Friday 6 October 1950**  0700 Relieved of fire support duty by USS MADDOX.

Unlike the battlewagons, aircraft carriers, and other floating hotels, we didn't have a barbershop. Nor did we have any professional barbers. A couple of entrepreneurial types who had their own barbering equipment were allowed to set up shop in whatever vacant space they could find to ply their trade. The rules were fifty cents a head, first come, first served, and no distinction as to rank.

Lt. C. D. "Chuck" Dvorcek, the *Borland*'s gunnery officer, was in the seat of honor when I got there. Three or four other guys were sitting around waiting their turns, noses buried in paperback novels.

Dvorcek was a big, muscular, blond-haired, slab-sided Bohemian of thirty-two, who had been a star football player at Texas A&M in 1940. His battered countenance clearly revealed the effects of having played too many quarters without a face mask. Though extremely well liked by his crew, Dvorcek was thought to be a little vain with regard to his muscular conditioning.

When he finished in the chair, Dvorcek flexed his muscles as he put his shirt back on. He started to leave.

Floyd Manders whispered to me, "Watch this." There was a twinkle in his eye. In a stage whisper just loud enough for the gunnery officer to hear, Manders exclaimed, "My, my, he sure is getting fat, isn't he?"

Dvorcek wheeled around and bellowed so loud he nearly shattered our eardrums, "Who the hell's getting fat!"

None of us dared laugh.

---

**Ship's Log: Saturday–Monday 7–9 October 1950**   Steaming as before on call fire support duty.

---

Shorty Hall's pride and joy was his personal coffee mug. It was absolutely the grungiest thing anyone had ever seen, but he never allowed it to be washed. Lord knows how many years it had taken for it to acquire its current patina. Shorty claimed, "Coffee doesn't really begin to taste good until the cup has built up a good 'cake' in it."

That day when Shorty reached for his cup, he barely recognized it. The mug was now bright and shiny and pristine. He stared at it for a moment as if unable to believe his eyes, then he let out a bloodcurdling yell: "Who in the goddamn hell washed my cup?"

"I did, sir," piped up a young seaman apprentice. "I thought you would want it cleaned." The kid had used Ajax cleanser, steel wool, and plenty of elbow grease to cut through the accumulation of stains. Obviously he thought he had done something to be proud of.

Shorty was not pleased. "Any goddamn idiot stupid enough to wash a goddamn coffee cup oughta have his goddamn head shot off!" With that, Shorty heaved the offending object over the side as far as he could throw it.

# 8    ON TO WONSAN

*October 10–26, 1950*

---

**Ship's Log: Tuesday 10 October 1950**    Steaming east coast Korea. Other ships include USS ROCHESTER (CA-124), USS MADDOX (DD-731), and USS THOMAS (DDR-833).

---

MacArthur's triumphal success with the Inchon landing had changed the outlook of the Korean War. Unification of the entire peninsula seemed imminently possible.

Now seeking to administer the coup de grace, MacArthur authorized a second assault landing to take place at Wonsan on Korea's eastern shore, some one hundred miles northeast of Seoul. The two armies would link up and encircle the enemy in a giant pincerlike maneuver. Thus trapped, the North Korean army would be forced to surrender or face annihilation.

The city of Wonsan occupied one of the most important strategic positions on the east coast of Korea. The harbor was large—nearly three hundred square miles—and relatively protected from storms. The city was the hub of both north-south and east-west rail routes. Moreover, it was the locus of highway communications. As an added bonus the city boasted an excellent airfield on the harbor island of Kalma Pando, originally developed as a Japanese naval air station.

The Wonsan operation was christened Operation Tailboard. D-day was set for October 20. That left even less time for planning than had been available for Inchon.

A small coastal plain in the delta of the Namdae River east of the city provided sufficient area for an amphibious landing. The three-mile-wide mouth of the harbor was guarded by the sentinel islands of Yo Do on the left, Ung Do on the right, and Sin Do, where a former Japanese fortress had been located, almost three miles dead ahead.

The harbor would have to be swept clear of mines before an amphibious landing could possibly take place. Shortly after sunrise, the minesweeping group began its work clearing the mines. Clearing an approach to the beaches would involve sweeping a thirty-mile lane—an area of more than fifty square miles. Ten days were allotted to do the job.

The minesweepers towed underwater devices called paravanes that "sweep" out from the sides of the ship and cut the anchor cables from the moored mines. The mines float to the surface where they can be exploded by gunfire.

By late afternoon, good progress had been made. Eighteen mines had been destroyed. Suddenly the voice of the helicopter pilot crackled over the radio: "One mine line directly ahead of *Pledge*. . . . Another line just beyond that. . . . Another. . . ." By the time he was through, he had reported five lines of mines directly ahead of the sweepers.

That disheartening discovery canceled out a whole day's work and raised the dire possibility that the sweep could not be accomplished within the allotted time. The sweepers turned back and filed out of the swept channel to anchor in safe waters while the planners plotted a new strategy.

---

**Ship's Log: Wednesday 11 October 1950**   1045 Relieved SWENSON on fire support station at entrance to swept channel, Wonsan, Korea.

---

In the light of the discouraging discovery the day before, attention now focused on clearing an alternate channel. Overhead, a slow-flying PBM seaplane circled, seeking out mine locations that were then plotted and communicated to the forces below. Navy frogmen were sent in to scout for evidence of controlled minefields. These were minefields that could be turned on and off electrically—turned off to allow friendly ships to pass; turned on to prevent hostile ships from coming through. The immediate danger, of course, was that if there were such controlled minefields, the North Koreans might be clever enough to turn them off while the minesweepers were doing their work—thus creating a false sense of security—then turn them back on when the invasion fleet sought to enter the harbor.

The day's sweeping went well. A lane was cleared to within four miles of the entrance islands.

---

**Ship's Log: Thursday 12 October 1950**   On fire support station, Wonsan, Korea.

---

A novel attempt at "countermining" was ordered. Carrier planes armed with 1,000-pound bombs flew in to bomb a five-mile stretch of harbor. The idea was that the explosions would blast loose or destroy enemy mines in their path. Although spectacular in the amount of water thrown up, the results were only moderately encouraging.

After the bombing, three minesweepers—the *Pirate, Pledge,* and *Incredible*—entered unswept waters at 11:12 A.M. to begin normal sweep operations. As they swung left around Yo Do, things began to happen. Two mines popped to the surface, their cables severed by the *Pirate*'s sweeping gear. Four more mines were cut and bobbed to the surface fifty yards apart. The *Pledge,* maneuvering through mines already cut by the *Pirate,* swept three more. The *Incredible,* still in formation, cut still another four.

Disaster struck. At 12:09 the *Pirate*'s stern rose high from the water, then sank back into a boiling sea of muddy spray. A mine had exploded directly beneath, breaking her main deck into two parts. Within four minutes she capsized and sank.

The *Pledge,* second ship in line, slowed, stopped, cut loose her gear, and lowered a boat to pick up survivors. Caught in an awkward position, she came under fire from previously undetected batteries on Sin Do, three miles inside the harbor. Counterbattery fire was returned by the *Pledge* and the destroyer-minesweeper *Endicott,* which was standing just outside the harbor. While this was happening, thirteen loose mines lay floating nearby on the surface. An untold number still lay undetected.

Rescue operations continued while the gunnery duel went on. Task Force 77 was called for an air strike. Ten minutes had gone by and enemy guns were finding the range. The skipper of the *Pledge* knew his position was untenable; he tried to turn back into waters that had already been swept.

At 12:20 the *Pledge* hit a mine amidships on the starboard side, causing extensive damage to the hull and injuring every man on board. She, too, began to sink.

Then the *Incredible* experienced complete engine failure. "Dusty, Dusty," she called on the radio, "my engines are dead."

By now, two ships were lost, with thirteen men missing or dead and seventy-nine wounded. A third was disabled and out of action. The rest of the day was spent picking up survivors and trying to figure out what to do next. The deadline for landing the marines was now only seven days away.

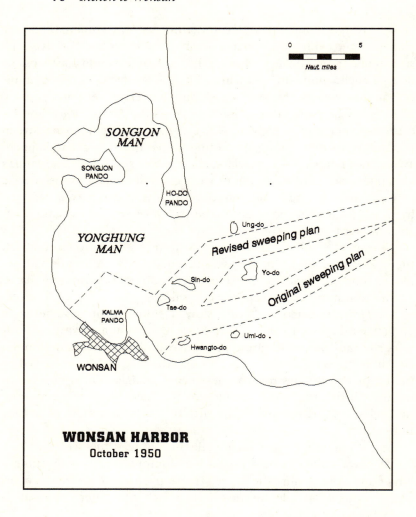

**WONSAN HARBOR**
October 1950

For the time being, at least, the U.S. Navy had lost control of the sea. Adm. Forrest Sherman, chief of naval operations, grumbled, "When you can't go *where* you want to, *when* you want to, you haven't got command of the sea."

---

**Ship's Log: Friday 13 October 1950**   0425 Relieved on fire support station by USS MADDOX (DD-731). 1214 Joined TOLEDO and USS THOMAS (DDR-833).

---

ROK troops moved up to capture Kalma Pando airfield, which brightened the picture considerably at Wonsan. Maj. Gen. Field Harris, USMC, flew in to inspect the landing field. After determining Kalma Pando was both secure and usable, he ordered up two marine fighter squadrons from Japan to be based there. The ability to use this facility for U.S. planes would greatly enhance the capability of providing close air support for troops moving inland.

The heavy cruiser *Toledo* and destroyer *Herbert J. Thomas* separated from the formation to range up and down the coast shooting up targets along a 120-mile stretch between Hungnam and Chongjin.

---

**Ship's Log: Saturday 14 October 1950**   0145 Joined USS ROCHESTER (CA-124) in company of USS DE HAVEN (DD-727).

---

The aircraft carrier *Boxer* checked in to the formation from a brief stint at the repair yard in Yokosuka, Japan. The month before, she had completed a high-speed round-trip to the West Coast of the United States to pick up an air group needed to support the Inchon landing. On recrossing the Pacific, she plowed through Typhoon Kezia. Speed and heavy weather had taken their toll, and one of her propellers had frozen up, thereby reducing the big ship to steaming on three shafts. Nevertheless, she remained at sea to provide air support for the Inchon landing, after which she retired to dry dock at Yokosuka to have the wayward propeller repaired.

---

**Ship's Log: Sunday 15 October 1950**   Steaming with USS ROCHESTER (CA-124) off Wonsan, Korea. 1430 Joined USS MISSOURI (BB-63) for conference.

---

MacArthur took time out from the war to fly to Wake Island for a highly publicized meeting with Pres. Harry S. Truman. The general was so certain of success—five days before the landing—that he assured the president organized resistance would end by Thanksgiving and U.S. troops would be home by Christmas.

Truman asked about the likelihood the Chinese might enter the war. MacArthur asserted that the likelihood of Chinese intervention, which was a matter of great concern in Washington, was very small.

MacArthur said of the Chinese, "We are no longer fearful of their intervention. We no longer stand hat in hand. The Chinese have 300,000 men in Manchuria. Of these probably not more than 100,000 to 200,000 are distributed along the Yalu River. Only 50,000 could have gotten across the Yalu. They have no air force."

He went on to say that if the Chinese did attempt to enter Korea, "there would be the greatest slaughter."

---

**Ship's Log: Monday–Wednesday 16–18 October 1950** Steaming on patrol, Wonsan, Korea.

---

The minesweepers reached the area of the landing beaches at Kalma Pando without further incident. Four days of magnetic sweeping began to calm fears about the harbor being seeded with magnetic mines. This seemed to contradict information gathered earlier from prisoners, which indicated magnetic mines had been laid in the harbor.

The sweepers *Mocking Bird, Chatterer, Redhead,* and *Kite* were making their last few sweeps near the beaches. Just when they thought it was safe to declare the harbor clear for landing craft, disaster struck again. In the words of the *Redhead*'s skipper, "The whole ocean started to erupt amid the sweepers." Two detonations astern of the minesweepers inflicted no damage. These were followed by a third explosion, a tremendous blast under the keel of the ROK *YMS-516,* which disappeared in a cloud of smoke and water.

Faced with irrefutable proof of the presence of influence mines (acoustic, magnetic, or pressure), Admiral Struble recommended that D-day be postponed. It was the disappointment of a lifetime to be within an hour of a completed mission and then to find a new kind of mine. They didn't know what *kind* of mines they were, they didn't know *where* they were placed, and they didn't know how *many* were there. But there was little choice; nothing short of a complete resweeping could ensure a safe channel for the landing craft.

---

**Ship's Log: Thursday 19 October 1950** 1505 Joined Task Force 77 consisting of USS PHILIPPINE SEA (CV-47), USS BOXER (CV-21), USS VALLEY FORGE (CV-45), USS LEYTE (CV-32), and 17 destroyers.

---

The ships carrying the attack force arrived on schedule in the operating area at midafternoon, ready for the next morning's landing. The transport group consisted of 7 APA attack transports, 10 AKA attack cargo ships, and 1 merchant ship. They were accompanied by a group of landing craft that consisted of 23 LSTs, 1 LSM, 3 LSDs, and 15 LSUs.

The discovery of new and deadly magnetic mines created a problem. They were forced to delay entrance to the harbor until a thorough magnetic sweeping could be accomplished.

The amphibious task force was ordered to steam southward for twelve hours at ten knots, then reverse course and steam northward so as to arrive back at the channel entrance at daylight the next day. Five destroyers provided an antisubmarine screen for these vessels and were instructed to maintain a sharp lookout for floating mines.

---

**Ship's Log: Friday–Monday 20–23 October 1950**  Steaming as before.

---

Further delays in clearing the harbor brought a repetition of previous instructions to maneuver so as to return at daylight the following morning—northward for twelve hours and southward for twelve hours.

General Almond, commandant of the attack forces, was so frustrated by the prospect of delay that he ordered the *Missouri*'s helicopter to take him and part of his staff ashore. Specifically, he wanted to direct the First ROK Corps, now under his command, which was rapidly approaching Wonsan from the south and threatening to take possession of that city before the amphibious troops could be landed.

Each day brought a continuation of the waiting game at sea. The amphibious force steamed northward twelve hours, then southward twelve hours.

---

**Ship's Log: Tuesday 24 October 1950**  Steaming as before.

---

Disgruntled marines labeled this Operation Yo-Yo. Five days of aimless wandering back and forth began to have serious deleterious effects: The long, undulating swells in the Sea of Japan caused the slow-moving troop transports to roll and pitch uncomfortably. Many of the marines and GIs became seasick during their five-day parade up and down the Korean coast. Food threatened to run short. Conditions were rife for the spread of epidemic disease. Dysentery broke out on the transport *Marine Phoenix*, afflicting 750 of the 2,000 embarked troops and a like proportion of the crew.

Boredom became the biggest problem for the GIs sardined into the amphibious shipping, as well as for us on the warships. We spent endless hours manning our battle stations waiting for something to happen.

---

**Ship's Log: Wednesday 25 October 1950**   Steaming as unit of Task Force 77.

---

Under the cover of naval bombardment, the ROKs had moved up and captured the city of Wonsan with no serious opposition. The North Korean army, though still a sizable force, had retreated into the hills and was moving along inland mountain tracks.

With Wonsan already in friendly hands, there was some question as to the need for an assault-type landing. It was still necessary, however, to put the troops ashore in order to accomplish MacArthur's main objective, which was for the Marine Corps to occupy the east coast of Korea and push inland to link up with the Eighth Army.

At 3:00 P.M., the ships moved in column through the swept channel to drop anchor in the southern part of the harbor, known as Yong-hung Man. Five LSTs were beached with advance parties of engineers and shore material. The main body of troops remained on their ships overnight.

---

**Ship's Log: Thursday 26 October 1950**   0623 Rendezvoused with gunfire support group providing protection for amphibious landing at Wonsan. Other units include USS HELENA (CA-75), USS ROCHESTER (CA-124), USS TOLEDO (CA-133), USS COLLETT (DD-730), USS DE HAVEN (DD-727), and USS SWENSON (DD-729).

---

General unloading began at first light. The 1st Marines went ashore across Yellow Beach and the 7th Marines across Blue Beach. Because of the shallow gradient, landing craft grounded some distance offshore and personnel had to wade the last few yards.

The operation proceeded smoothly and efficiently. Of the more than twenty-five thousand men in the division and attached units, well over half were ashore by evening, along with more than two thousand vehicles and two thousand tons of cargo. Once ashore, the marines started moving out in strength, striking northward through some of Korea's highest mountains toward the northern border.

The landing had been delayed six days by the mining effort. Except for that, the operation was unopposed and, therefore, economical. A major port had been seized and opened, and a major force was ashore in eastern North Korea. North Koreans were in rapid retreat with the main battle lines some fifty miles to the north, and still moving.

For the marines, the only casualties were the eighty-four dysentery victims who had to be hospitalized. Even after factoring in the loss of four minesweepers, the bill in military terms was comparatively small.

Operation Yo-Yo was over.

## 9    NORTH TO THE BORDER

*October 27–November 23, 1950*

**Ship's Log: Friday 27 October 1950**   Moored to buoy 8, Sasebo, Japan. Assigned to technical availability USS DIXIE (AD-14) for minor repairs.

The cheerful prospect of an imminent end to the fighting hung in the air. On land, at sea, and in the air it was harvest time. The armies rolled forward almost at will. The navy cruised undisturbed along the Korean coasts. The war was uncontested in the air.

With the war winding down, ships were being sent home. Destroyer Division 31 *(Eversole, Higbee, Kyes,* and *Shelton)* was released to the West Coast for overhaul. The *Philippine Sea* and *Boxer* left for Yokosuka. The *Valley Forge* and *Leyte* retired to Sasebo. The *Boxer* was routed onward to the States for overhaul. Plans were made to withdraw the escort carriers from Korean waters.

Dear Rusty: I hope this doesn't upset you, but I read a recent State Department survey that said 1/3 of all the people in the world now believe that the U.S. started the war in Korea. Score one for Russia's propaganda machine—and the ineffectiveness of ours. Unfortunately, I'm afraid that a lot of American citizens feel the same way. There seems to be a rising tide of dissatisfaction toward the American involvement in Korea. They want us out. I really do wish people appreciated more what you're doing there, and how much their future depends on it.   Love, Anna

---

**Ship's Log: Saturday 28 October 1950**  Moored as before. 1000 Ship's inspection by ComDesRon 7.

---

Our captain and the commodore didn't get along very well. That was no secret, and it became more evident this day during Commodore's Inspection.

The title *commodore* was an honorific title bestowed on a squadron commander.[1] Therefore, Capt. Samuel R. Lang, Commander Destroyer Squadron Seven (ComDesRon 7), was commonly addressed as "Commodore Lang."

Lang was a short man with a curly mustache and curly black hair. He strutted with an air of aggressive self-importance. In the minds of many, Lang had "stars in his eyes," meaning that he looked on this job as his passport to an admiral's star.

One of the first things Lang did upon taking command of DesRon 7 in his flagship, the *Lofberg* (DD-759), was establish a new radio circuit exclusively for the use of the ships in his squadron. He dubbed this circuit RonCom, short for Squad*ron Com*munications.

Every time Lang became exercised about something he would send a message by blinker light ordering all the skippers to come up on RonCom. Then he'd get on the circuit and start reading them off . . . how stupid they were, what they had done wrong, and so forth. The skippers didn't know what to do about his intemperate behavior. They were getting tired of being called "stupid sonofabitches" and other offensive epithets over the air.

Commander Buaas devised a scheme to cook Lang's goose. He had a wire recorder mounted in CIC right above the plotting table with a selector switch that could record any circuit that came into CIC. Thereafter, whenever Lang got on RonCom, Buaas would record what he said.

As Lang was winding up his inspection tour this particular day, Buaas said to him, "Commodore, I want you to see our CIC."

He showed him the wire recorder, saying, "You know, Commodore, just to be sure I make no mistakes on what you've told us to do, I record everything you say."

Lang blanched, turned on his heel, marched off the ship. He never again set foot on the *Borland* as long as we remained with the Seventh Fleet.[2]

---

**Ship's Log: Sunday–Tuesday 29–31 October 1950**   Moored buoy 8, Sasebo, Japan. Ready for sea.

---

The fantail of the ship had become a beehive of activity, surrounded, as it was, by a score or more Japanese sampans. Each was hawking a different ware or offering a different service. Some tradesmen sold souvenirs, some sold jewelry; others were cobblers who repaired shoes or tailors who mended uniforms.

These tradesmen were not allowed to climb up onto the ship, nor were our sailors allowed to climb down to the sampans. All matters of trade, including payment of money and transfer of goods, were conducted by raising and lowering wicker baskets tied to the ends of rice-straw ropes. All of this activity was accompanied by a noisy din of shouts as people tried to make themselves understood in poorly spoken pidgin English.

Some guys took wicked delight in confounding these tradesmen's intense desire to learn English. From time to time a tradesman would hold up an object and ask what it was called. Most guys would tell him the right word, but every once in a while some wiseacre would deliberately give a wrong word.

One leatherworker held up a rivet, a common ordinary steel rivet, and asked what it was called. Unfortunately, he asked one of the ship's inveterate pranksters, a seaman named Manion. Manion told him it was called an "asshole plug." For the remainder of that day, this poor soul went around proudly holding up his rivet, grinning widely, and solemnly repeating the words he had been taught, "Asshole plug. Asshole plug."

**Ship's Log: Wednesday–Saturday 1–4 November 1950**
Moored buoy 8, Sasebo, Japan. Ready for sea.

Indications that Chinese Communists were entering the war began to appear. Nationalist sources reported an ominous buildup in the level of military activity in North China and Manchuria. Fearing an imminent all-out effort, they expressed concern that UN forces were in grave danger.

Beginning October 28, ROK troops began encountering Red Chinese troops wearing North Korean uniforms. At first blush, these troops did not appear to be a dangerous adversary. On November 2, the Chinese publicly acknowledged their presence in a radio broadcast, calling them a "volunteer corps." They claimed they were there to "protect dams and power complexes" along the Yalu River.

This presence was not taken seriously at General MacArthur's headquarters in Tokyo. The general would not entertain the prospect of a full Chinese intervention. Maj. Gen. Charles Willoughby, MacArthur's chief intelligence officer, speculated the Chinese were attempting to "save face" by characterizing their troops as volunteers. That way, he said, they would not risk loss of prestige if their army should be defeated, but they could claim credit for helping neighboring North Korea in their time of need.

It was a different story in Washington. The Joint Chiefs of Staff (JCS) *were* becoming alarmed. They asked for MacArthur's appraisal of the situation. He reassured them that he did not expect the Chinese to enter the war, saying, "I recommend against hasty conclusions which might be premature and believe that a final appraisement should await a more complete accumulation of military facts."

Dear Anna: It's noontime, and I have a few moments to be alone with my thoughts of you. Outside, it is snowing . . . great big, fluttery, fantastically beautiful snowflakes . . . and I think how cozy it would be to snuggle up with you before a nice, roaring fireplace. The letters you sent were so marvelous. You are such a fantastic person. But you do enjoy tantalizing, teasing me, don't you? In a few hours we will be leaving this haven to return to the war zone. It's not the danger I fear but the loneliness. I long for the day when we can be together. Love, Rusty

**Ship's Log: Sunday–Tuesday 5–7 November 1950**  Screening Task Force 77, conducting air strikes against North Korean Communist Forces.

The first Chinese openly entered the war. They wore brown, padded uniforms over their summer uniforms and rubber shoes. They had no weapons heavier than light mortars and machine guns. Most carried old Japanese .25-caliber rifles left over from the Kwantung Army of 1945. About 20 percent had no weapons at all. Their training was minimal. General MacArthur exhibited enormous contempt for them.

Major General Beiderlinden, MacArthur's chief personnel officer, was not so complacent. In a communiqué to the Joint Chiefs of Staff, he gave his rundown on the situation as he saw it:

1. The casualties would continue to mount.
2. The Chinese armies were well trained and highly disciplined.
3. The danger now faced was as great as that at the Pusan Perimeter.
4. The winter weather would make the fighting far more difficult for the UN.
5. The Chinese intervention was no "flash in the pan."[3]

MacArthur's relationship with the Joint Chiefs of Staff was becoming increasingly strained. He didn't like their interference in his conduct of the war. On their part they regarded him as a pain in the ass, as evidenced by events of November 6.

One of MacArthur's little tricks for getting around the JCS was to create a confusion of messages.

He was alarmed by reports from aerial observers that a steady stream of Chinese was crossing the bridges over the Yalu River into North Korea, so he ordered air force lieutenant general Stratemeyer to send up his B-29s to bomb the bridges. "Combat crews are to be flown to exhaustion if necessary," MacArthur ordered.

But they were bound by a UN resolution that held the Yalu River border inviolate. Further, the United States was in the midst of trying to secure UN condemnation of the Chinese for entering the war. Failure to achieve that condemnation would weaken our position in calling for military participation of other UN members.

Not even MacArthur would have dared violate the directive without at least pretending to inform the JCS. So he made sure the information arrived after the fact. He sent it out over a routine teleconference program designed to convey nonurgent material. Because of the difference in time zones, he could count on nearly a day before Washington would deal with this message. In the interim, of course, the first raid would have been carried out.

War was escalating, but MacArthur seemed oblivious to the warning signs. One sign was the increasing numbers of Chinese troops, for which American intelligence sources still had no idea of how many. Estimates ranged from thirty thousand to one hundred thousand.

Another sign was a flurry of diplomatic signals sent through friendly embassies that the Chinese were not eager to pick a fight, but they feared the Americans would soon be invading Manchuria and carrying on a war against China.

Nothing MacArthur did allayed those fears. His own views on Red China were widely communicated. He fully expected to carry the war against China and, if necessary, to fight the Soviets then and there. He also proposed using the atomic bomb.

---

**Ship's Log: Wednesday 8 November 1950**  Continued to screen while Task Group 77.3 conducted air operations.

---

A new and dangerous threat stormed across the border into North Korea. Stubby swept-wing jet fighters taking off from bases in Communist China immediately rendered obsolete every U.S. fighter then in the theater. A potent new plane entered the skies that put the U.S. Air Force in danger of losing control of the air to another power—a concept Americans had come to regard as unthinkable.

That stubby, swept-wing jet fighter was the Soviet-built MiG-15—a bold, new design that would revolutionize military aviation.

History's first jet-to-jet battle pitted a Soviet-built MiG-15 against the Lockheed F-80 Shooting Star—a straight-wing jet fighter developed but not used during World War II. Less maneuverable and 100-mph slower in level flight, the F-80 was no match for the MiG. But skill and experience counted for more. One MiG pilot made the mistake of trying to dive away from the heavier F-80 of Lt. Russell Brown. Brown caught up with him and poured a stream of .50-caliber fire into the MiG. The enemy plane flipped over and crashed into the ground.

---

**Ship's Log: Thursday 9 November 1950**  Proceeded to rendezvous with USS BADOENG STRAIT (CVE-116) and USS SICILY (CVE-118).

---

Following the air force's lack of success in destroying the bridges across the Yalu River, the navy got a crack at the job. For the next three days, planes from the *Valley Forge, Philippine Sea,* and *Leyte* struck the bridges. They destroyed the southern ends of the highway bridge at Sinuiju (site of the interim North Korean capitol) and the two smaller bridges at Hyesanjin at the headwaters of the Yalu. The railroad bridge at Sinuiju still stood, however.

These were extremely difficult targets, since the approach had to be made either up or down stream. All attacks had to be carried out through predetermined airspace and subject to unimpeded antiaircraft and fighter opposition from the Manchurian side. Moreover, this angle of attack brought the pilots across the narrowest dimension of the bridge, making it an extremely difficult target to hit. The slightest error in range or deflection would ensure a miss. For top cover, eight or more F9F Panther jets accompanied the attack planes.

A flight of MiG-15s came up to meet them during the attack at Sinuiju. Lt. Comdr. W. T. Amen of the *Philippine Sea* got locked in a battle with a MiG. They chased each other from four thousand to fifteen thousand feet and down again before the enemy spun in. Again, training and gunnery made the difference, because the F9F was no match for the MiG in speed, maneuverability, or rate of climb.

---

**Ship's Log: Friday 10 November 1950**  1033 Anchored in berth D-25, Wonsan, Korea. Commenced work on gyro compass.

---

The gyro compass, known simply as the gyro, is the nucleus of a number of automatic systems on a ship. Without it we were as worthless as tits on a bull. Ours crapped out in the middle of the night, and we had to enter calm waters in order to balance and realign it.

First, the gyro provides the reference to "true" north, which is the basis for all task force commands. For example, if the task force commander issued orders to "come to heading 270 degrees," then all ships better have the same reading of 270 degrees on their compasses. Otherwise they would have a terrible mess on their hands, particularly at night.

Second, all of the radar and sonar screens throughout the ship are oriented to true north by the gyro. Thus, for example, if an operator reports a "bogie" at bearing, say, 135 degrees, that is with reference to true north. Everyone needs confidence that the direction he calls out is a reasonably accurate one.

Third, the gyro provides the "stable platform" for controlling the ship's big guns. It electronically compensates for the pitching and rolling of the ship so that no matter how heavy the weather or rough the seas, the guns will track level in the direction they are aimed.

Wonsan Harbor was still a dangerous place. Mines were strewn everywhere, and the North Koreans were laying new ones nightly.

Entering the harbor, we had as many as five mines at a time on the sonar scope. It was a sobering thought to realize four ships had been blown up and a fifth damaged in this same harbor, all within the past month.

More recently, we had seen the terrible damage a mine can do when the *Brush*'s keel was broken and the *Mansfield*'s bow blown off.

My bunk was in the forward crew's quarters. That's where a mine would hit. If it happened in the predawn hours, casualties would be horrendous—a dozen dead chiefs and fifty dead crewmen. Assuming they were able to find and identify our remains.

---

**Ship's Log: Saturday 11 November 1950**  Anchored Wonsan, Korea. Continued work on gyro compass.

---

Our two IC electricians, Pete Hoffman and J. J. Phillips, were tired, frustrated, and groggy. All night they worked to repair the gyro. But it wouldn't hold enough vacuum.

A crew came over from the USS *Kermit Roosevelt* (ARG-60), a repair ship anchored in Wonsan Harbor. Those technicians fiddled around all day until finally they broke off the vacuum valve. Now we were in deep shit.

"Don't worry," they insisted. "We'll just drill it out and put in a new one."

Brimming with confidence, the *Roosevelt*'s technicians drilled out the broken valve, rethreaded the hole, and installed an oversize valve in place of the one they had broken. All to no avail. In fact, it only made matters worse. Thanks to them, the recalcitrant gyro now refused to hold any vacuum at all. They threw in the towel.

---

**Ship's Log: Sunday 12 November 1950**   0700 Underway to rejoin Task Group 96.8.

---

Even without a gyro, we were ordered back out to sea. We were clearing the outer end of the swept channel when a yell came down from the signal bridge, "Holy shit! Would you look at that!"

Entering the channel was the USS *Buck* (DD-761). The first thirty-one feet of her bow were almost severed. Both anchors and capstans were swept away, mount 51 was knocked askew, and she had a gaping hole in her side. At first we assumed she had hit a mine. Then we found out the damage was caused by a collision.

Minutes later, the USS *John W. Thomason* (DD-760) hove into view, escorted by the USS *Chandler* (DD-717). The *Thomason,* too, had a smashed bow. Her damage was not nearly as extensive as the *Buck*'s.

Commander Buaas called all the officers to the bridge. "See what happens when you don't pay attention!" he said.

Information was sketchy, but we were able to piece together a general outline. Earlier in the day, the *Buck* and four other destroyers departed formation to refuel in the replenishment area. About 8:00 P.M. the *Buck* returned to the task force and was ordered to proceed independently to take station number five in the screen. Midway through the maneuver, the formation was ordered to change course.

The *Buck*'s skipper was a real hot rod. He often bragged he could get his ship on station faster than anyone else. The weather was awful that night. He took off at flank speed. Comdr. Chung Hoon, skipper of the *Thomason,* didn't take off as fast. Had he been going at the same speed as the *Buck,* there wouldn't have been a collision. As it was, the *Thomason* wasn't out of the way when the *Buck* went crashing through. They plowed into each other. Fortunately, no one was killed.

Both ships were ordered to Wonsan, where emergency repairs were made by the USS *Kermit Roosevelt,* and then on to Sasebo. The *Thomason*'s damage would be repaired at Pearl Harbor; she would return to action in March. The *Buck* would go to Bremerton, Washington, to have a new bow installed before returning to Korean waters in April.

Commodore Lang was fit to be tied. Two of his ships were out of action. The *Borland* was a "sick chick." That left him only the *Lofberg*. Not much of a fighting force to earn an admiral's star.

As if to rub salt in the commodore's wound, the *Lofberg* was pulled out of formation to baby-sit with the *Borland*.

---

**Ship's Log: Monday–Tuesday 13–14 November 1950**   0700
This vessel with the USS LOFBERG (DD-759) detached to escort the
USS SICILY (CVE-118) to Wonsan, Korea.

---

It was Operation Yo-Yo all over again. Hardly had we rejoined the fleet when we were ordered back to Wonsan. This time as baby-sitter for another cripple, the carrier *Sicily*.

We were instructed to navigate through the fifty-mile-long minefield, not by fixed landmarks but by following the marker buoys placed there by the minesweepers. We were told that the minesweepers themselves used no landmarks to guide them when they swept the channels, so the only safe passage was to follow the buoys they left as markers.

About halfway down the channel and—oops!—the next marker wasn't there. After slowing down to search the area, lookouts spotted it quite a distance off to port. It made no sense that the buoy should be in that location—that was a crazy way to sweep the channel. Commander Buaas decided the buoy had come loose from its mooring and was drifting freely. He sent a message to the skipper of the *Sicily* to tell him what he thought the problem was. The *Sicily* agreed, and we proceeded straight on through.

Hero one minute, goat the next. Amid the flurry of getting out a report to warn other ships about the errant minefield buoy, Buaas forgot to make out an arrival report. Commodore Lang was pissed . . . again.

---

**Ship's Log: Wednesday 15 November 1950**   Proceeding to
Sasebo, Japan, with the USS SICILY. At 1836 moored alongside USS
DIXIE (AD-14) in Sasebo Harbor for gyro compass repairs.

---

MacArthur's mood swung to expansive optimism as parka-clad marines of the 7th Division fought through four-degree-below-zero weather to reach the key transportation town of Hagaru. They were now only sixty-five miles from the Manchurian border. Only light resistance was encountered. MacArthur said it was essential to reach the Yalu before it froze over, which was predicted to occur between November 24 and December 10. If his attack beat the freezing, the war would be over.

The Eighth Army intelligence organization warned of a new buildup of Chinese forces in North Korea.

MacArthur did not believe this information to be accurate. He continued his planning for the end-the-war offensive as if it were going to be a cakewalk into occupation.

President Truman's attitude was far from that of MacArthur's. At a press conference Truman pledged he would "take every honorable step to prevent any extension of the hostilities in the Far East." He followed up later with a statement that the U.S. "never at any time entertained any intention to carry hostilities into China."

MacArthur labeled the order restraining him from hot pursuit across the Yalu as, "the most indefensible and ill-conceived decision ever forced on a field commander in our nation's history."

---

**Ship's Log: Thursday–Friday 16–17 November 1950**  Moored alongside USS DIXIE, Sasebo, Japan.

---

Fireworks were popular in Japan, but regulations made it illegal to bring them aboard ship. Nonetheless, some foolhardy souls couldn't resist the temptation to sneak them on board anyway.

One such soul was Robert Beisheim, radarman third class. He brought back a sack of pyrotechnic pellets called "torpedoes." These were about the size of chickpeas, and they exploded on impact when thrown against a hard surface. Although harmless, the bang could be startling when you weren't expecting it. Beisheim made a pest of himself by popping them off at people's feet.

Suddenly we heard a ripping explosion. It sounded like a string of firecrackers going off. The CIC filled with a cloud of acrid, blue smoke. Silence. Then peals of laughter. Poor Bob Beisheim was standing there, dumbfounded, the left leg of his dungarees shredded and in tatters. Wisps of smoke still curled from the tattered threads.

It seems he had a pocketful of those damn torpedoes when he accidentally banged into the corner of the plotting table, setting them off. The whole batch went up in smoke and noise, blowing the pocket clean off his pants. Apart from a bruised ego and a ruined pair of pants, he was unharmed. Chastened and wiser, perhaps, but OK.

---

**Ship's Log: Saturday 18 November 1950**   Moved from alongside USS DIXIE (AD-14) to SSK dry dock No. 4, Sasebo, Japan, to balance and set gyro compass.

---

Technicians from the *Dixie* worked three days on our gyro. They tore it down piece by piece, then reassembled it, hoping to undo the previous damage caused by the *Kermit Roosevelt*'s technicians. But it still wouldn't balance properly.

Eventually, they had to move us into dry dock and swing a new gyro on board.

It was vindication for Hoffman and Phillips. All along, Commodore Lang had been bitching that the *Borland*'s technicians weren't competent. Now, with all the problems the *Dixie*'s technicians were having, he had to acknowledge that the problem was not with our people but the equipment.

Meanwhile, up north in the battle zone, two more MiG-15s were shot down by pilots from the *Valley Forge* and *Leyte* flying F9F Panther jets. So far, the results of these engagements were encouraging. Though the MiG was a hotter plane, our pilots more than made up the difference with their extensive experience and superior training.

---

**Ship's Log: Sunday 19 November 1950**   Moored alongside USS DIXIE (AD-14), Sasebo, Japan.

---

Shorty Hall came back aboard ship after an evening of drinking in Sasebo. He was silly drunk.

"Hey Gamble," he said with a grin on his face, "Look what I've got." With a flourish, he pulled out from beneath his topcoat a magnum of champagne. (A magnum holds two fifths.) How in the world that little runt of a man managed to sneak a bottle that big past the SPs and the OOD (officer of the deck) was beyond me. "We'll save it till New Year's," he said, "and then we'll have ourselves a party."

Shorty's saving grace was that he was a helluva good navigator. That's probably why skippers tended to turn a blind eye to his drinking escapades. Shorty was the ship's chief quartermaster, the enlisted man chiefly responsible for the ship's navigation and signaling.

Other duties of the quartermaster were to keep all navigational charts up to date, check the accuracy of the ship's compass, maintain the chronometers, and generally advise the captain on weather and sea conditions. Oft times, when summoned hurriedly to the bridge, Shorty could be heard to mutter under his breath: "When in danger, when in doubt, run in circles, scream and shout, 'Quartermaster, take a bearing!'"

---

**Ship's Log: Monday 20 November 1950**   Underway to rejoin Task Force 77.

---

The day was made memorable by the Secretary of the Navy Francis P. "Frank" Matthews landing on the Wonsan airstrip with an inspection party. Admiral Doyle had sailed down from Hungnam the day before to meet the distinguished visitors and to welcome them aboard his flagship, the USS *Mount McKinley.*

Matthews, already eighteen months into his job and never having set foot on a naval vessel, was a Washington hack who was thoroughly despised throughout the navy and an object of ridicule. He was known contemptuously as "Rowboat Matthews."

On the deck of the *Mount McKinley,* Matthews delivered a short speech to the ship's company in which he acknowledged that this was the first visit he had ever paid to any ship of the U.S. Navy.

Many years earlier, during the presidency of Ulysses S. Grant, much had been made by writers of that era regarding the secretary of the navy, a man who was said to have been surprised by the discovery that ships were hollow. Likewise, the footnotes of history should memorialize a secretary who on November 20, 1950, aboard *Mount McKinley,* had been in office for more than a year and a half and had never bothered to find out for himself what a navy ship was like.

---

**Ship's Log: Tuesday 21 November 1950**   0730 LEYTE sighted possible periscope; HAMNER and CHANDLER detached to investigate.

---

Experts couldn't agree on what the Chinese were really doing or how many of them were doing it. Were there thirty thousand or three hundred thousand? MacArthur was still holding to the former estimate despite mounting evidence to the contrary. "Any larger number than that," he insisted, "would have been detected from the air."

Yet Chinese prisoners of war spoke of 45 divisions of 10,000 men each—that would have been 450,000 troops. But our intelligence officers routinely ignored this information because it came from noncommissioned officers and private soldiers. It was unthinkable to them that low-ranking soldiers would possess such vital information. What we did not understand about the Chinese army was that their commanders regularly shared basic information with the common soldiers as a part of their technique for instilling loyalty and inspiring effort.

---

**Ship's Log: Wednesday 22 November 1950**   1230 until 1730 controlled AEW and AD planes.

---

Another example of the *Borland*'s capability and versatility was demonstrated on this day. For a period of five hours, we were the eyes and ears of Task Force 77.

The choice of our destroyer to run this experiment can be attributed, in large part, to the performance of our SPS-6 radar and the ingenuity of our operations officer, Lt. Frank Howland. Compared with older air search radars, the SPS-6 could literally "knock your eyes out," and Lieutenant Howland had redesigned CIC so as to maximize its capabilities.

At midmorning we detached from the main body of the task force and proceeded northward to a position some fifty miles off its beam. At 12:30 Task Force 77 shut down its radars and radios and we took command of its strike aircraft.

From 12:30 to 5:30, the *Borland* directed all strike operations for planes flying from the *Leyte* and *Philippine Sea*. This was an amazing feat, considering we possessed no more than one-tenth the CIC capability of the carriers. Throughout, Task Force 77 maintained full radio and radar silence.

The operation was a success. Although no official explanation was passed down to the crew, it wasn't hard to figure out the purpose of the exercise. The arrival of Russian-built MiG-15s two weeks earlier had added a whole new dimension to the war. As yet, we didn't know what kind of threat the MiGs would pose, but we did know that we had no planes in the fleet that were their equal. Further, we could fairly assume that the Russians would be using radio and radar detection equipment to locate the fleet.

Therefore, if the fleet were to maintain complete radio and radar silence while actual flight operations were directed from another location fifty miles away, enemy planes or missiles might be decoyed to the strike control ship. That would afford the fleet an extra margin of safety in putting up its own defenses.

---

**Ship's Log: Thursday 23 November 1950**   Steaming with Task Force 77 off east coast of Korea.

---

Dear Anna: Thanksgiving Day. General MacArthur's confidence is so complete and persuasive the war is almost over that Thanksgiving Day was celebrated all up and down the battle line in an atmosphere of rejoicing. Even in the frozen wastes of North Korea, the soldiers and marines fed on shrimp cocktail, roast turkey with sweet potatoes, stuffed olives, cranberry sauce, fruit salad, fruit cake, and mince pie. For a few minutes they might as well have been at home.

The U.S. 7th Infantry Division troops reached the Yalu at Hyesanjin on Tuesday, making MacArthur's glory complete. His lackey, General Almond, flew up to the area and had his picture taken overlooking the Yalu, which has confirmed the worst fears of the Chinese.

Tomorrow is the day that MacArthur has announced to launch his final offensive. Am longing to see you.   Love, Rusty

*November 24–December 8, 1950*

---

**Ship's Log: Friday 24 November 1950**   1440 Joined Escort Carrier Group 96.8 consisting of the USS BADOENG STRAIT (CVE-116), USS HANSON (DDR-832), USS MACKENZIE (DD-836), and this vessel. The Marine Air Group in the USS BADOENG STRAIT is engaged in close tactical air support of United Nations forces in North Korea.

---

Instead of believing the Eighth Army's warnings of a new and dangerous buildup of Chinese forces, General MacArthur made ready for his final "cakewalk to the Yalu."

The great offensive began with a stirring communiqué in which MacArthur concluded, "If successful, this should for all practical purposes end the war."[1]

All along a broad front the soldiers moved quickly, meeting virtually no opposition. By the end of the day, the advances ranged from six to ten miles. MacArthur was elated.

The 7th Marines, supported by the marine aircraft from the *Badoeng Strait,* were preparing to act as the right arm of the pincer. Moving west from Hagaru to Yudam-ni, they were meeting only light resistance. Two of my friends, Sgt. James Cotton and Pvt. Bill Cockrell, both from Oklahoma, were with 2d Battalion, Dog Company. In fact, Cockrell celebrated his nineteenth birthday at Hagaru.

General MacArthur flew up to Eighth Army headquarters on the Chongchon River for a press briefing and photo opportunity. We all believed him when he spoke glibly of "getting the boys home by Christmas."

The only sour note came from the British press, which commented that this was a strange way to fight a war—in the glare of a publicity campaign that gave the enemy a good insight into the details and objectives of UN military operations.

Dear Anna:  It started snowing last night about 9 o'clock and was still snowing at dawn GQ. The sea has been very rough since yesterday afternoon. Still snowing at 10 A.M. Around 11:00 came within sight of N. Korea and the land is covered with snow. Has stopped snowing at sea and the sun has finally decided to show itself. Temperature around 34 degrees. Love, Rusty

---

**Ship's Log: Saturday 25 November 1950**   At 0758 sighted empty Chinese junk; attempted to sink boat; stove in sides and bottom, but could not sink it.

---

On the second day of the attack, the UN forces began to encounter heavy resistance. During the morning, the Chinese launched some strong probes against the ROK troops on the western front. With nightfall, the Chinese attacked in force. They were accompanied by the nerve-shattering sound of bugles that sounded like no other bugles in the world; whistles screamed, flutes screeched, cymbals clanged, and drums rattled as they came by the thousands.

The Chinese had not 34,000 soldiers but 300,000—ten times as many as MacArthur thought they had. Another 300,000 remained poised across the Yalu.

How were they able to conceal that massive a buildup? For one thing, 120,000 had been in North Korea since mid-October, having entered under the cover of smoke and haze of deliberately set forest fires. Second, new divisions had streamed across the Yalu night after night, starting after nine and marching until three in the morning, artfully concealing their locations from American reconnaissance planes flying overhead. Third, captured Chinese soldiers gave misleading unit names they had been taught to give: armies became divisions, divisions became regiments, and so forth, thereby creating the impression there was a much smaller force in the area. UN commanders had been talking in terms of Chinese divisions when they should have been talking about whole armies.

---

**Ship's Log: Sunday 26 November 1950**   Steaming as escort for BADOENG STRAIT.

---

During the night, the Chinese waded the Chongchon River and overran the 61st Field Artillery, killing many men and capturing many others. Only a handful made it out. They abandoned every vehicle and every weapon. One man was barefoot, having been surprised in his bedroll.

When daylight came, the ROK divisions on the right began to crumble under Chinese pressure. Whole regiments began fleeing through UN lines. The U.S. 2d Division was ordered to pull back several miles, but the road was so jammed with vehicles that it was nearly midnight before the battalion could move out.

That night the wind howled and the temperature dropped to zero. Lacking shelter, the men could not sleep. When they were not on the firing line, they sat huddled around gasoline stoves or went out in all the clothing they could find to move ammunition.

Still the Chinese attacked.

---

**Ship's Log: Monday 27 November 1950**   Steaming as escort for BADOENG STRAIT.

---

November 27 dawned cold. Very cold. Thick layers of ice covered the ship's mast and superstructure. Rough sea conditions forced the suspension of all air operations.

Inland, temperature dropped to twenty degrees below zero. On the hills and in the valleys, the troops shivered and ached with the cold. And from all directions, attacking, probing, came the Chinese soldiers.

At Yudam-ni, marine sergeant James Cotton was leading a patrol up one of the two little hills north of the village, not expecting to encounter enemy activity. The Chinese opened up on them as they reached the top. They dug in just below the ridge line. The platoon lieutenant crawled up and said, "One of our men fell down the other side when they shot him. I'm going up to get him."

"You'd better not," Cotton warned, "They'll blast you." The lieutenant stood up anyway. Sure enough, they shot him right through the chest. The platoon spent the day on the hill, pinned down, able to retreat only under cover of darkness. When they rejoined the regiment, the men were told they got off easy—some of the platoons were hit much harder. "Expect some company tonight," the captain warned.

Cotton was then sent to take over Third Platoon, all of whose officers and noncoms had been killed. The men took positions along a frozen creekbed, but the ground was frozen so solid they couldn't dig foxholes. They lay atop their sleeping bags as insulation from the snow, peering into the dark for an enemy they knew inevitably would come. No fires, no food, and what water they had was frozen.

Around ten o'clock, they could hear the Chinese advancing over the frozen ground. Cotton raised up and saw some along the skyline as they crossed one-by-one through a saddle between two small hills. He fired on one and hit him. The Chinese opened up on Cotton with a burp gun, but they were firing over his head. A few seconds later, another Chinese appeared, and Cotton fired on him too.

As he was taking aim to fire on yet a third one coming through the saddle, Cotton thought to himself, "Boy, when I fire this time, they're going to know where I am from the muzzle flash, and they're going to open up on me." Nevertheless, he did fire; and the Chinese fired back. This time, they found their mark. It felt like a sledgehammer.

Cotton didn't know how long he was out. When he regained consciousness, he couldn't see a thing. He thought, "Boy, it's even darker than it was a while ago." He called out for some of his men. No one answered. He decided to strike out for the command post (C.P.). Right off, he banged into a tree. "Man, it is dark!" he said to himself. Every time he tried to move, he banged into another tree.

Another marine called out a warning, "Watch out for that tree!"

"I'm trying to," Cotton replied. "But how can I watch it when I can't see it?"

"Hold on to me," the other marine said. "I can see better than you can." It wasn't until they got down to the C.P. that Cotton discovered he'd been shot in the face, right between the eyes. The slug was still lodged in his forehead. He was totally blind.

A quarter of an inch lower and the bullet would have gone in his eye socket. Cotton figured it just wasn't his time to die.

---

**Ship's Log: Tuesday–Wednesday 28–29 November 1950**
Steaming as escort for BADOENG STRAIT.

---

Eighth Army was in full retreat. The 2d Division was desperately trying to extricate itself from a position of the gravest peril. The confusion of disaster was beginning. Retreating troops were slowed by the litter of disabled and abandoned trucks and tanks along the roads.

MacArthur reported to Washington that the UN Command had met "conditions beyond its control and strength," that it had shifted into a defensive posture, and that "we face an entirely new war."

The navy had already begun to react. At 3:34 P.M. on November 28 Admiral Joy alerted Rear Adm. James H. Doyle, Commander Amphibious Force Far East, for a possible general emergency that would require removal of ground forces from Korea to Japan. Doyle and his staff began at once to work out preliminary plans for deploying half the amphibious craft to west coast operations and half to the Wonsan-Hungnam area. All ships were alerted to the possibility of air attack and placed on six-hour notice.

Task Force 77 expanded its area of reconnaissance. Throughout the day the *Philippine Sea* and *Leyte* kept eight F4U Corsairs and six AD Skyraiders over the border strip.

The U.S. 2d Division became entangled in a five-mile roadblock north of Sunchon. Cut off, cut up, swept with fire from the hills, and blocked by its own vehicles, the division became disorganized. In a two-day ordeal, it lost 40 percent of its personnel and most of its guns and gear.

Courageous navy pilots kept these losses from being greater. Task Force 77 sent seven Corsairs and five AD Skyraiders across the peninsula to provide close support.

---

**Ship's Log: Thursday 30 November 1950**   Steaming as escort for BADOENG STRAIT.

---

The successes of the Chinese ended all thoughts of advancing to the Yalu. The army's 3d Division was ordered to pull back to the coast and reassemble at Wonsan. Farther to the northeast, the ROK I Corps was ordered to retire to Songjin, and there to prepare for further movement by land or sea. The UN was pulling out of North Korea.

The 7th Marines began an orderly pullout from Yudam-ni back toward Hagaru, bringing their dead stacked in trucks and their wounded by whatever means possible. Those that could walk, walked. Sergeant Cotton, still blind, trudged alongside one of the trucks by hanging onto a rope someone had tied there for him. Just one tank remained, and keeping it on the icy road was difficult—it kept wanting to slip off.

Traveling the seven miles back to Hagaru would take three days and three nights. It was a constant battle all the way, meeting resistance at every turn. The marines had no food, and their only water was snow they melted in their mouths. The vehicles had to be kept running day and night because anything that was shut down would freeze up.

Despite blinding snow and rough seas, the aircraft carriers continued to provide close air support for troops ashore. Icy conditions on the flight decks made the work of flight crews miserable and extremely dangerous. It was a wonder to us that we didn't lose somebody overboard.

---

**Ship's Log: Friday–Saturday 1–2 December 1950**   Steaming as escort for BADOENG STRAIT.

---

On the first day of December the weather over eastern Korea was very bad. Morning flights from the carriers met a solid cloud cover over the plateau and were diverted to the Eighth Army area where three missions totaling twenty-three aircraft successfully attacked large concentrations of enemy troops and blew up an ammunition dump at Sinanju. But the weather that had altered their assignment also prevented their return to the carriers whence they came, for the task force had been obliged to cease flight operations late in the morning. Unable to get home, the aircraft landed at Wonsan. Then they were kicked out again because of enemy ground fighting in the neighborhood. They refueled and flew on to Kimpo where they finally spent the night.

During the morning hours, army troops were ordered to break out southward from Chosin Reservoir and were advised that maximum air support would be provided. Bad weather, however, plagued the withdrawal. Although marine pilots from *Badoeng Strait* got through to napalm the Chinese enemy, the early flights from Task Force 77 were weathered out of the reservoir. Eventually the fast carriers were forced to cancel air operations altogether. Without the promised air cover, a combination of heavy attacks and enemy roadblocks fragmented the retreating column; most officers and key NCOs became casualties. By the time darkness fell, total casualties reached almost 75 percent.

The destroyers *Eversole, Higbee, Kyes,* and *Shelton,* on their way to the West Coast for overhaul, received orders to reverse course and return to the battle zone. Escort carriers *Sicily* and *Bairoko* were rushed to the battle line. All available deck space was needed for marine pilots.

Maximum effort was directed toward evacuation from the Chosin Reservoir. As the 5th and 7th Marines continued their move toward Hagaru, Task Force 77 put two-thirds of its sorties into the reservoir area. They attacked troop positions at Toktang Pass and provided fighter cover to transports flying in supplies. Chinese attacks on the marine column were heavy throughout the night and into the next day, but without disorganizing the advance.

It snowed most of the day. Landing conditions aboard the carriers were perilous. Aircraft were instructed to divert to an air base near Wonsan, but apprehensions of enemy attack prevented them from staying overnight. They had to hazard a shipboard landing during a heavy snowstorm.

U.S. mail left the ship for the first time since November 20.

---

**Ship's Log: Sunday 3 December 1950**   1050 Detached from Task Group to investigate sonar contact. 1102 Evaluated as non-submarine.

---

At midafternoon the Eighth Army sent an urgent dispatch for the navy to send as many large ships as were available to Chinnampo on the west coast for evacuation of troops. Three transports and two cargo ships were already in Yellow Sea waters and immediately headed northward in that direction. The British carrier *Theseus* and four British destroyers were also moved up to cover the evacuation.

The destroyer escort *Foss* was providing the city with electrical power. Offshore, a minesweeping group was standing by with their guns to provide escort through the tortuous channel.

At Wonsan, outloading of UN personnel and materiel also began. Covering fire was furnished by the cruiser *Saint Paul* and destroyers *Sperry* and *Zellars*. Shellfire from these three ships effectively isolated the city from enemy attack during the day, and at night they fired starshells to keep the enemy on the defensive.

Naval gunfire was so effective the entire operation was completed without loss of a single life or the necessity to sacrifice any of the UN's valuable munitions or equipment.

By late afternoon the marines from Yudam-ni were inside the Hagaru perimeter. Between the frostbite and enemy action, Dog Company had suffered 100 percent casualties. Just before they got into Hagaru, my friend Private Cockrell got blown off an artillery piece by a mortar. Receiving a severe concussion in addition to the frostbite, he was evacuated by C-47 to Tokyo and thence back to the States.

A total of 117 sorties were flown by marine pilots from Yonpo and the *Badoeng Strait* to support the movement. Task Force 77 put an additional 80 sorties into the Chosin area.

---

**Ship's Log: Monday 4 December 1950**   0724 Left formation to investigate floating mine, sank same.

---

Ensign Jesse Brown, the navy's first black pilot, was one of eight Corsairs on a flight from the USS *Leyte*. They were skimming the snow-covered terrain north of the Chosin Reservoir searching for targets of opportunity.

Suddenly, Brown called out, "I'm losing power!"

The other pilots watched helplessly as Brown's plane glided toward the ground. He nursed his powerless plane toward the levelest spot he could find. The impact was hard. It tore the engine loose from its mountings and twisted the fuselage just forward of the canopy.

The other pilots watched as Brown slid open the canopy and waved feebly at them. They would fly protectively overhead while awaiting a rescue helicopter. With luck, Brown would be picked up safely.

Brown's wingman, LTJG Thomas J. Hudner, noticed smoke coming from Brown's plane. Brown wasn't climbing out. Hudner surmised he was either trapped in the wreckage or was too badly injured to move.

"I'm going in," Hudner radioed his flight leader. He cut power, dropped flaps, and went in for an emergency landing. Hudner hit the mountainside a hundred yards away. Nearly a foot of snow covered the ground. He ran over to Brown's plane and tried to pull him out.

He worked frantically to free his buddy. But Brown's legs were trapped in the twisted wreckage under the instrument panel. He had severe internal injuries. And he was already suffering badly from subzero temperatures.

Brown was groggy, in a lot of pain, and bitterly cold, but he did not utter one word of complaint as they waited for the rescue helicopter to arrive.

The helicopter crew brought a fire axe. But their efforts were futile. The axe simply bounced off the metal plate that trapped Brown's legs. Meanwhile, the fire still smoldered. Brown was growing weaker. His speech slurred.

Brown knew his situation was hopeless. It was growing dark. The helicopter would have to leave. He knew he could not survive the night. But he knew he was not alone. His wingman was there to comfort him. He gave Hudner a message for his wife, then lapsed into unconsciousness.

Tearfully, Hudner and the helicopter crew left the dying pilot.

When Hudner returned to the *Leyte,* he was called to the bridge. He expected to be chewed out for crash-landing his plane. Instead, the captain told him he was being recommended for the Medal of Honor.[2]

---

**Ship's Log: Tuesday 5 December 1950**   1046 Observed plane crash, proceeded to scene. 1102 Recovered two pilots from the water. Pilots and three of ship's company treated for exposure. 1720 Transferred pilots to BADOENG STRAIT.

---

Loading continued throughout the morning at the west coast port of Chinnampo. The destroyer escort *Foss* kept the electrical power on. An ROK Navy shore party took over guarding the docks following the planned withdrawal of the Eighth Army's service party. Sailboats packed with refugees slipped down the river.

At 5:30 P.M. the *Bexar,* last of the transports, headed downstream escorted by the *Foss.* One final emergency developed when the *Bexar,* having made both inward and outward voyages in darkness, grounded north of Sokto. But she got herself off without damage, and with morning the destroyers and LSTs made an uneventful downstream passage to reach Cho Do at noon and anchored in a blinding snowstorm.

Another evacuation was getting underway at Songjin, a hundred miles up the coast from Wonsan. The transport *Noble* and two merchantmen were ordered to outload elements of the retiring ROK I Corps. Covering fire was provided by the destroyers *Maddox* and *Moore,* and everything went by the book. The ships finished loading and sailed for Pusan.

Midmorning, the fast carrier *Princeton* joined Task Force 77 and began launching aircraft. The result was a record 248 sorties in support of the U.S. Marines at Hagaru.

---

**Ship's Log: Wednesday 6 December 1950**   1436 Began search for man overboard from BADOENG STRAIT. 1730 Concluded search, man not recovered.

---

The U.S. Marines started their southward trek over the winding road from Hagaru leading toward Koto-ri. Disengagement at Hagaru required hard fighting; the Chinese troops previously sighted to the north had now arrived. Morning fog hampered air operations, but more than a hundred offensive sorties were sent up by the *Princeton, Leyte,* and the marine squadrons from the *Badoeng Strait* to strike against Chinese troops in ridges along the road. All day and throughout the night the march continued amid heavy casualties, the marines bringing their dead with them.

Sergeant Cotton was evacuated to the navy hospital at Tokyo where the doctors cleaned the frozen mud and blood from his eyes. Gradually his vision returned, and within three days he was seeing clearly.[3]

---

**Ship's Log: Thursday 7 December 1950**   Steaming in company with USS BADOENG STRAIT. USS SICILY (CVE-118) and USS HANSON (DDR-832) joined the formation.

---

The return of the *Sicily* doubled the capacity of our light carrier group to provide close air support for the withdrawing marines. Despite bad weather in the afternoon, the fast carrier group of the *Philippine Sea, Princeton,* and *Leyte* put 125 offensive sorties into the Koto-ri area in support of the marine withdrawal.

Farther to the south, Wonsan was evacuated of all friendly forces by the end of the day. The outloading included 3,834 military personnel, 1,150 vehicles, and 10,000 tons of cargo.

One empty cargo ship, the SS *Lane Victory,* was left over. The embarkation officer, Capt. Albert Jarrell, packed it with Korean refugees who were likely to be classified as "enemy" by the North Koreans and then slated for execution. Originally, Jarrell expected to board about a thousand civilians. It soon became apparent this was a gross underestimate. He continued loading the ship to capacity, cramming in something in excess of seven thousand Koreans. Sadly, he had to leave another twenty thousand still on the dock clamoring to get out. Jarrell concluded that the entire population of Wonsan and outlying towns wanted desperately to leave.

Dear Anna: Words cannot describe the let-down we felt when the USS *Hanson* returned from Sasebo without bringing any mail. It appears our mail was placed aboard one of the oilers which, hopefully, we'll rendezvous with one of these days. It's lonesome out here. Two weeks without mail is two weeks too long. I miss reading your sweet words. The sea is very rough and heavy today, which mirrors my present state of mind.   Rusty

---

**Ship's Log: Friday 8 December 1950**   1615 Sank large floating mine by gunfire, no detonation.

---

The *John J. Borland* (DD-855) became the AKA-855 for about four hours. (AKA is the designation for an armed cargo vessel.) We transferred approximately 3,100 pounds of napalm from the *Sicily* to the *Badoeng Strait*. The operation took four hours in driving sleet and snow.

The cruiser *Saint Paul* and destroyers *Zellars* and *Sperry* provided covering fire for the final withdrawal from Wonsan. By 10:15 P.M. the beach was clear. Everything had been taken out; no destruction of supplies or gear had been necessary. The total Wonsan lift was 3,800 troops, 7,000 refugees, 1,146 vehicles, and 10,000 tons of cargo.

Two east coast evacuations had now been accomplished, and a third was shaping up. Naval gunfire had held the North Korean forces at bay, and the entire operation was completed without the loss of life or equipment.

The Wonsan evacuation provided a miniature dress rehearsal for the Hungnam evacuation that was soon to follow.

The USS *De Haven* (DD-727) plows through heavy seas while refueling from an aircraft carrier off the coast of Korea.

Winter's cold blast forms four-inch layer of ice on gun mount on the USS *Oriskany* (CVA-34) in Korean waters.

Three ships refuel simultaneously from the USS *Salamonie* (AO-26): the USS *Power* (DD-839), USS *Newport News* (CA-148), and USS *Hanson* (DDR-832). The author served aboard the *Hanson*, 1953–55.

A hillbilly band aboard the USS *John A. Bole* (DD-755) serenades the admiral. The author is shown holding a cup of coffee. (photograph by Charles T. Hampton)

Navy Unit Citation is presented to the destroyers *Collett* (DD-730), *Lyman K. Swenson* (DD-729), *Mansfield* (DD-728), and *De Haven* (DD-727) for outstanding action at Inchon, Korea.

Burial-at-sea ceremonies for LTJG David Swenson are held aboard the USS *Toledo* (CA-133) on September 14, 1950, at Inchon Harbor. Lieutenant Swenson was the nephew of Lyman K. Swenson for whom the destroyer DD-729 was named.

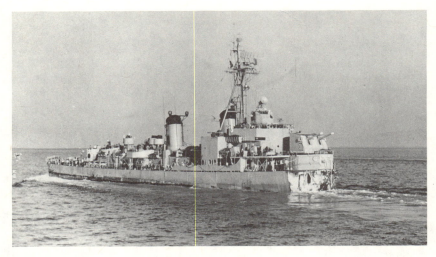

The USS *Ernest G. Small* (DD-838) grew smaller when she struck a mine off the coast of Korea on October 7, 1951, blowing eighty-five feet off her bow. The ship backed slowly to Japan, where emergency repairs were made.

U.S. Marine and Army troops land at Wonsan after a six-day wait while the harbor was cleared of twenty-five hundred mines.

F4U Corsair fighter planes line up for takeoff from an aircraft carrier of Task Force 77 off the coast of North Korea.

F9F Panther jet fighters from the USS *Boxer* (CV-21) fly by ships of Task Force 77 on their way to strafe military installations in North Korea.

Raging seas and pitching decks make dangerous work of transferring a seaman via highline from the USS *Tolovana* (AO-64) to the USS *Valley Forge* (CV-45).

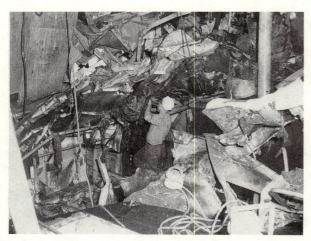

A navy repairman inspects damage to the USS *Walke* (DD-723), which was mangled by an underwater explosion on June 12, 1951, off the coast of Korea. Twenty-six men died in the explosion; seven were wounded.

Smoke billows hundreds of feet into the air as the last troops withdraw from Hungnam, North Korea, December 24, 1950.

The USS *Mansfield* (DD-728) arrives with temporary wooden bow at Bremerton, Washington, after being struck by a mine while searching for a downed air force B-26 pilot.

A smoke ring is formed by the muzzle blast of a 5-inch gun as the USS *Toledo* (CA-133) fires salvo at enemy installations in Wonsan, Korea.

Four destroyers steam in formation: the USS *John W. Thomason* (DD-760), USS *Taussig* (DD-746), USS *John A. Bole* (DD-755), and USS *Beatty* (DD-756). The author served aboard the *Bole,* 1949–51.

## 11 EVACUATING HUNGNAM

---

**Ship's Log: Saturday 9 December 1950**  Steaming with Marine Air Group in USS SICILY (CVE-118) and USS BADOENG STRAIT (CVE-116) making air strikes in close support of UN troops in North Korea.

---

In November General MacArthur thought he had the world by the tail. In December he was staring disaster in the face. His troops were spread too thin and their lines of supply were stretched beyond the ability to provide needed reinforcements and supplies. Bitter cold and harsh weather severely restricted mobility on the ground and in the air.

On December 6 he sent a dispatch to Washington saying that unless he received massive reinforcement almost immediately he would have to evacuate Korea.

MacArthur's dispatch had a chilling effect. Not only did the Pentagon conclude that the UN forces were in danger of being annihilated, but they became even more fearful that the Chinese intervention might be the first step leading the Soviet bloc into a third world war.

The Joint Chiefs of Staff directed MacArthur to evacuate his troops from North Korea. The embarkation port was decreed to be Hungnam.

The marines broke out of a potential trap at Hagaru on December 7 and fought their way down the road to Koto-ri, their main staging area, some seven miles south. There they established a strong defensive perimeter. Night temperatures at times reached twenty-five degrees below zero.

On the following day they began the eleven-mile march across a high mountain pass and down to the town of Chinhung-ni. For a brief period the convoy extended over the entire distance between the towns, but air support kept the Chinese under control until the movement was completed. From Chinhung-ni it would be another thirty-two miles to the sea. This route was described by General Shepherd as "a defile through which no military force should ever have to fight."

They also had to fight the bad weather. A swirling snowstorm moved down around Koto-ri on the morning of the eighth, reducing visibility to zero and making air support impossible. But the weather lifted on the ninth, and the carriers got back at work. Sorties mounted to a record 479.[1]

---

**Ship's Log: Sunday 10 December 1950**   Screening and lifeguard duties with USS BADOENG STRAIT.

---

At sea, a soft snow began falling about 8:00 A.M. It continued throughout the day. But the navy was ready. Admiral Doyle had assembled one of the mightiest naval forces ever mobilized for short-range support of ground forces.

This operation would have every attribute of a major amphibious landing—but in reverse. On shore, supplies were being packed up, moved down to the beach, and made ready to be lifted out to the anchored cargo ships. Troops would be retiring from a steadily shrinking perimeter to the embarkation points where they would be ferried out to transports at sea.

Initial estimates of the task at hand called for the removal of between 110,000 and 120,000 men, some 15,000 vehicles, and about 400,000 tons of cargo.

A total of 109 naval vessels were assembled for the evacuation. These included 38 LSTs, 8 troop transports, 3 attack cargo ships, 4 repair ships, and various command, escort, and commercial cargo vessels. Some of these ships were to serve double duty by shuttling back and forth to Pusan with their cargoes.

For protection, fire support ships were assigned to lay down a curtain of steel around the Hungnam perimeter. This group consisted of the cruisers *Saint Paul* and *Rochester;* the destroyers *Forrest Royal, Norris, English, Hank, Lind,* and *Massey;* and three LSMR rocket ships. Estimates of enemy strength suggested that the Chinese could throw between six and eight divisions against the perimeter. Accordingly, defensive positions were laid out ashore to permit naval gunfire to bear upon the attacking Chinese.

For air support, Task Force 77 was expanded from two to four fast carriers, with the *Valley Forge* (hastily recalled from the United States) and *Princeton* being added to the *Philippine Sea* and *Leyte,* which had already been on station. In addition, the escort carrier group of *Sicily* and *Badoeng Strait* was now augmented by the light carrier *Bataan,* to provide additional air cover for ground forces and ships in the port area.

Finally, because the hills north of Hungnam tended to block the radars of the ships in the harbor, thus leaving them vulnerable to air attacks from low-flying aircraft, the destroyer *Duncan* was stationed fifty miles to seaward as a radar picket ship.

---

**Ship's Log: Monday 11 December 1950**  Assigned to various screening stations with USS SICILY and USS BADOENG STRAIT.

---

In one of history's great successful retreats, the leading elements of the marines reached the staging area at Hungnam. The 1st Marine Division had made the trek from Koto-ri to Hungnam, pelted by snow and icy winds, sometimes moving as much as twenty hours at a stretch, carrying packs, parkas, sleeping bags, and weapons across frozen roads and hillsides. At a cost to the enemy immeasurably greater than to itself, the marine division, under its canopy of marine and naval air, had been extricated from an impossible situation.

Marine losses had been 4,418 battle casualties—3,500 of whom were wounded—and 7,300 nonbattle casualties, most from frostbite. Instead of destroying the 20,000-man marine force, as the Chinese had set out to do, they had themselves suffered about 35,000 casualties.

---

**Ship's Log: Tuesday 12 December 1950**  1242 Gained sonar contact bearing 313T, distance 6,000 yards. 1330 Sonar contact evaluated as non-submarine.

---

We received our first mail since November 20. Fifty-seven bags of it. I got a trickle of Christmas cards from relatives and four cans of nuts from my mom and stepdad. Nothing from my honey. I was crushed! My disappointment was so overwhelming that tears welled up in my eyes and I had to go off by myself so people wouldn't see me crying.

I think that's when I first realized I had fallen in love. Slowly, imperceptibly, almost without realizing it, Anna's letters had become such an important part of my life that now I couldn't bear the thought of being without them. What's more, I could not imagine a future without her in it. What started out as a passing fancy was turning into a lasting love.

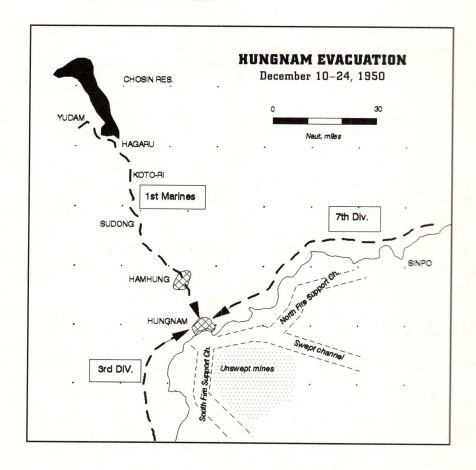

**Ship's Log: Wednesday 13 December 1950** 1725 Unidentified aircraft detected, went to general quarters. 1740 Aircraft intercepted and identified as friendly.

Received the rest of our mail. Sixteen bags. Nine of the sweetest, most precious letters from my Anna. Happy days were here again.

Sea smooth and calm. Temperature warm. First day we could go out without foul weather gear. Sure did feel good not to be weighed down. Our deck wasn't under water once all day.

Delivering mail to ships at sea can be a logistical nightmare, particularly if the ship is being shuttled from one assignment to another as often as we were. Our mail might be put aboard an oiler, a carrier, or

another destroyer that was expected to rendezvous with us somewhere at sea, only to find that we were somewhere else by the time
they arrived. Perhaps half a dozen ships might be carrying packets of
our mail at the same time.

---

**Ship's Log: Thursday 14 December 1950**   Steaming in company
with USS BADOENG STRAIT (CVE-116) and USS SICILY (CVE-118).

---

Rough and heavy seas again. Temperatures hovered right
around the freezing point. Would have felt wonderful to stay curled up
in a nice, warm bunk.

I had to put my first man on report for doing just that—oversleep-
ing. Seaman Charles Kelley failed to show up for dawn GQ. That was a
real no-no.

In the navy's system of justice, the captain's mast—so-called because it was traditionally held at the base of the ship's main mast—was
the lowest order of disciplinary proceeding. The captain could either
mete out punishment directly in the case of minor offenses, or he
could bind the offender over for a deck, summary, or general court
martial, depending on the severity of the offense.

Commander Buaas showed great ingenuity in meting out punishment to Seaman Kelley. He sentenced him to being awakened one
hour before reveille for the next five days.

---

**Ship's Log: Friday 15 December 1950**   1725 Proceeding independently to gunfire support at Hungnam.

---

The marine convoy of twenty-two thousand troops sailed
from Hungnam. Among those evacuated was Harold "Muley" Mul-
hausen, marine private from Oklahoma City, who had landed in Korea
in early November. During that month Muley had seen enough killing
to last him a lifetime.

No naval gunfire was requested until this night. But the navy was
ready and had been for days. The evacuation was supported by the
battleship *Missouri,* with her 16-inch guns, two cruisers, seven destroyers, and three rocket craft. *Saint Paul* commenced 8-inch call fire at
ranges up to ten miles for deep support and for interdiction of enemy
movements. As soon as the perimeter contracted within range of 5-

inch guns of the destroyers, these bombarding ships were able to move closer ashore to obtain better firing positions. On two occasions, the rocket ships were used to fire barrages on the high ground overlooking Hungnam where enemy troops were reportedly concentrated.

---

**Ship's Log: Saturday 16 December 1950**   On fire support station covering evacuation of UN troops, area of Hungnam, Korea.

---

The Army 3d Division pulled back from Hamhung to Hungnam, and the ROK Capital Division moved down from the northeast. The perimeter was narrowed to the Hungnam area alone.

The chief worry was that the enemy might launch an attack on the shrinking perimeter. Bad weather inland limited fast carrier offensive sorties to a mere forty-one. The North Korean IV and V Corps attempted a simultaneous attack on the northeast side of the perimeter. They launched a few desultory mortar barrages, but their effort was repelled by naval gunfire.

---

**Ship's Log: Sunday 17 December 1950**   Screening while carriers launched air strikes against enemy forces in area of Hungnam.

---

Subfreezing temperatures hit shortly after midnight, accompanied by heavy seas. We awoke to about six inches of ice covering every exposed surface of the ship. The *Borland* looked like a picture out of Currier and Ives.

The ice was beautiful—and hazardous. The deck crew rigged hand ropes, but walking anywhere on an open deck was virtually out of the question, particularly since heavy seas and freezing spray continued to wash over the ship.

We spent a lot of time with our foredeck under water. Waves and freezing water crashed over mount 51. Icy spray reached as high as the radar antennas at an eighty-five-foot elevation. We shut down the radars to minimize torque on their antenna motors.

The bad weather added woes to the already complicated evacuation at Hungnam. Temperatures dropped below freezing and westerly winds reached forty knots. Four LCMs broke loose from their moorings and were blown out into the minefields. From 5:00 P.M. until after midnight small boat traffic had to be halted. Working around the clock and exposed to cold, spray, and wind, many of the boat cox-swains had to be carried aboard their ships after returning from long trips.

---

**Ship's Log: Monday 18 December 1950**   Steaming with USS BADOENG STRAIT.

---

The ships were still covered with ice, but the sea was not as rough as it had been. At midmorning, the sun made an appearance and stayed out for the rest of the day, giving a fairylike luminescence to the ice.

With improving weather, the outloading of troops resumed at Hungnam. When the Army 7th Division was safely loaded, the perimeter was then shrunk to a radius of three miles from the center of the city.

One of the most difficult problems was presented by a Korean LST loaded with seventy-four hundred Korean refugees. It fouled a shaft with manila line and was unable to retract from the beach. The snarl was cleared by personnel from the rescue ship *Conserver*. But when the LST tried to get underway again it fouled both shafts. Despite the cold, divers from the *Conserver* freed the port shaft and the cripple got underway again. She was accompanied by the USS *Diachenko*, which was rigged for towing.

---

**Ship's Log: Tuesday 19 December 1950**   Screening and acting as plane guard for the USS BADOENG STRAIT. 1524 All hands to general quarters, manned ASW stations, investigated sonar contact. 1540 Evaluated as non-submarine.

---

Air and surface radars were out of operation in the aftermath of the ice storm. Apparently they got twisted out of alignment by the heavy ice. Reluctantly, we shut them down to prevent further damage. Until we could get back to port, we would have to get by without that vital equipment.

As the perimeter around Hungnam contracted, the Chinese and North Koreans surrounded the city. Naval artillery continued to thunder day and night, and navy planes swarmed over the city like angry hornets.

They hit Communist troop movements on the roads and bombed any concentrations of supplies or ammunition that they found.

The plan was to get everything out—not just personnel and loaded vehicles, but everything. They nearly succeeded.

To deprive the enemy of salvage possibilities even broken-down vehicles were outloaded. Inoperative machinery filled our Liberty ships. Col. Edward Forney, control officer for the evacuation, found his responsibilities steadily increasing: an original count of 5,000 drums of lubricating oil ended up in the onloading of 29,500 drums, with 200 left behind; almost 9,000 tons of ammunition were taken out. Of the 1,000 tons of ammunition remaining, half was frozen dynamite too dangerous to handle. These leftover commodities were used in the final demolition of the port.

---

**Ship's Log: Wednesday 20 December 1950**   1431 Unidentified aircraft overhead, crew to general quarters. 1441 Aircraft identified as friendly.

---

A very annoying, not to say unsanitary, habit was that of bumming a sip of coffee from somebody's cup. Elbert Garwood, QM3, a tall, gangly lad from Texas who had a reputation of stumbling over his own feet, thought he had found a way to cope with the annoyance. When someone would ask him for a sip of coffee, he replied, "Okay, but I spit in it." That usually put the fellow off.

Garwood met his match one day in Sam Stock. Garwood was coming out of the charthouse bearing a steaming cup of coffee. "Hey, Gar," Stock asked, "How about a sip of your coffee?"

"Okay," Garwood said reluctantly. "But I spit in it."

Sam took a sip, then went ptooey! "That's okay, I spit in it too," he said, handing it back to a startled Garwood.

---

**Ship's Log: Thursday 21 December 1950**   1320 Exercised crew at general quarters to test fire all automatic weapons; expended 72 rounds of 40MM ammunition.

---

Destroyers have often been called "the greyhounds of the sea." The metaphor is apt. Like the greyhound, they depend on speed and agility. Also like the greyhound, excess weight is a hindrance that can reduce their fighting effectiveness. And, just as the greyhound is capable of only short bursts of intense activity and must rest between forays to restore its energy, destroyers must periodically replenish sources of food and fuel.

After thirty days of steady steaming, we were beginning to run short of just about everything. The galley was out of such staples as potatoes, pork, and green vegetables. Breakfast was reduced to powdered eggs, green with age—surely one of the gosh-awfulest concoctions ever foisted on man. For the most part, the crew took these deprivations in stride.

The item whose absence caused the most discomfort was *toilet paper.* That's one of nature's little necessities a person doesn't think about until he doesn't have any. People were reduced to scrounging anything that would serve as a substitute. Paperback novels worked best; their pages were of the right size, strength, and texture—and they were readily available. Thus it became common to see a guy sitting on the john attending to the call of nature, reading a novel, and hearing someone clamor, "Hurry up and finish that page."

That's how I learned to be a speed reader—trying to keep ahead of the demands for potty paper.

---

**Ship's Log: Friday 22 December 1950**   At 1225 detached from Task Group and proceeding independently to Sasebo, Japan.

---

One aspect of the evacuation developed into wholly unanticipated proportions. That was the problem of the North Korean refugees. It presented both a tragic spectacle and a military menace.

For the inhabitants of North Korea, the miseries of war had been compounded by the arrival of an alien army from across the Yalu. Villagers were dispossessed, their houses taken over by the Chinese. Whether because of dissatisfaction with their own repressive government or distaste for the invader from the north, countless thousands cast their preference for the "invader" from across the ocean. In any event, a veritable tide of humanity flowed southward toward Hungnam.

An original estimate of 25,000 refugees requiring evacuation had quickly to be expanded. Early in the operation Colonel Forney found himself with 50,000 people in hastily constructed camps and more pouring in; at Hamhung more than 50,000 had attempted to board the last refugee train for Hungnam. The exodus involved an incredible packing of humanity; LST loads were never less than 5,000, and in one case reached 10,500; a total of about 14,000 were taken out in the chartered *Meredith Victory*.

As evacuation preparations were being completed, Forney brought in three victory ships and two LSTs on which he loaded 50,000 Koreans. The final tally showed 91,000 taken out, not counting children in arms, in knapsacks, or in utero. Despite this remarkable accomplishment no one congratulated himself overmuch, for as Forney's report concluded, "at least that number had to be left behind for lack of shipping space."

---

**Ship's Log: Saturday 23 December 1950**   At 1140 moored alongside the USS JASON (ARH-1) at buoy 14, Sasebo for repairs to air search radar antenna.

---

Some guys seem to have a knack for beating the system. No liberty for the crew, but Claude Gray, gunner's mate second class, managed to get ashore anyway. He used the excuse of needing to get his glasses fixed. Along the way, he managed to go by the canteen and belt away two or three shots of Japanese Suntory whiskey.

On a sadder note, it was announced that Gen. Walton Walker, commander of the U.S. Eighth Army, had been killed when his jeep swerved off the road and overturned. Ironically, like his World War II idol, Gen. George S. Patton, Walker died not on the field of battle but in a traffic accident.

That evening, as Gen. Matthew Ridgway was at dinner with some old army friends at Fort Myer, he received a telephone call. It was from the army chief of staff informing him he had been selected as Walker's successor.

Ridgway had hoped to spend Christmas with his family, but after a hurried briefing the next morning at the Pentagon, he boarded a plane that evening for the Far East. He would arrive on Christmas Day.

Off Songjin, the USS *Sperry* (DD-697) was hit by three enemy shells while on shore bombardment duty. No casualties, and only minor damage.

---

**Ship's Log: Sunday 24 December 1950**  1713 Underway from Sasebo, Japan, to rejoin Task Group in operating area off Korea.

---

At Hungnam, all was in readiness for the final evacuation of the remaining forces. The Army 3d Division had been given the responsibility as rearguard and, as such, was the last to leave. H-hour was set for 11:00 A.M.

The most ticklish problem was how to get the men off the beach without an enemy attack. Gunfire ships maintained a zone barrage covering a mile-wide area outside the three-thousand-yard perimeter.

Everything went as planned. The only difficulties were caused by an accidental explosion of an ammunition dump, which destroyed some landing craft and resulted in a number of casualties.

At 2:10 P.M. the real fireworks display began. UDT personnel set off demolition charges and blew up all the munitions that had to be left behind, including several hundred 1,000-pound bombs and four hundred tons of dynamite. Piers, cranes, and walls of the inner harbor disappeared in a blast of smoke and flame.

The statistics of the evacuation are worth noting: 105,000 U.S. and Korean military personnel, 91,000 refugees, 350,000 tons of cargo, 17,500 vehicles. For fifteen days in December, Hungnam was one of the world's busiest ports.

Evacuations can hardly be counted as victories, but the evacuation from Hungnam was nevertheless impressive. Under the severest possible conditions, the march to the sea was successfully accomplished; only the barest minimum of equipment and supplies had to be destroyed; the evacuation was a deliberate, orderly, and controlled process.

Dear Anna: We're to leave Sasebo around 5:15 P.M. on our way to rejoin the task force. The crew is bitterly disappointed that we didn't get to stay in port over Christmas. Merry Christmas.   Love, Rusty

# 12 ESCORTING THE ESCORTS

*December 25, 1950–January 28, 1951*

---

**Ship's Log: Monday 25 December 1950**   0800 Rejoined Task Group 96.8. Passed mail, movies, and passengers for Task Group 96.8 to the USS HANSON (DDR-832), USS TAUSSIG (DD-746), USS SMALL (DD-838), USS SICILY (CVE-118), and USS BADOENG STRAIT (CVE-116).

---

Along the war front Christmas was eerily quiet. Intelligence sources kept reporting on a buildup of enemy forces—an estimated 167,000 North Koreans and 276,000 Chinese in North Korea, with 300,000 more Chinese across the border. But nothing was happening. It was like waiting for the other shoe to drop.[1]

Except for being served a Christmas turkey with all the trimmings, we didn't have much to indicate that this day was different from all the others. We spent until eight in the evening passing men, mail, and movies that we had hauled out of Sasebo for delivery to other ships in the fleet.

I was still so dad-gummed ticked off at our having to sail on Christmas Eve I ended up doing something really stupid. Along with our meal, each man was offered a choice of a fine cigar or a pack of Camel cigarettes. Although I had quit smoking more than a month before, I said to myself, "If the damned navy can afford to give me a pack of cigarettes, the least I can do is smoke the damn things!" I guess it was a case of cutting off one's nose to spite one's face because by the time I finished that pack of cigarettes I was hooked again.

---

**Ship's Log: Tuesday 26 December 1950**   Steaming with Task Group 96.8 in operating area off west coast of Korea to provide air support for UN forces.

---

Because the *Borland* was what was called a short-hull *Sumner,* the top brass did not want us running with the fast carriers.[2] The problem was that we had less fuel capacity than the fourteen-foot-longer *Gearings* and therefore had to be fueled more often. Whenever possible they assigned us to the slower escort carriers.

These baby flattops were initially designed to combat the U-boat menace in the North Atlantic during World War II. Built on converted tanker hulls, they steamed with the convoys to provide an effective air defense against the German submarines, which until the arrival of the escort carriers, had been decimating the fleets of merchantmen. The baby flattops saw their role expand as the Second World War progressed, and by war's end they had seen extensive service in the Pacific.

---

**Ship's Log: Wednesday–Friday 27–29 December 1950**   Acting as plane guard for USS SICILY (CVE-118) during air operations and conducting sonar and mine search in ASW screen between air operations.

---

The winter in Korea remained bitterly cold. Howling winds whipped down from the vast empty plains of Siberia with a furious intensity. Subfreezing temperatures at sea and winds exceeding forty knots were not uncommon. Salt spray was turned into four-inch-thick layers of ice on the decks and rigging of ships. High winds made work on the destroyers particularly uncomfortable. Topside tasks were arduous, uncomfortable, and dangerous.

The officer whose fate it was to have the most absurd name was George Washington Stubblefield Jr., lieutenant, USN, our engineering officer. A tall, slender man with a sharp face, red-gold hair, and a pencil-thin mustache, he was known throughout the ship as a fantastic, but excitable, engineer who was not afraid to get down in the sweat and grime of the enginerooms with his men. His trademark was a battered officer's hat that had been burned on one side. He smoked like a chimney and was a prime candidate for lung cancer.

For some damn-fool reason, the guys in the radio shack had nothing better to do one night than to joke about Stubblefield's name. They invented new ways to pronounce or spell it. Silliness set in, and they began making up names like "Shistlefinger," "Shistlepisser," "Pistolshisser," "Thumbsucker," and some even grosser. Each variation provoked peals of laughter that forced the next guy to try to top the last one.

When it came time to carry the message routing board around to the officers to read and sign, the assignment fell to Roy Pippin, radioman striker. These silly names were still ringing in his ear as he climbed down the ladder to step onto the main deck. Whom should he bump into but Stubblefield himself. Pippin was so flustered at this unexpected encounter that he saluted awkwardly and blurted out, "Uh, hello there, Mr. Shistlefinger."

A mortified Pippin beat a hasty retreat back up the ladder. A perplexed Stubblefield was left to wonder what in the world was going on.

General MacArthur threw down the gauntlet to the Joint Chiefs of Staff. He fired off a cable to Washington in which he urged four actions; "(1) blockade China's coast; (2) destroy China's industrial warmaking capacity, through air and naval bombardment; (3) reinforce the UN Command with Nationalist Chinese; and (4) allow the Nationalists to undertake diversionary action against the mainland."[3] He also requested four more divisions be sent to Japan.

In effect, MacArthur was arguing that given the continuing restrictions on his operations, UN withdrawal from the Korean peninsula was an inevitable consequence.

---

**Ship's Log: Sunday 31 December 1950**   1100 Took passengers aboard via high line for transfer to USS BADOENG STRAIT. Broke fueling hose due to heavy seas.

---

Very few of us bothered to stay up to see the old year out and the new one in.

Shorty Hall, however, broke out the magnum of champagne he'd been hoarding. It was amazing, knowing Shorty's proclivity for potation, that he hadn't already tapped it. He was in his glory, still reveling in his feat of having smuggled a whole two-quart bottle of booze aboard without being detected.

Lieutenant Dvorcek was the OOD. In keeping with tradition, he wrote the first entry of the new year in poetry—of a sort. It began:

At sea this a.m. in the John J. Borland, off the Korean west coast,
We pause for a moment from duties assigned, and offer a heartwarming
    toast
To men and the ships of the Task Group we're in, number nine-six-point-
    eight,
With Admiral Ruble, the OTC, directing our fortunes and fate.

His doggerel, which ran for another forty-five lines, would never win any literary prize.

---

**Ship's Log: Monday 1 January 1951**   Acting as plane guard for designated carriers.

---

General Ridgway's "honeymoon" was short-lived. Hardly had he landed on Korean soil then the Chinese launched a major attack in the early morning hours. Ridgway articulated a new philosophy by which he would fight this war: "Real estate" was irrelevant. In this he differed sharply from MacArthur. Ridgway was not interested simply in occupying a few square miles of land for the sake of newspaper headlines—land the Chinese might take back from him later. What he wanted most of all was dead Chinese.

His men were instructed to "seek every opportunity to punish the enemy, . . . to seek occasions where the enemy may be drawn into a trap where strong forces on his flanks may counterattack and cut him up."[4] Ridgway intended to make the war so costly to the Chinese they would have to begin thinking about their own withdrawal from the political trap that Korea had become.

---

**Ship's Log: Tuesday 2 January 1951**   USS BATAAN (CVL-29) joined Task Group. Rescued Major K. L. Reuser, USMC, when his F4U aircraft crashed off port beam. Transferred him via high line to the USS SICILY (CVE-118).

---

Picking up downed pilots was by now refined to a high art. We had to move fast.

These guys had about twenty minutes to live once they hit those frigid waters. That was all. The water was so bitterly cold that within minutes the hands were frozen. Then the face. Ten more minutes of immersion in those fearful waters and the arms became immobile. By the twentieth minute all life functions ceased.

Jamie Passarelli was our resident body builder. A boiler technician third class, Passarelli was the reigning holder of the title "Mr. San Diego, Upper Body."

From Chicago, Passarelli stood about five-seven, weighed in at 155 pounds, and boasted characteristic Latin good looks. He had married a San Diego girl shortly before we left the States. Passarelli's station was the after fireroom that powered the starboard engine and screw.

Boiler technician (BT) was a skilled position that carried responsibility for generating the steam that powered the ship's main propulsion engines. Keeping the boilers full of water was tricky even under normal conditions, and it was particularly difficult when in a storm at sea. When the ship was rolling violently from port to starboard and bouncing up and down, the BTs almost never knew where their water level was.

---

**Ship's Log: Wednesday 3 January 1951**   Escort for carriers SICILY, BATAAN, and BADOENG STRAIT.

---

General Ridgway decided to abandon Seoul. As the army moved out, he personally stood on the north bank of the bridge across the Han River and watched the last of the tanks and artillery cross, followed by thousands of refugees swarming after the departing soldiers. Ridgway expected the Chinese and North Koreans to follow with another attack, but they chose not to cross the Han.

---

**Ship's Log: Thursday 4 January 1951**   Steaming as before as unit of Task Element 96.84.

---

The *Borland* narrowly escaped being cut in two by the USS *Bataan*. It happened when we were steaming darken ship and the carriers turned into the wind to receive returning planes in a night landing.

The weather was lousy. In fact, it was snowing. To give the pilots a better shot at finding the carriers in the snowy overcast, the task force commander ordered all ships to turn on their lights. Lights came on everywhere. They created a lot of disorientation among the screen ships who were not used to seeing that many lights at night. It was hard to judge how far we were from other ships.

Lieutenant (j.g.) Melesky was the OOD on the bridge. Captain Buaas came up to the bridge to observe the maneuver. As he looked out the port side, he saw the bow of an aircraft carrier bearing directly down us. It was the *Bataan*. Collision was imminent.

Instantly Buaas jumped into the pilot house, grabbed the engine order telegraph, and yelled "Right full rudder! Starboard engine back full! Port engine ahead full!"

The *Borland* swung around and cleared the area of that carrier. But just barely![5]

If things seemed hectic on the bridge, that was nothing compared with what was going on belowdecks in the ship's enginerooms and firerooms. Jamie Passarelli was in charge of the after fireroom. All hell broke loose down there when, out of nowhere, the order came, "flank," then "stop," then "full reverse." Throwing a ship into reverse isn't as simple as backing up an automobile. It has to be done systematically, in order, and with extreme caution.

At the time, we were running "split plant"; that is, the forward engineroom and forward fireroom ran the port screw, and the after engineroom and after fireroom ran the starboard screw.[6] The superheaters were on, generating nine-hundred-degree temperature and six hundred pounds of steam. A jet of steam from a broken pipe could cut a man in two.

When the screw went to full reverse, the engine placed a sudden, huge demand for steam. This demand caused the amount of steam to diminish, which in turn, sucked water out of the boiler. Without water, the boilers would blow sky high.

Passarelli watched the water gauge with a growing sense of panic. The boiler casing was expanding like a huge lung gasping for breath. The crew, galvanized into action, ran every pump they had trying to get fresh water into the boiler. And it had to be hot water; cold water might have formed a "slug," which if it passed through the steam lines to the turbines, would hit those hot blades and knock the turbines out.

One minute passed, then two, then three. Still no water showing in the gauge. The whole fireroom was about to blow. Four minutes. Passarelli was on the verge of ordering the crew to evacuate the fireroom when he saw water creeping up in the gauge. Five minutes. The gauge filled up.

During those five minutes, Jamie Passarelli aged fifty years. He was only eighteen years old.

---

**Ship's Log: Friday 5 January 1951**   Screening the USS BATAAN in operating area off west coast of Korea.

---

The Eighth Army now started retreating south again. At Inchon, destruction of the port facilities was begun in what could be only termed a "scorched earth" policy. Admiral Smith argued that was a dumb thing to do, inasmuch as the Chinese weren't shipping anything by sea and the facilities wouldn't be of much use to them anyway. On the other hand, if our armies moved north again we would have great need for a functioning port.

The sea lift from Inchon was a sizable one. Thirty-two thousand troops, more than a thousand vehicles, and fifty-five thousand tons of cargo were moved out. Port facilities were blown before the Chinese entered the town.

Throughout the period of retreat, Task Force 77 flew strikes against enemy concentrations in the central mountains and westward to the area of Seoul. At Inchon, the cruisers *Rochester, Kenya,* and *Ceylon* supported the evacuation of the port and bombarded Kimpo Airfield. From the Yellow Sea the marine fighter pilots from the *Sicily* and *Badoeng Strait* flew in to provide protective patrols, strike the advancing enemy, and burn quantities of abandoned supplies at Kimpo Airfield.[7]

---

**Ship's Log: Saturday 6 January 1951**   Screening and plane guard operations for the carriers of Task Group 96.8.

---

Sadness tinged with envy characterized our farewell to Lieutenant Dvorcek. He was transferred via highline to the USS *Graffias* during a fueling operation for transfer to Pacific Reserve Fleet, San Diego. He was headed home.

A highline transfer was not for the faint-hearted. The delivering ship rigged a heavy manila line high in its superstructure—hence the term "highline"—and then fired a shot, with a small messenger line attached, to the receiving ship, which in turn, secured the line to its own superstructure. The individual being transferred then took his seat in a canvas bos'n's chair that hung from a pulley-wheel mounted on the manila line, and a group of line handlers then hauled him across until he was safely on the deck of the receiving ship.

The ships must match speed for speed, and their superstructures are moving with the motion of the waves—sometimes leaning toward each other, sometimes swaying apart. If the two ships rolled toward each other at the same time, the passenger would take a dunking. If they rolled apart, the line could separate.

Dvorcek made it across safely. There had been some good-natured kidding beforehand that the guys were going to dunk him on his way across. But the sea was too rough and the water too cold for them to risk taking a chance with a man's life.

---

**Ship's Log: Sunday–Monday 7–8 January 1951**   Screen and plane guard operations for Task Group 96.8.

---

Dear Anna: I guess they've given up on the weather here and are sending us back into port. Flight operations have been shut down for three days now, with no improvement in the forecast. This makes 50 days we've been continuously at sea—except for those few hours in Sasebo on Christmas Eve during which no one got liberty.   Love, Rusty

---

**Ship's Log: Tuesday–Saturday 9–13 January 1951**   Moored in Sasebo, Japan, for one week availability alongside USS HAMUL (AD-20).

---

Our new executive officer, Lt. Comdr. James W. Roddy, reported aboard. He replaced John Maddox who was leaving to command his own destroyer. Roddy was a reserve officer called back to active duty. Above average height, strong and wiry, and damnably good looking, Roddy ran an advertising agency in San Francisco.

We had our first captain's personnel inspection in several weeks. It was snowing, and the enlisted men's peacoats were almost white. Afterward, a photographer posed everyone with a beard in front of mount 51 and took their picture for the cruise book.

Like many sailors, I once tried my hand at growing a beard. Guys like Claude Gray and Hale Beard had grown full, luxurious beards. Arend Folkens sprouted a pointy goatee to cover up his receding chin. Even LTJG Chuck Reeves cultivated the dashing look of a Prussian officer with his short-cropped chin whiskers and spike mustache.

My own attempts at achieving such hirsute splendor met with ignominious failure. My facial growth came out all red and scraggly. I was the butt end of so much teasing and ridicule that I finally gave up and shaved it off after the first month. But I kept the upper lip hair, which I hoped to nourish into a handlebar mustache.

The difficulty with cultivating a handlebar mustache was that I didn't have any mustache wax to hold it in the desired shape. I tried everything—paraffin off milk cartons, beeswax, even shoe polish—all to no avail. I got damned tired of whiskers drooping into my food.

Before going ashore on Saturday, I shaved off my mustache. Later, as I was puttering around one of the old-fashioned shops in Sasebo, I came across a tiny tin of mustache wax. It had probably been there since the 1890s.

Feeling as if I had just discovered a gold mine, I dashed off to the nearest rest room where I might find a mirror. Only when my reflection stared back at me in the mirror did I realize I had shaved the damned thing off less than an hour before.

---

**Ship's Log: Sunday 14 January 1951**   Moored in Sasebo, Japan, alongside USS HAMUL.

---

Dear Anna: Sunday. Went to Nagasaki today. Left the ship at 10:30 A.M., back aboard at 11:00 P.M. It's a beautiful city which, for more than two centuries, was the most important port in Japan. Visited the Glover mansion, the home of an English merchant who married a Japanese woman. The story for Puccini's opera *Madame Butterfly* is said to have been set here. We also visited Peace Park, built on the exact center of the August 9, 1945, atomic blast that, in a blinding flash, killed 75,000 people and destroyed a third of the city. That A-bomb really had a destructive blast. Made me realize how terrible the A-bomb really was . . . and still *is*.   Love, Rusty

---

**Ship's Log: Monday 15 January 1951**   Moored in Sasebo, Japan, preparing to get underway.

---

The SPS-6 radar crapped out on us as we were running equipment tests. It was the transmitter (TR) tube. Great as the SPS-6 was, it had a nasty habit of burning out TR tubes when running at high power. The damn things cost twelve hundred dollars apiece.

Ensign MaCamont was running scared on costs. He was afraid Commodore Lang—who was something of a martinet—would blow a gasket when he found out we had overspent our budget. We talked with Commander Buaas.

"Captain," I said, "we have a problem. We have a radar that's capable of doing tremendous things, but it's burning out the TR tubes. If we run it at the power ratio we're supposed to in order to get the results we're supposed to be getting, we're going to be burning them up and have to replace them."

His reply was terse and to the point. "We're in a war now. Don't worry about that!"

So that's what we did—ran full power and damn the costs. I hoped the commodore wouldn't get on our ass for overspending our budget. But that was the captain's worry now.

---

**Ship's Log: Tuesday 16 January 1951**   Underway to join Task Force 77 in operating area off east coast of Korea.

---

We fired 40-mm AA practice at towed sleeves for two-and-a-half hours. But our gunners weren't hitting anything.

These guns spit out 1.75-inch, 2-pound high explosive projectiles at a rate of 160 rounds per minute per barrel. With four barrels per quad mount, that's an incredible amount of metal. They became enormously popular in the Pacific during World War II as a defense against approaching Japanese kamikaze planes. Now, however, they were outmoded against modern high-speed jets and could rarely be counted on to defeat an attacking jet before the pilot released his weapon.

Our new exec, Lieutenant Commander Roddy, got so mad at the inability of our 40-mm gunners to hit the sleeve that he stormed off the bridge. "For Chrissake," he yelled at them, "somebody throw a rock at the goddamn thing!"

---

**Ship's Log: Wednesday 17 January 1951**   Screening heavy units of Task Force 77 while conducting air operations against enemy forces in Korea.

---

New operational orders switched us from sunrise GQs. From now on, general quarters would begin at sunset and continue for one hour. Whatever the military reason, the crews were pleased. It meant they wouldn't have to get up so early.

\*   \*   \*

The temperature was so cold that not even the electric heaters inside our enclosed gun director station could stave off the chill. Ensign White commented, "I don't know which is worse, being frozen or being scared."

The guys who manned the 40-mm gun mounts had it much worse. They had to stand out in the open air, unprotected from the bitter cold and the icy wind.

Floyd Manders was in a pensive mood. "Mr. White," he asked, "how did we get into this goddamn mess?"

White seemed taken aback. "What do you mean by 'this mess'?"

"I mean, this is a fight in which we have no interest; there's no incentive to fight; and the people back home don't support it. Hell, they won't even dignify what we're doing by calling it a war."

White thought for a moment, then responded, "Well, first of all, we didn't start the war. Joseph Stalin did."

"Why, what's in it for him?"

"Someone once described Stalin as being like a hotel burglar. He walks down the corridor and turns the handles of the doors; if he finds an open door, he goes in and ransacks the place. Well, in much the same fashion, the Soviets have shown a proclivity for probing weak spots they can exploit at minimum risk to themselves. They're perfectly willing to support proxy wars fought by client states. For them, it's the best of both worlds—they have everything to gain and nothing to lose."

Manders still was not convinced. "Yes, but couldn't we find a better way than going to war?"

"In my opinion," White continued, "Truman had three choices, none of them good: One, mount a massive invasion from the shores of a reluctant Japan; two, use atomic weapons on the North Korean capital of Pyongyang; or three, simply walk away."

He concluded, "The worst thing a great power can do is get caught in a bluff and not be willing to back it up. Joseph Stalin chose the time and the place. Truman responded. Failure to meet Stalin's challenge would be so morally derelict that it might fatally endanger America's leadership and ability to avert a third world war."

---

**Ship's Log: Thursday–Sunday 18–21 January 1951** Steaming with Task Force 77.

---

Shorty Hall cursed up a storm. A sudden lurch of the ship had caused his coffeepot to slop brown liquid all over his charts.

Ground coffee was provided gratis from the galley, but each unit had to provide its own coffeepot—such as Shorty's. Folklore had it that navy chaplains led a move back in the 1840s for the government to take away the daily grog ration theretofore enjoyed by U.S. sailors and substitute in its place a daily coffee ration. Ever since, coffee has traditionally been available at all hours of the day and night.

Vowing never again to contend with spilled coffee, Shorty's fertile brain came up with a creative solution. Borrowing an idea from the ship's compass, he suspended the coffeepot inside a set of gimbals. Those are a pair of rings pivoted so that one swings within the other, thereby allowing the compass—or in this case, the coffeepot—to remain horizontal regardless of the movements of the ship.

Shorty's invention worked like a charm. No matter how violently the ship rolled, Shorty's coffeepot remained serenely in an upright position. No more spills.

---

**Ship's Log: Monday–Friday 22–26 January 1951**  Steaming in company with Task Force 77.

---

The ship was covered with ice again, even worse than before. Air operations were brought to a near standstill.

It is said that necessity is the mother of invention. That proved to be true in our case. The necessity was being out of range of any radio station that played American music. The invention was our own shipboard radio station.

Entertainment loudspeakers were spread throughout the ship and fed from a central radio receiver. Out there in the middle of nowhere, we couldn't get even one decent channel. Mostly we heard unintelligible static.

Meanwhile, up in the ET shack, we had a stack of fourteen-inch platters that were transcriptions of old radio programs dating back to World War II. How they got there and how long we'd had them, no one seemed to know.

We matched a "resource" with a "need." By hooking up a record player to the ship's entertainment system, we were able to pipe music throughout the ship. We broadcast four hours every evening.

Gradually we added other features. A second unit could play regular LPs and 45s that people brought us. A microphone allowed us to originate a nightly newscast.

We named the station WORGB. People wondered how we came up with a *five-letter* call sign rather than the usual four. The answer was simple: Above our workbench was a sign that read WORGB. That was the color-coding on the wiring of radio handsets—white, orange, red, green, and blue. Technicians were continually having to repair handsets that had been jerked off their cords, and we posted the sign to remind ourselves of the proper color coding.

The sign, which began as a simple reminder, became our radio call letters.

---

**Ship's Log: Saturday 27 January 1951**   1051 Left formation at speed 27 knots to investigate possible plane crash, reported 20 miles northwest of formation center. 1118 Ordered to rejoin screen, pilot picked up by helicopter.

---

Still cold. Still ice on the ship. Seas not as rough as before. Carriers resumed flight operations. Sun broke out around 10 A.M. The deck crew was out chipping ice off rigging and superstructure. Gunners cleared their guns of ice. High atop the mast, the air search radar antenna sat immobile, encased in ice.

About midmorning, Lieutenant Commander Roddy called me up to CIC. "I know I can't rightfully ask anyone to do this, but we're on our way to pick up a downed pilot. It would really help to have that air search radar back in operation. Do you think, under the circumstances, one of your men would volunteer to go up and see if he could get that antenna rotating again?"

Without thinking, I blurted out, "I'll do it." Ingrained in me was the philosophy, Don't ask someone else to do something you're not willing to do yourself.

"We'll try to hold the ship as steady as we can, but we're not going to be able to slow her down for you," Roddy said.

I buckled on my tool belt, stuck a paint scraper and chipping hammer under my belt, donned my cold-weather gear, and set out to climb the mast. God, but that wind was cold!

Once on the platform, I hooked up my safety harness. That made me feel more secure. Then I began chipping away at the ice around the rotating mechanism. When I thought I had the mechanism freed up, I called on the phone for the radarman to give it a try. The unit shuddered and groaned, but it wouldn't budge. I banged away on the thing some more, hoping to break it loose. Still nothing.

Then the ship started slowing in speed and making a wide turn back in the direction whence we came. I was told that I could come back down because the pilot had been picked up by helicopter. Roddy thanked me for my efforts.

Now I knew how rescued pilots felt. I was never so cold in all my life. One good thing to come out of it was that "Doc" Combest gave me a shot of medicinal brandy to help thaw out my frigid digits.

**Ship's Log: Sunday 28 January 1951**   Continued screening Task Force 77.

As January neared its end, a tally was made of the days when the effectiveness of the carriers was severely limited by the month's foul weather. Twelve of the first twenty-eight days brought icy conditions and winds exceeding thirty knots.

Dear Anna: Sunday. We refueled and received 21 bags of mail. Received the most beautiful pictures (2) from the sweetest girl there is. Also received freight and mail for USS *Juneau*, gave them their mail, etc.

## 13   FEIGNING AN INVASION

*January 29–February 14, 1951*

**Ship's Log: Monday 29 January 1951**   Detached from Task Force 77 in company with USS FRANK KNOX (DDR-742), USS LOFBERG (DD-759), and USS MISSOURI (BB-63). 1715 Sighted object in water on port beam, sank same.

Intelligence sources indicated the Chinese were fearful of a landing on their rear flank. Vice Admiral Smith, commander of the amphibious force, conceived the notion that even if no such landing was carried out, one could always pretend. He proposed relieving pressure on the ground troops by mounting a fake amphibious attack in the Kansong-Kosong area, some fifty miles beyond the front line. A coastal plain provided a logical objective for an assault from the sea. This enterprise was dubbed Operation Ascendant.

At about 4:40 P.M. we left the task force with the *Missouri* and two other tin cans *(Frank Knox* and *Lofberg)* to rendezvous with Admiral Smith's amphibious group off Kansong. Word passed throughout the ship that we'd be taking part in an amphibious invasion. Gunners were told to break out enough ammo to fire sixty rounds of 5-inch every hour, two-gun salvos every two minutes. Reveille would be at 5:00 A.M. with shooting to begin at 7:00.

---

**Ship's Log: Tuesday 30 January 1951**   At 0705 commenced firing neutralization fire, 5-inch battery salvo fire, into assigned sector. At 1745 closed to beach area and made 40MM machine gun sweep of area.

---

Minesweepers were busily at work inshore from us, sweeping the area clear of mines in preparation for the landing craft. The USS *Montague* (AKA-98), USS *Seminole* (AKA-106), and several LSTs put their boats in the water and went through their prelanding activities.

Parked about four thousand yards beyond us were the battleship *Missouri* and two cruisers, lobbing their shots over our heads. The might of the Big Mo's 16-inchers was awesome. The shells rumbled like freight cars as they passed overhead. We could actually see the orange glow from the butt-ends of the projectiles as they seemed to float lazily toward their appointed destinations.

The *Iowa*-class battleships had been retired after World War II because of their high cost of operation, but the Korean War brought renewed interest in their capability. The value of the battleships centered on two key features, their massive destructive power and their enormous survivability.

The battlewagon's 16-inch guns deliver a massive amount of ordnance on target. These guns can shoot a 2,700-pound armor-piercing projectile to a range of twenty-five miles or more, which can be quite devastating. I doubt there was any ship on the high seas that could withstand a hit from a 16-inch armor-piercing projectile. At first glance, the guns seemed quite small in proportion to the rest of the ship. But the bulk of these massive gun turrets was largely hidden.

They extended as far as a four-story building deep into the bowels of the ship.

As the day progressed, we had a hard time understanding why the landing craft waited so long to go into shore. It was late in the afternoon before we learned that the whole exercise was an elaborate hoax. A landing was never intended, merely that the Chinese *think* there would be one.

---

**Ship's Log: Wednesday 31 January 1951**  0505 Proceeded with bombardment group to fire support off Kosong, Korea. At 0700 commenced firing 5-inch battery, firing neutralization fire in assigned sector. At 1730 laid smoke screen to cover withdrawal of elements of Task Force 95. Ammunition expended during 30 and 31 January: 808 rounds 5″ AAC, 914 rounds 40MM projectiles.

---

After retiring seaward during the night, we moved forty miles up the coast to Kosong to repeat the bombardment effort. Question: Why repeat the exercise a mere forty miles away from the first feint? Answer: Deception. Admiral Smith wanted the Chinese to think Kosong was the real landing. Typically, in amphibious warfare, the first area bombarded is a feint; the real landing occurs somewhere else—as, for example, when the Allies landed at Normandy, causing the Germans to think we were coming ashore at Calais.

This day's shoot contained an added attraction, namely, LSMR rocket ships. These vessels are a sight to behold. They unload those rockets at the rate of 1,440 a minute—Whoosh! Whoosh! Whoosh! When those critters take off, the launching craft practically disappears in a solid sheet of flame.

At 2:00 P.M. the USS *Dixie* (AD-14) got into the act by unleashing 204 rounds from her 5″/38s. This was the first time in the annals of naval history that a destroyer tender served as a flagship and participated in beach bombardment.

During a smoke-laying exercise, we came perilously close to disastrous collision with the cruiser *Manchester*. In laying smoke, the lead destroyer is nearest to shore; she lays smoke in a direction parallel to the beach. A second destroyer, now screened by the first line of smoke, lays a second line of smoke. Then comes a third destroyer laying a third line. The whole operation is performed at high speed.

In this case, the first two destroyers, *Lofberg* and *Frank Knox*, had already laid their lines of smoke. We were making the third run. Suddenly, the nose of the *Manchester* came poking through the smoke line, barely a hundred yards off our starboard bow. Both ships went all engines back full. A collision was narrowly averted. But it was close. Damn close!

---

**Ship's Log: Thursday 1 February 1951**   Proceeding in company with the USS MISSOURI and USS LOFBERG to rejoin Task Force 77 after gunfire support mission.

---

Task Force 77 was being used as a mobile "home base" for ships coming off the firing line. That is to say, whenever we were not on some specific assignment, we generally returned to Task Force 77 to await our next mission. It afforded a less strenuous routine, an opportunity to take on fuel and supplies, and a chance for our mail to catch up with us.

In my mind the men on the minesweepers were the most unheralded heroes of this war. Their work remained arduous, uncomfortable, and dangerous. The short winter daylight hampered operations. The winter weather, with high winds and freezing spray, made their work particularly difficult. There was always a chance of new minefields or of replenishment of those previously swept. The continued possibility of influence mines increased the danger. Moreover, intelligence reports indicated that the enemy was preparing a new mining campaign.

---

**Ship's Log: Friday 2 February 1951**   At 0825 anchored to seaward of the USS MISSOURI in outer harbor at Pusan, Korea. Maintaining sonar and condition 3 watch screening the USS MISSOURI.

---

The day was spent at anchor in Pusan Harbor while Admiral Struble, commander of the Seventh Fleet, held a conference with the *Missouri*'s skipper, Capt. Irving Duke. Our squadron commander, Capt. Samuel Lang also participated.

The USS *Partridge* (AMS-31) hit a mine about a mile off Sokcho, just north of the parallel. She sank in ten minutes. Ten men were killed or missing and six severely wounded. The *Partridge* became the fourth

U.S. minesweeper sunk, plus one Japanese and five South Korean sweepers.

---

**Ship's Log: Sunday 4 February 1951** 0830 Entered harbor Sasebo, Japan, fueled, loaded ammunition and stores. At 1700 left Sasebo, Japan, with the USS MISSOURI and USS LOFBERG en route to east coast Korea.

---

Although Sunday, and supposedly a day of rest, this was, in fact, a working day. We took on 800 rounds of 5-inch AAC, 800 cans of smokeless powder, and 111 cans of 40-mm. We also replenished our food supply.

A rumor got started that we were going to leave Japan and escort the Big Mo to New York by way of the Red Sea. That was totally fictitious. It started as a lark, a joke, and it made no sense whatsoever. But people believed it because they so desperately *wanted* to believe it.

---

**Ship's Log: Tuesday 6 February 1951** At 0805 proceeded at maximum speed to Yongdok, Korea, to furnish call fire support for United Nations ground troops.

---

A high-speed, solo run was made to Yongdok in response to an urgent call for fire support from troops ashore. However, the army unit ("Clawhammer 60") was nine miles inland, too far for our 5-inch to do any good. We had to content ourselves with destroying a couple of floating mines.

As soon as darkness fell, we edged closer toward shore, threading our way into the mouth of the river in an attempt to bring our guns within range of enemy troop concentrations. Lt. Frank Howland had the conn; Sam Stock was on the SG-6 precision radar. Visibility was only a few hundred yards.

At about 9:30 Stock advised the bridge, "My radar shows we're getting too close to shore."

"Roger," bridge responded, seemingly unconcerned. "We see it on our chart."

Again, Stock called the bridge. "Either there's something wrong with the radar, or we're getting too close."

Again, bridge responded, somewhat annoyed at Stock's effrontery,

"We have visual contact." Still, the ship kept moving closer and closer.

Alarmed that the bridge wasn't taking his warning seriously enough, Stock yelled into his microphone, "Goddammit, I have it on my radar, and we're about to crash!"

At that moment the lookout saw looming through the gloom the object Stock had been warning them about. It was an outcropping of rock that stood directly in their path, not at all where the charts showed it to be. The bridge shouted back down to CIC, "We're getting too close!"

Howland's order, "All engines back full!" came just barely in time to avoid running aground. He backed us the hell out of there into deeper water. As we learned later, the ship came so close to grounding that it actually tore up the sonar dome and scraped a section of the fantail.

---

**Ship's Log: Wednesday 7 February 1951** Lying to, 4,000 yards from the coast. Fired 14 rounds 5″ AAC on ranging targets called by SFCP.

---

Enemy resistance, which had stiffened at the start of the month, suddenly gave way. The Chinese were retiring from the area around Yongdok.

The weather at sea was abominable, even worse on land. Troops ashore were moving through wretched terrain, their movement hindered by the beginning thaw and by heavy rains that turned all roads into mudholes. By the end of the day, however, the coastal territory north from Yongdok to Ulchin was thoroughly under UN control.

Some ninety miles to our north at Kangnung, the *Missouri*'s big 16-inchers with their reach of twenty-five miles were still doing effective shooting in support of ROK troops.

---

**Ship's Log: Thursday 8 February 1951** Steaming independently off east coast of Korea in vicinity of Yongdok. 0252 Joined formation with USS MISSOURI (BB-63) and USS LOFBERG (DD-759), proceeding to Inchon, Korea, for fire support mission.

---

Admiral Smith now believed the time was ripe for the recapture of Inchon. He successfully argued that heavy naval bombardments should be made as soon as possible in the Inchon area. At the very least, he said, it would deceive and confuse the enemy and force him to divert some of his ground strength to defend the area. Inchon's recapture, of course, would return a valuable port and supply base to the UN forces. This new enterprise also had the code name Operation Ascendant.

Shortly after midnight we took off with the *Missouri* and *Lofberg* at twenty-seven knots on a run to the west coast of Korea. The seas were rough, and the two destroyers pounded heavily—wham! wham! wham!—as they plowed doggedly through the waves.

Sweet Love: I want this letter to find you full of happiness and joy in the sheer act of living out your life's goals. Had a little mishap on the ship today and ended up on the "binnacle list." (That's Navy lingo for people excused from duty because of illness or injury.) The ship was pounding heavily through rough seas when it took a sudden lurch, and I slipped on a slick deck and busted open my scalp. I can use the couple days rest. Besides, it will give me more time to think sweet thoughts of you. You are my strength and inspiration.    Rusty

---

**Ship's Log: Friday 9 February 1951**  Refueled from HMS WAVE KNIGHT at sea off Inchon, Korea. 1726 Anchored in harbor Inchon, Korea, to furnish AA protection for auxiliary vessels and standing by for fire-support missions.

---

We refueled from the HMS *Wave Knight*, the same Chinese-crewed Limey ship we had fueled from last time we were here. The seas were so rough that we broke the fuel lines, spraying oil all over the place. We were then forced to cast off all lines and maneuver around to the starboard side of *Wave Knight* in order to complete fueling.

The cruiser *Saint Paul* had already arrived on the scene, having been at Inchon since January 25, together with the destroyer *Hank* (DD-702) and the British cruiser *Kenya*. They were greeted by some short salvos from Wolmi Do, which were quickly neutralized with some help by air strikes from the British carrier *Theseus*. The *Saint Paul* group kept the Kimpo-Kumpo area under intermittent bombardment.

The amphibious landing group, consisting of two AKAs and an LSD reached Inchon on the eighth. The landing of two transport divisions was scheduled for the afternoon of the tenth.

　　＊　＊　＊

Upon our arrival, we received mail from a British Corvette, but none of it was for our ship; all was for the *Saint Paul* and the *Hank*. What a disappointment! We changed anchorage four times running a mail delivery service.

**Ship's Log: Saturday 10 February 1951**   Gunfire support, Inchon Harbor, Inchon, Korea.

The landing was set for the afternoon tide. The *Missouri* had prepared the way with two days of heavy bombardment. Shortly before the scheduled embarkment, however, we heard voices screaming over the radio, "Stop shooting! Stop shooting!"

The voices were ROK Marines. The Chinese had retired from the area, and a party of ROK Marines from Tokchok To had moved up under our shellfire and were now occupying the city where the *Missouri*'s shells were landing.

It seemed evident that the Chinese did not welcome the prospect of a second invasion at Inchon. Our presence made their evacuation of the area more urgent and rapid. By nightfall U.S. troops had reached the banks of the Han River and were only a few miles from Seoul.

**Ship's Log: Sunday–Tuesday 11–13 February 1951**   Lying to as before, Inchon Harbor, Inchon, Korea.

The reoccupation of Inchon was more than welcome. For the past month, Pusan had been the only port of supply, and both it and the supply lines were being taxed to the limit of their capabilities.

The wisdom of having demolished the port during the January 5 evacuation was now coming into question. In retrospect, the Eighth Army's "blow-and-go" strategy seemed not to have been a wise move. It would take a lot of work to get the port back into working order.

Rear Adm. L. A. Thackrey was the man charged with getting the port facilities up and running. He decided against letting his LSTs get hung up on the mudbanks during Inchon's famed low tides, so he limited the rate of unloading to an amount that could be picked up inside of twelve hours. That limitation posed no problem because the Eighth Army only had enough trucks to accept a mere five hundred tons a day.

We remained at anchor in Inchon Harbor for another three days without firing a shot. The ground fighting was beyond the nine-mile range of our guns, but the Big Mo, with her range of twenty-five miles, kept up a steady barrage in support of troops on their march toward Seoul. Plenty of starshells lit up the night. Artillery fire could be heard from the battle being waged inland. The Chinese had regrouped and were not going to give up Seoul without a fight.[1]

Despite the seemingly serene setting of the harbor, these were still mighty dangerous waters. All islands were still in enemy hands. We posted fifteen lookouts scattered throughout the ship over main and 0–1 decks. Our days were punctuated with frequent GQs every time someone thought he saw something moving on one of those islands.

---

**Ship's Log: Wednesday 14 February 1951** Underway in company with USS MISSOURI and USS LOFBERG, proceeding to east coast Korea to rejoin Task Force 77.

---

The second "invasion" of Inchon was over. It was never planned to be a full-scale amphibious operation such as the one accomplished the previous September. Its aims were first, to open a second port through which to supply the advancing Eighth Army, and second, to throw a scare into the Chinese and cause them to redeploy their forces. Both aims were accomplished.

Now, back to Wonsan.

# 14 SETTING THE SIEGE AT WONSAN

*February 16–25, 1951*

---

**Ship's Log: Friday 16 February 1951**   At 0400 detached from
Task Force 77. Formed special bombardment element under operational control of Commander DesDiv 112 in USS OZBOURN. Proceeding to naval gunfire area Wonsan, North Korea. Ammunition
expended: 180 rounds 5-inch AAC, 180 rounds 5-inch smokeless.

---

For the first time since December 7, U.S. warships entered the
harbor at Wonsan. Everyone now agreed it was a mistake to have
abandoned Wonsan back in December. At that time, Admiral Doyle
had argued that it would be possible to form a perimeter at the waist
of Korea and to defend this position on the coast throughout the winter. Doyle felt "that with the Navy's surface and air power available
we should have held the Wonsan area indefinitely." But his sugges-
tion had fallen on deaf ears.

In order to undo the effects, at least to some extent, Admiral Smith,
commander of Task Force 95, proposed a heavy bombardment of Wonsan. This would be accompanied by seizure of Yo Do and Ung Do,
which guarded the harbor. Smith was convinced an unremitting naval
bombardment of North Korea's exposed transportation complex by day
and night, fair weather and foul, "could get 75 percent or 80 percent
stoppage of traffic."

In company with the destroyers *Ozbourn* and *Sperry*, we began a
schedule of round-the-clock bombardment of targets ashore. Our arrival had been preceded by four days of minesweeping operations,
which created a six-hundred-yard-wide clear channel.

The mission had two purposes: (1) to harass and damage enemy rail
and road communications through Wonsan, and (2) to make the enemy think an invasion was imminent, thereby causing him to draw
forces away from other sectors in order to defend this important facility.

The siege of Wonsan began on my twenty-first birthday, an event
that passed unnoticed by anyone on the ship. However, I had been
saving a letter from Anna marked, Do Not Open Until Your Birthday.
She had written me a love poem:

Your love is like a gentle rain, nourishing the little flowers—caressing
them 'til they blossom fully, stretching up to heaven in tribute to God
and all his glory.

Your caring is like a ray of sunshine that warms the coldest days, sending sunbeams dancing 'til all they touch turns to gold.

Your laughter is like a cool breeze on a summer day, lifting the leaves 'til they meet the soaring birds in their flight of happiness.

Your mind is open and your thoughts flow forward like a river that has no end, winding through all the earth—creating its own course and giving currents of renewed life to all that touches its shores.

Your heart is like the magic of the sky, open to all the universe—yet enclosing it without boundaries.

Your soul is like the mystery of each day's sunrise and sunset, free to compose its own music with songs that sing the melodies of life—with sweet refrains of love echoing through the heartbeat of eternal joy and peace.

---

**Ship's Log: Saturday 17 February 1951**   1615 Returned to firing line Wonsan Harbor. Conducted night interdiction selected targets. Ammunition expended: 46 rounds 5" AAC, 46 rounds 5" smokeless, 1012 rounds 40MM.

---

After a long string of grade-B shoot-em-up movies, Pete Hoffman finally hit the jackpot. He worked a swap with the *Cimarron* for a first-run Doris Day movie, *My Dream Is Yours.* Jack Carson starred with Doris Day in this 1949 flick about a hard-working agent (Jack Carson) who pushes a young new singer (Doris Day) to the top of the charts in the days of live radio variety shows.

But this movie created a helluva problem for the crew. There was no way on God's green earth that all the men clamoring to see the movie could possibly squeeze inside the cramped quarters of the mess hall where movies were ordinarily shown. A delegation went to ask the captain for permission to show the movie topside, something not ordinarily done except when in port and during clement weather—and certainly not in a combat zone within range of enemy guns. Nevertheless, after quite a bit of haggling, Buaas gave his OK provided the projector be set up on the seaward side, away from the beach.

Accordingly, everyone traipsed up to the main deck, port side, where the movie was shown against the flat bulkhead of the bridge superstructure. The weather was colder than hell. Men were bundled up in their foul-weather gear. But it was a full house and no one complained.

Every six minutes, as regular as clockwork, the projector would shudder. Blam! Another round of 5-inch was lobbed over toward the beach. It seemed so very incongruous that we should be launching missiles of deadly destruction while escaping into flights of frivolous fantasy.

About halfway through the film, the tide shifted. The ship swung around at anchor so we were now on the leeward side, facing toward the beach. That was not a healthy situation. A hundred and fifty American sailors illuminated by the light of a movie projector offered a tempting target for enemy gunners. What to do? We dismantled the projector, moved everyone over to the starboard side, and continued with the show.

Stupid? Yes. Was it worth the risk? Yes. That movie did more for our morale than anything short of going home. Sitting out on deck in freezing weather, inside an enemy-held harbor, and within easy range of hostile guns—only for Doris Day would we have risked that.

---

**Ship's Log: Sunday 18 February 1951**   On gunfire station Wonsan Harbor. 1206 USS OZBOURN (DD-846) taken under fire. Returned counterbattery fire. At 2200 detached from bombardment group, proceeding to east coast gunfire area.

---

We were anchored at short stay in the swept channel in the vicinity of buoy number 3 next to the southern flank of the firing line. The *Ozbourn* was to the north near buoy number 7; the *Sperry* was between us at buoy number 5. A group of minesweepers, *FSS-699*, *YMS-510*, and *YMS-514*, were anchored eastward in the vicinity of Yo Do.

It had been snowing steadily since early morning. The *Ozbourn* and *Sperry* were firing intermittently at targets ashore, using indirect fire.

Suddenly, at high noon, *Ozbourn* was taken under fire. Shells from three or four 3-inch batteries were coming from the direction of Kalma Gak peninsula and Sin Do. The first shot landed 150 yards short on the port beam. The next two hit the ship—one amidships in the athwartships passageway, the other through the Mark 56 gun director.

The *Ozbourn* immediately slipped her anchor and got underway. Flashes were observed in a gun revetment located on Sin Do, range four thousand yards. The targets were taken under fire. Direct hits were scored on this position with three six-gun salvos. Subsequently, another revetment was identified nearby and destroyed.

By 12:44 all ships were out of range of the shore batteries. An estimated twenty-five gun splashes were observed. The *Ozbourn* escaped with only three casualties, none serious.

The *Ozbourn* was not yet through for the day, however. About 4:15 P.M., Ensign Ralph M. Tvede, an F4U pilot from the *Valley Forge,* lost power in his Corsair and had to ditch in the water off Wonsan. He landed unhurt, but the weather was bitter cold and the seas were heavy. Worse, the spot where Tvede landed was in the midst of a minefield. This precluded sending a destroyer or similar steel-hulled vessel into the mine-infested waters. Rescue would have to be by small boat.

Despite having been shot up at Wonsan, the *Ozbourn* immediately responded to the distress call. Rescue was complicated by the fact that the destroyer could not come closer than thirteen miles offshore because of the mines. Moreover, her motor whaleboat had been holed by North Korean shore battery fire earlier that day. The only boat available was the captain's gig.

LTJG John Moriarty was the boat officer. He and his crew braved the cold and icy sea, and with guidance from airborne observers they reached the downed airman at 7:30 P.M. By that time, Tvede was suffering from hypothermia. The airman was in such bad shape that he lapsed into delirium, then unconsciousness, during the hour-long return trip. The boat crew was almost as cold and wet as he was. Tvede regained consciousness around midnight, and the next morning he was transferred via highline to the supply ship USS *Chara* (AKA-58) for transfer back to the Happy Valley, with hardly a chance to thank his rescuers. Lieutenant (j.g.) Moriarty was awarded a bronze star for his action.[1]

---

**Ship's Log: Monday 19 February 1951**  Screening the USS MISSOURI against submarines in naval gunfire area.

---

We were seeing mines with increasing frequency now. It was apparent that the North Koreans were stepping up their mine-laying activities, particularly in sections of the east coast where invasion was possible. Sampans and fishing boats were used for this purpose. Also, mines that had a self-planting mechanism were recovered in Wonsan Harbor. With this device the enemy was using river currents to float mines into the harbor buoyed by oil drums, logs, and kegs.

\*   \*   \*

Anna's birthday fell just three days after mine. Not to be outdone by her touching tribute, I was inspired to try my own hand at the poet's art.

On the special day that you were born
    the universe gazed in silent wonder.
On the special day that you were born
    the angels celebrated a new addition to their number.
On the special day that you were born
    the earth became a more beautiful place.
On the special day that you were born
    mankind received a new quality of grace.
On the special day that you were born
    my spirit leapt with quickened beat.
And my heart knows it would never rest
    until united with yours in eternity.
On that special day when you were born.

---

**Ship's Log: Tuesday 20 February 1951**   Screening the USS MISSOURI (BB-63) in gunfire area, Tanchon, Korea. 1424 Transferred to MISSOURI via whaleboat Silva, Raymond C., FN for acute appendicitis. 2142 Commenced firing on targets of opportunity. Expended 90 rounds 5-inch AAC.

---

General MacArthur made a photo-op trip to Korea. Ostensibly the trip was to confer with General Ridgway but really it was to show himself to the public and announce to the press that he was still running the show.

He blew the element of surprise in Ridgway's upcoming battle by grandiosely announcing, "I have just ordered a resumption of the offensive." Having revealed the secret Ridgway was trying to preserve, MacArthur mounted his command plane and flew back to Tokyo, leaving the responsibility for defeat with Ridgway but preparing to take the credit for victory himself.

In company with the *Missouri* and *Lofberg,* we arrived at Tanchon around 6:00 A.M. Situated a couple of miles up an estuary at the point where two rivers join, Tanchon offered tempting rail and highway bridge targets, a marshaling yard, and some minor industrial facilities. Throughout the day, the Big Mo dispensed 16-inch shells against the multiple bridges that spanned the double river at Tanchon, while the destroyers protected her to seaward from submarine attack. Big Mo shot up boxcars, power plants, and a railroad bridge.

We got in our licks too. Our targets included railroad tracks, two grade crossings, a tunnel, and lights on the road leading south.

At Wonsan, the destroyers *Lind, Ozbourn,* and *Sperry* engaged in the rescue of a pilot who had crash-landed in the harbor. While the three ships were attempting rescue operations, shore batteries opened up on them, and the *Lind* successfully returned fire.

---

**Ship's Log: Wednesday 21 February 1951** Proceeding to gunfire area with USS MISSOURI and USS LOFBERG.

---

The last we saw of Lt. George Washington Stubblefield was when he climbed into the bos'n's chair—battered, burned hat set jauntily atop his head—and was whisked away via highline to the oiler *Mispillion*. From there he would be transferred to the Fleet Gunnery and Torpedo School, San Diego.

Instinctively Stubblefield lifted his legs above the roiling seas, knowing the engineering gang had promised him a dip in the drink. He steeled himself against the icy shock he knew would inevitably come. "Now!" a voice called out. Amid the cheers of half a hundred onlookers, the chair dipped just low enough for him to get slapped on the fanny by the crest of a wave. Then they hauled him up and aboard the oiler.

Moments later he reappeared on deck. As a parting gesture, he took off his trademark hat that had been the object of so much derision and sailed it across the water back toward his former shipmates.

Lt. G. N. Selby reported aboard as our new gunnery officer, replacing Lieutenant Dvorcek who had departed in January. Selby came from a minesweeper where he had been awarded the silver star for bravery. A tall, rugged, heavy-set man, Selby exuded an air of competence and self-confidence, but he was hard to get to know and lacked the "people" skills that had made Dvorcek so well-liked by his crew.

The departure of Stubblefield occasioned a small celebration that evening in the main battery director. We presented Ensign White with a small cake decorated with a miniature SOPA flag.

In the navy's lexicon, SOPA is the senior officer present afloat—defined as the senior line officer on active service, eligible for command at sea, who is present and in command of any unit of the operating forces afloat. Whichever ship has the SOPA signifies his presence by flying a blue triangular flag.

White was baffled.

"Congratulations!" we told him. "Now that Stubblefield has gone, you have had more time aboard the *Borland* than any other officer."

White had reported aboard June 24, 1949. Of course, it was a stretch to suggest that made him the senior officer. But he went along with the gag.

---

**Ship's Log: Thursday 22 February 1951**  Screening the USS MISSOURI in gunfire area Songjin, Korea. 1532 USS MISSOURI completed scheduled firing.

---

Political interference in the Korean War was nowhere better illustrated than in an exasperating experience in mid-February. On February 18 General Ridgway drafted a plan for his March offensive that, in colorful military language, he labeled Operation Killer. It was intended to exploit the gains made in the earlier drive.

When that title reached Washington, it caused an enormous flap. Groups of every sort jumped on the bandwagon of criticism. Republicans in Congress charged that all the Democrats wanted to do was to kill Chinese. The State Department complained that the name would make it harder to reach a diplomatic arrangement with China. The Joint Chiefs of Staff protested that it was a public relations gaffe.

The March offensive was renamed Operation Ripper, a name calculated not to offend anyone. The whole episode was a reflection of the growing media disenchantment with the war and the U.S. military. The major problem was the failure to convince a broad spectrum of the American public that Korea was worth the effort. In short, the war lacked "sex appeal."

---

**Ship's Log: Friday 23 February 1951**  En route to Sinpo to conduct shore bombardment.

---

Snow appeared very deep on the mountains when we arrived at Sinpo (fifty miles south of Tanchon) for shore bombardment. We arrived on station about 6:00 A.M. Before we got into action, however, we were instructed to rush back to Songjin—which we did in short order. At Songjin, the Big Mo fired for about three hours. Then we left to rejoin Task Force 77.

The *Missouri* had been averaging an expenditure of 166 rounds of 16-inch per day. This firepower was approximately equivalent to that of a hundred aircraft sorties, and at far less monetary cost and risk to pilots' lives.

---

**Ship's Log: Saturday 24 February 1951**   Steaming in company with TF-77 in operating area off east coast of Korea.

---

On the morning of the twenty-fourth, two destroyers, a frigate, and an ROK LST landed 110 Korean marines on Sin Do. Lacking a shore fire control party, arrangements to support the Sin Do landing were somewhat complex. The Koreans had been given a portable radio, but the only interpreter was on the cruiser *Manchester* several miles offshore. Messages to the supporting destroyers had to be relayed. *Manchester*'s helicopter, which provided aerial observation, was in communication with the destroyers but not the landing party. But all went well, and the island was soon declared secure. UN forces were back at, if not in, Wonsan.

Under cover of darkness, the *English* (DD-696) put a fire control party ashore on Tae Do, which lay close to the city of Wonsan. This operation allowed gunnery ships to fire on targets in Wonsan with good results, their gunfire being corrected by spotters on Tae Do.

Concerned that fleets of wooden junks presented numerous small targets, hard to hit and impossible to sink, ComNavFE directed that eight sixty-foot captured Korean junks be brought to Yokosuka for practice purposes. Extensive tests conducted by Rear Adm. Edgar A. Cruise, commander of the Hunter Killer Task Group, demonstrated that their destruction was excessively costly in ammunition expenditure. Equally unsatisfactory results were obtained in trying to sink a one-hundred-tonner and a six-hundred-tonner.

---

**Ship's Log: Sunday 25 February 1951**   1330 Proceeding independently to Pusan, Korea, to pick up Commander Seventh Fleet and furnish transportation for him to USS MISSOURI.

---

Dear Anna: We refueled from the USS *Missouri* today. You cannot believe how small a destroyer appears alongside a battleship. Pulled into
Pusan around 2 P.M. Dropped hook in harbor. No mail. Tomorrow we
get underway for Yokosuka. Be there on the 28th. Here's hoping we
go on to the States from there. In the meanwhile, I am loving you
with a love that flows beyond the confines of this universe.   Rusty

## 15   TANGLING WITH TYPHOONS

*February 26–March 15, 1951*

**Ship's Log: Monday 26 February 1951**   Canceled arrangement
for transporting Commander Seventh Fleet due to bad weather.
0810 Underway with USS MISSOURI and the USS LOFBERG en
route to Yokosuka, Japan.

In another of our many roles—this time as "water taxi"—the
*Borland* was scheduled to shuttle Adm. A. D. Struble, commander of
the Seventh Fleet, out to the *Missouri* for the trip to Yokosuka and a
conference with General MacArthur. Because of an approaching typhoon, however, the admiral called off his short destroyer junket. The
storm made ship-to-ship transfer unsafe. Winds had picked up to a
sustained twenty knots, gusting to thirty-five. Seas were rough.

When the Pacific Ocean whips into the fury of a tropical typhoon,
the power of the sea is awesome. Man-made objects toss about like
tiny toys on the surface of the deep. Brave men tremble when faced
with the reality that their puny efforts can do nothing to tame the angry waters.

A typhoon is a great tropical storm that comes roaring in from the
central Pacific. Nearly circular in shape, it covers an area about five
hundred miles in diameter. Wind speeds range up to two hundred
miles per hour and beyond. High winds, coastal flooding, and torren-
tial rains cause enormous damage.

Rumors were rampant that we were going home from Yokosuka.
We'd been in the Far East for six months and were due for a rotation.

On this jaunt, the *Missouri* seemed to be a "lady in a hurry." She really hauled ass out of there. I don't know why the rush—unless it was to try to outrun the storm. We plowed through the heavy seas at twenty-two knots. The *Borland* was laboring greatly in the heavy seas and taking a terrible pounding. We were critically low on fuel, which caused the ship to ride light in the water and roll badly. At 2:30 P.M. the engineers began ballasting the forward tanks with seawater to improve the ship's stability by reducing its buoyancy.

The captain ordered the weather decks secured. The deck crew rigged lifelines on the entire topside and lashed down all loose gear. Ammunition was removed from the ready-service racks and upper handling rooms and transferred to magazines below.

At 10:20 P.M. we passed Bono Misaki Light at the southwestern tip of Kyushu and made our turn to the east. That's when things really started to get rough. The seas were now coming at us from off our starboard beam—nearly at right angles to our ship's course. The ship rolled and pitched violently in the long cross swells. We were heeling over to thirty-five or forty degrees. Still, the *Missouri* plowed ahead, seemingly oblivious to either the condition of the sea or the pounding of the destroyers. It was all we could do to maintain formation course and speed.

About midnight I hit the sack. To stay in my bunk proved to be a struggle. Falling asleep was even more difficult. The constant shrieks and groans of the seas incessantly pounded against the ship's hull and threatened to tear her apart at the seams.

---

**Ship's Log: Tuesday 27 February 1951**   Steaming with USS MIS-SOURI en route to Yokosuka, Japan. Forced to reduce speed to 7 knots by high wind and very heavy seas.

---

February 27 was my mother's birthday. It got off to a bad start. At 4:30 A.M. a tremendous roll to port tossed me unceremoniously out of my bunk. Further sleep was impossible. I dressed in the dark and made my way up to CIC to see what was going on.

The storm was closing in on us. Wind speed was now thirty-eight knots from a point or two off the starboard bow, gusting to sixty to sixty-five knots. Barometer reading was 29.71 and falling rapidly. Estimated distance to the storm's center was 220 miles to our southwest and moving in a westerly direction. On paper it appeared our course speed and direction should take us away from the storm's fury. Inexplicably, sea conditions continued to worsen and wind force intensified.

At 4:49 A.M. the *Missouri* dropped formation speed to eighteen knots. This reduction had little effect on the buffeting. The *Borland* still labored greatly. Forty-five minutes later, at 5:34, a further reduction in speed was ordered to fifteen knots, to be followed at 5:44 with another reduction to twelve knots.

I had never seen the sea this rough. Sixty-foot waves about six hundred feet apart rolled over us. Up on the bridge, Lieutenant (j.g.) Melesky, who had the OOD watch, jokingly rechristened the *Borland* the USS *Borefish* (SS-855). He reckoned that since we were spending so much time with our forecastle submerged we might as well be reclassified as a submarine. Mountainous waves crashed over mount 52 and as high as the pilot house. It was extremely dangerous for anyone to venture out onto the bridge wings.

A careful muster of the crew was taken at 8:00 A.M. to make sure no one had been washed overboard during the night. Commander Buaas passed word that all hands not performing an essential task should remain below decks. "Rescue in these seas would be impossible," he warned.

Despite the warning, I toted my Kodak Pony camera out onto the boat deck aft of the radio shack passageway where there was an overhang. Facing aft, I took several pictures of walls of water cascading over the superstructure. It was like being on the underside of a waterfall.

Later, I went up to the main battery director to get pictures of the stormy sea from that high vantage point. Even at that elevation I had to duck the stinging spume and spray that shot up from the bridge. It hit with such force ugly red welts were raised on the exposed flesh of my face.

Thirty-five hundred yards to port, the *Lofberg*, at 2,200 tons and 379 feet long, was tossed around on the ocean like a cork. No wonder they called these things tin cans! The waves were so huge that when the *Lofberg* was down in a trough she would completely disappear from view except for the radar antenna atop her mast. Other times, riding the crest of a wave, her entire bottom would be exposed.

Meanwhile, the battleship *Missouri* plowed straight ahead on an even keel. At forty-two thousand tons—nearly twenty times our displacement—she was unfazed. Her huge underwater hull and small superstructure gave her an advantage over the top-heavy destroyers.

Even though gigantic waves crashed over her 16-inch gun mounts, she shrugged them off with the nonchalance of an elephant sauntering through the bush. We rolled and writhed like a wounded gazelle.

At 10:45 A.M. we reduced formation speed to ten knots. The captain ordered ballasting to begin in the two aft fuel tanks. We shut down our SPS-6 air search radar as a precautionary measure. The SG-6 surface radar was so cluttered with echo as to render it useless for short-range targets.

Below decks, things were in a terrible mess. Every item not bolted down came crashing out of shelves. Locked cabinets sprang open and spilled their contents onto the deck. Drawers slammed open and shut again as the ship lurched first to one side and then to the other.

W. W. Hoisington, damage controlman second class, received severe lacerations on his head from falling on a slick deck. He was carried to the officers' wardroom, which doubled as a battle-dressing station. Hardly had "Doc" Combest sewn him back together when another casualty was carried in. Before the day was out, four men were injured by the storm.

The cooks didn't bother to prepare a hot meal. Instead, they made sandwiches and kept the coffee brewing. Anyone who had the stomach for food could come by the galley and pick up rations. Eating in the mess hall was impossible.

The storm continued to worsen. At 9:58 P.M., formation speed was reduced to nine knots. At 10:29 it was reduced to eight knots, then to seven knots at 10:40—just barely enough to maintain steerageway and avoid broaching in heavy seas.

---

**Ship's Log: Wednesday 28 February 1951**   Steaming as before en route to Yokosuka, Japan.

---

The savage fury of the storm was full upon us.[1] The ship now rolled fifty degrees and more, the amplitude increasing. The worst times came when the ship heeled over to port. The wind, coming from our starboard side at a sustained sixty-five to seventy knots, drove against the destroyer's superstructure with such force it threatened to push the ship on over. We would hang there for what seemed like an eternity. Then with a shudder and a lurch, the ship would right itself again. Each time we wondered, "Will she come back?"

Maintaining one's footing was like engaging in hand-to-hand combat, and nearly as exhausting. During one particularly vicious roll, Bos'n's Mate Don Hanley, who was helmsman on the morning watch, lost his hold on the ship's wheel and sailed across the pilot house. He crashed up against the steel bulkhead and was knocked unconscious. He had to be carried below.

The bridge watch personnel kept their eyes riveted on the clinometer, which measured the degree of roll. With each roll, it went farther and farther—55, 57, 58 degrees. Quartermaster third-class Dennison swore he actually saw it hit the peg at 70 degrees. We hung over there for what seemed like forever before another wave came along and lifted us back into an upright position.

At 8:00 A.M. the gale remained unabated. The storm center was estimated to be 220 miles southwest of us. By noon, it was just 170 miles away. That meant it had reversed course and was now traveling east at about twenty knots. In four hours, it had closed the distance on us by 50 miles even though we were steaming away from it at seven knots. Hell's bells, the damn thing was chasing us!

Three more men were injured in storm-related accidents. Miraculously, we had not lost anyone overboard. Rescue would have been well-nigh impossible.

Around 4:00 P.M. the gale abated slightly and the ship began riding more easily. At 6:00 P.M. the storm center was almost due south of us at 130 miles and losing intensity. At 10:00 P.M. it still moved on a parallel course with us, now 120 miles to the south.

Winds were still strong. They came from straight ahead, allowing the ship to ride more easily. At 6:06 A.M. we were able to increase speed to eight knots, then at 8:16 P.M. to nine knots. We were now twenty-four hours behind our scheduled arrival at Yokosuka.

---

**Ship's Log: Thursday 1 March 1951**  Attached to Fleet Activities, Yokosuka, Japan, for maintenance, dry docking, and recreational period.

---

Dear Anna: Never had I seen the sea so rough. Just about everybody on the ship got sick but me, including the "old salts" who've had many more years of sea duty than I. Soda crackers seemed to be about the only food many guys could keep down.

When I failed to get sick, one guy grumbled, "Gamble, you never

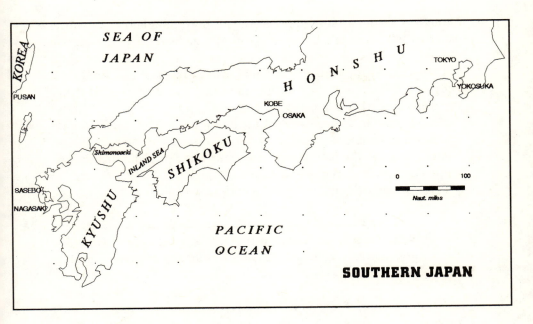

know up from down anyway!" He probably wasn't far from the truth. Seasickness originates in the inner ear. People who have a good sense of direction and balance—both due to the workings of the inner ear— tend to be prone to seasickness. As for me, I have such a lousy sense of direction and balance I can get lost three blocks from home.

The inner ear theory makes good sense. A ship at sea moves in five directions at the same time, roll, pitch, yaw, vertical, and lateral. Briefly, a roll occurs when the ship tilts left or right; pitch is a tilt for- ward or back; yaw is a twist left or right; vertical is an up-and-down movement; and lateral is a sideways movement. People who have a very sensitive inner ear also have a strong spatial orientation. Their systems get disoriented and become upset by this constant motion. Most are able to adjust to the motion after a few hours, or at most a few days. But when sea conditions become as violent as we experi- enced the past three days, anyone can fall victim.  Love, Rusty

Yokosuka enjoyed a reputation as one of the really great liberty ports in the world. She was blessed with fine restaurants, posh hotels, pretty girls, and plenty of sight-seeing opportunities.

Shorty Hall and I went ashore together as soon as liberty was an- nounced. We ended up at the NCO club, quite a posh place. We ran into a few sailors from the *Missouri*. Man, they complained about the rough seas! I couldn't believe it, considering what a pounding we took.

I asked if anyone had ventured up topside to look at the destroyers. They said, "Yeah, we saw you tin-can sailors bouncing around there. We wondered what it was like."

"Well," I said, "it got so rough at one point that we had to shut down the pool table."

One guy took the bait. "Pool table?" he asked incredulously. "How in the hell do you play pool on a tin can?"

"We use square balls," I replied with a straight face.

---

**Ship's Log: Friday 2 March 1951** Attached to Fleet Activities, Yokosuka, Japan, for maintenance, dry docking, and recreational period.

---

A team of divers from the *Jason* went down to make a visual inspection of our sonar bell. They discovered the trouble—a big gash along one side. Water rushing through that hole caused "noise" on the screen that masked the echoes. That, of course, meant we'd have to go into dry dock to get the thing replaced.

By the luck of the draw, I ended up with shore patrol duty. My partner was Kenneth Paton, machinist second class. At 11:30 A.M. we left the ship to report in to SP headquarters. We thought we'd be on for a regular eight-hour shift and return to the ship in the evening. It came as a surprise when, at the end of our shift, they told us to turn a second shift at Fleet Landing.

What we found there was total chaos. Sailors were penned in like cattle in a stockyard. A couple hundred sailors from a dozen ships milled around as they waited for boats to carry them back to their ships in the harbor. Many were drunk, some falling-down drunk. As the effects of the alcohol wore off they tended to get belligerent.

There were too few boats for the number of sailors trying to get back. The LCTs could carry seventy-five to a hundred men at a time. But it took each boat half an hour to make the round-trip.

It was freezing cold, damp, and miserable. There was no place to sit down.

Getting back to the ship was only half the problem. Getting *on* the ship was the other. The *Jason* had thrown cargo nets over the side. Instead of being able to walk up the gangway, the returning sailors—some drunk, some loaded with packages—had to climb hand-over-hand up the cargo nets to reach the deck.

Claude Gray was the victim of bad luck. He had managed to make it this far with a fifth of Japanese Suntory whiskey. If discovered, this could get him a stiff punishment. The bottle was crammed down into his sock, hidden from view by the flare of his bell-bottom trousers. He walked like a guy who had crushed nuts.

Gray made it all the way to the top when disaster struck. As he snapped to attention to salute the OOD, a muffled thump was heard. His sock gave way and the bottle slid out onto the deck. Cool as a cucumber, Gray stepped over the upright bottle and continued on his way as if nothing had happened. The OOD was too stunned to act until it was too late.

We often speculated about what the OOD did with that booze. Did he turn it in or keep it for himself?

---

**Ship's Log: Saturday 3 March 1951**   Attached to Fleet Activities, Yokosuka, Japan, for maintenance, dry docking, and recreational period.

---

Dear Anna: I know you didn't want me to, but I went ahead and reenlisted on board today for another four-year hitch. I did it for two reasons: one, my enlistment was already extended at least another year by the Korean War—and who knows how much longer. Second, I want to make the most of the situation by applying for Officer Training School, which requires a minimum of 30 months after graduation. Besides that, I pocketed $1,400 reenlistment bonus which, with the money I'm saving here, should help to build quite a nest egg.

---

**Ship's Log: Sunday 4 March 1951**   Attached to Fleet Activities, Yokosuka, Japan, for maintenance, dry docking, and recreational period.

---

The ship was pulled into dry dock to replace the sonar bell. Once out of the water, they discovered we needed repairs to the fantail as well.

Liberty was canceled for the deck gang. They all had to go over the side and scrape paint up to the waterline. You never heard such bitching and screaming in your life. This was a helluva way to spend a Sunday, particularly when they'd been out at sea for two months.

All power on the ship was shut down except for emergency lighting pulled in from the dock. The temperature was down around freezing. We had neither heat nor running water. As if that weren't enough, the head was down the dock at the end of the pier—a real thrill when nature called in the middle of the night. Some of us just didn't answer the call.

---

**Ship's Log: Monday 5 March 1951** Attached to Fleet Activities, Yokosuka, Japan, for maintenance, dry docking, and recreational period.

---

Four guys—sonarmen Roger Stone and Hale Beard and radarmen Grady Breed and Robert Cooper—went partying at a small hotel on the outskirts of Yokosuka. No military personnel were allowed on the streets between midnight and 6:00 A.M.

These guys fell asleep and didn't awaken until Stone heard roosters crowing the next morning. He roused the other guys and they beat a hasty path back to the ship. It was critically important that they get back before morning muster, at which time they would have been listed as AWOL.

When they arrived back on the dock, they saw the OOD and the Petty Officer of the Watch (POOW) manning their stations at the head of the gangway. The fearful foursome hid behind a shack and waited for the OOD and POOW to leave the quarterdeck. They shivered in the cold morning air for half an hour while they waited. Muster was getting closer and closer.

At long last, both the OOD and POOW disappeared from view. The four AWOLs made a mad dash up the gangway. It was only twenty yards but it seemed like twenty miles. They thought they'd made it.

The POOW hove back into view. He heaved a big sigh and was heard to mumble, "Aw shit." Then he turned his back and pretended to see nothing. Unbeknownst to them, he'd already written up seven other guys who were hauled in by the shore patrol. He had no stomach for writing up four more. The gods of the sea were very forgiving that day.

**Ship's Log: Tuesday–Thursday 6–8 March 1951**   Attached to Fleet Activities, Yokosuka, Japan, for maintenance, dry docking, and recreational period.

My turn came for a little R-and-R. This stood for rest and recreation. Thirty of us left for three days at a camp owned by the navy at Karuizawa, Japan. I wasn't enthusiastic about going, but it was supposed to be good for the soul. Besides, the navy was picking up the tab and it wouldn't count against our accumulated leave.

Karuizawa was a resort town in the Mikumi Mountains about a hundred miles northwest of Tokyo. It was a lot like Aspen without the skiing. (The nearest slopes were twenty-five miles away at Shiga Heights.) Formerly, it had been a fashionable alpine retreat for Japanese nobility seeking to escape the summer mugginess of Tokyo.

Mount Asama, a triple-cratered active volcano, soared 8,399 feet above the town. Lately, it had been making grumbling sounds, and an ever-present wisp of smoke curled upward from its crater. Villagers didn't seem overly concerned about an imminent eruption.

My biggest complaint was that the place was as boring as hell. There wasn't anything to do but eat, drink, play cards, and sleep. I did more of the latter than anything. The only bar in town was at the hotel, and that was filled with the same sailors I saw every day aboard ship. No floor show or entertainment. No movies. Not even any B-girls.

Our resident letch, Joe Medway approached me. "Hey, Gamble, we're getting up a group to go to a Japanese bathhouse. Want to come along?" He named a town about ten miles away. "The cost is twenty dollars," he added.

The idea didn't appeal to me. "No, I think I'll pass."

I missed out on a real whingding. Eight guys signed up. When they rolled in at midnight, they were eight of the most spent, worn out, and used up sailors I had ever seen. Their twenty-dollar fare bought not only transportation and admission to the bathhouse but also all the sake they could drink and some *very* attentive girls. The wine, women, and warm water had drained every last vestige of tension from their bodies. They were as limp as rags.

Four letters from my honey were waiting for me when I got back to the ship. What sailor's heart would not be warmed by these endearing words?

Why, my love, have we been drawn to each other? I choose to believe that in some impossible-to-explain reality we are walking hand-in-hand up the path of life that takes us to the edge—and beyond—of the universe. I believe our love has become a meaningful part of that which makes up the fullness of life before death—and the glory of life after death.

---

**Ship's Log: Friday–Sunday 9–11 March 1951** Attached to Fleet Activities, Yokosuka, Japan, for maintenance, dry docking, and recreational period.

---

If there's one thing that will drive the navy nuts it's for someone to have a name that doesn't fit the specs. For example, a reserve hospitalman apprentice arrived aboard whose name was simply R. B. Jones. No first or middle name, just R.B. That's what his parents named him.

Having been in transit for several weeks, he was behind on receiving his pay. R.B. filled out his pay chit exactly the way he was christened, "R. B. Jones." A terse note came back saying initials were not allowed and he should fill out the chit in a proper fashion using his full name. He wrote across the note, "This is my full name," and returned it to the sender.

Back came another note instructing him that if that was the case and the initials didn't stand for anything, then he should write the word "only" beside each initial to so designate. Dutifully, he complied with the instructions. He filled out the chit with the words "R(only) B(only) Jones."

Wonder of wonders, he got a paycheck. But in typical bureaucratic fashion, it still wasn't right. The name to which the check was issued was *Ronly Bonly Jones.*

---

**Ship's Log: Monday 12 March 1951** Steaming in company with Task Element 70.11 en route to operating area off east coast of Korea.

---

Since the first week in February, the destroyer *Lind* had been involved in clandestine reconnaissance operations in and around the vicinity of Wonsan. These intelligence operations proved to be extremely rewarding. Known by the code name Comber, these clandestine operations involved putting South Korean agents ashore behind enemy lines and receiving back from them reports on enemy troop movements and concentrations.

They used the ship's standard 26-foot motor whaleboat equipped as follows: a radar reflector; four empty 5-inch powder cans with three heated fire bricks in each; SCR-300 radio handset; compass; submachine guns; Very's pistol with flares to be used in emergency (white to indicate boat's position, green to indicate trouble requesting help, and red to indicate trouble but keep clear); inflatable landing raft; and a reel and line to tow the raft. Another important piece of equipment proved to be a spare bucket, inasmuch as the agents being landed invariably got seasick.

All operations took place at night. After the boat left the ship, it towed the empty raft seventy-five to one hundred yards off the beach, at which time the "combers" were loaded into the raft with their equipment (money, papers, food, radio, etc.). The combers would then paddle the raft onto the beach while the boat's crew paid out the attached line. After the combers had landed, the empty raft was then hauled back to the motor whaleboat and the return trip started. The normal round-trip for the ship's boat and crew lasted five to six hours in freezing cold and wetness.

With agents ashore at Wonsan, Chongjin, Suwon Dan, and Iwon, the *Lind* was able to gather valuable intelligence information, which it passed on to ComNavFE for processing. On March 1, for example, agents reported that the enemy was unloading new Soviet mines at the Kalma railroad siding, which, on the seventh, was blown to smithereens by the light cruiser *Manchester.* On March 12 agents reported the presence of enemy troop concentrations at assembly areas in the neighborhood of Wonsan. These reports were followed up with rapid-fire bombardment by the *Manchester* and *Lind* resulting in six thousand to eight thousand enemy casualties.[2]

---

**Ship's Log: Tuesday 13 March 1951**   1140 Joined Task Force 77 in operating area east coast Korea.

---

We bid farewell to the Mighty Mo. We had been through a lot with her the last couple of months. I felt a twinge of jealousy as I watched our lady sail over the horizon with two new escorts, the *Hollister* and *Ozbourn.*

The three ships roamed the North Korean coast from Songjin to as far north as Chongjin on the Siberian border, wrecking every bridge their shells could reach. Over the next four days, they were credited with the destruction of eight railroad bridges and seven highway bridges. Rail traffic along this east coast line was choked off and brought to a virtual halt through this program of systematic destruction.

---

**Ship's Log: Wednesday 14 March 1951**   ASW screen and plane guard with Task Force 77. 0628 Sighted a floating mine and was detached to destroy it.

---

Pilots from the USS *Princeton* carried out a raid that became known as "the Battle of Carlson's Canyon."[3]

Earlier, on March 2, Lt. Comdr. Clement M. Craig, commanding officer of Fighter Squadron 193, spotted the bridge as he was returning from a strike at Kilchu. He described the bridge as long and high, measuring six hundred feet in length, and having a maximum height above the terrain of sixty feet. Five concrete piers supported six steel spans across the canyon. It was located at a point where three rail lines from Manchuria joined. If the bridge could be destroyed, the flow of traffic southward would be seriously impeded.

That same afternoon an unsuccessful attempt was made to destroy the bridge. The following morning, Lt. Comdr. Harold C. "Swede" Carlson of the *Princeton* led a squadron of AD Skyraiders in a spectacular raid over the target. They dropped one span, damaged a second, and twisted two others out of alignment. In honor of his bravery, the other pilots dubbed the locale "Carlson's Canyon."

The Communists, working by night, promptly commenced repairs. By March 14 a reconnaissance plane from the *Princeton* reported Carlson's Canyon bridge was largely restored and would be back in operation within a few days.

Accordingly, pilots from the *Princeton* launched another devastating strike. When they finished, the new wooden structures beneath the originally damaged spans were obliterated; a third original span was destroyed and a fourth seriously damaged. Of the original six spans, only two now remained standing.

---

**Ship's Log: Thursday 15 March 1951**   In ASW screen and plane guard with Task Force 77. 2016 USS BRADFORD in station 4 picked up sonar contact bearing 090T, distance 1,000 yards, evaluated as submarine. OTC gave permission to attack and directed USS BORLAND to assist. 2029 BRADFORD dropped a pattern of depth charges, contact was not regained.

---

The fleet was placed on a high level of alert as to possible intervention by Soviet submarines. In an unusually bellicose interview in *Pravda,* Joseph Stalin reinforced speculation that the Soviets might overtly intervene in the war if the Chinese manpower and air resources were not sufficient to defeat what he called the "interventionists." Peking had already demonstrated that it was willing and able to commit unlimited manpower to the war. Recently, we had seen a tremendous buildup of the Chinese air force with Soviet jet fighters. That left only the sea where the U.S. remained unchallenged. Only the awesome might of the U.S. Navy was what had been keeping the UN forces viable in Korea.

With that somber warning firmly fixed in our minds, the *Bradford* caused more than a little excitement when she reported a sonar contact shortly after sunset positively evaluated as a submarine. Three big carriers in the task force would make a juicy target.

The *Bradford* was given permission to run it down. We were designated to assist.

As soon as our sonarmen confirmed the contact, the *Bradford* initiated her depth charge attack. We held station five hundred yards away. If a second run was called for, we would have made a crossing pattern. Neither ship, however, was able to reestablish sonar contact after the *Bradford*'s initial run. Nor were we able to spot any floating debris that could have confirmed a kill.

The South Korean capital of Seoul was finally recaptured by U.S. Eighth Army forces. It was a Pyrrhic victory, however; two conquests and two liberations had taken a frightful toll on that metropolis, and hardly a tenth of the city's original population still lived amid the ruins.

# 16 PATROLLING THE STRAIT

*March 16–April 7, 1951*

**Ship's Log: Friday 16 March 1951**   0703 Proceeding to Keelung, Formosa, in company with USS LOFBERG. 1435 Alongside USS CIMARRON (AO-22) to transfer FISHER, E.R. MMFN for further transfer to U.S. Naval Hospital, Yokosuka, Japan.

Formosa moved onto the world stage in 1949 when the Nationalist Chinese government of Chiang Kai-shek was ousted from the mainland by the Chinese Communists, and the exiles shifted their base of operations to Formosa. Somehow, this improbable island nation, comprising barely three-hundredths the area of mainland China, presented itself as the *Republic of China* and claimed to be the one, true, legitimate government of China. Naturally, the Communist regime of Mao Tse-tung was annoyed by the continued presence of this thorn in its side and made repeated threats to cross the channel to annex this redoubt. Conversely, Chiang Kai-shek and his generals harbored dreams of launching their own attack across the channel to regain their lost territories.

For its part, the United States was committed to preventing an attack either on Formosa from the mainland or an invasion of China by the forces of Chiang Kai-shek. Toward this end, the Seventh Fleet was directed to maintain a constant naval presence in the strait that separated the two adversaries.

At Wonsan, the siege was now entering its twenty-ninth day. Naval bombardment kept three to four divisions of Chinese troops pinned down, defending against a possible invasion, which otherwise would have been available for the front. But things were getting more dangerous. The destroyers *English, Lind, Walke, Zellars,* and HMNS *Evertsen* got involved in a "shoot-out" with enemy shore batteries.

At 5:30 P.M., the *English* was straddled by three splashes of 3-inch gunfire, the nearest splash about thirty-five yards from the ship. HMNS *Evertsen* in the next berth was also straddled by near misses. Both destroyers were forced to cut loose their anchors in order to get underway in a hurry.

Counterbattery fire was opened by the destroyers in a matter of seconds. They saturated the area with 5-inch AAC and white phosphorous. Subsequently, the helicopter reported complete and heavy coverage in which all enemy batteries were silenced.

---

**Ship's Log: Saturday 17 March 1951**   Steaming en route Keelung, Formosa. Conducted full power trial and smoke prevention exercises.

---

Washington was increasingly concerned that our policies in Korea might inadvertently lead to a third world war. Peking had almost unlimited manpower and had shown no hesitation to commit this manpower to Korea indefinitely. Moscow was lurking in the background and might overtly intervene in the war if Chinese manpower proved to be insufficient. The Soviets had already supplied large numbers of planes and munitions to bolster the Chinese air force.

Speculation about Soviet intervention intensified after Joseph Stalin's bellicose statement that "the war in Korea can only end in a defeat of the interventionists." This, plus numerous reports of Soviet "volunteers" being recruited for service in Korea, caused the Pentagon to warn Tokyo: "It must be emphasized that the USSR military forces in the Far East are considered to be currently organized, equipped and disposed in such a manner to permit initiation of action without warning."[1]

The destroyer *English*, now in her thirteenth consecutive day on the firing line at Wonsan, was taken under fire for a second time from concealed gun positions on Kalma Gak. She swung around to bring all 5-inch guns to bear on target and silenced the enemy batteries.

Just a few miles to the south, the *Lind* went in to investigate a reported enemy shore battery at the lighthouse of Suwon Dan, near Kosong. She moved in close aboard the lighthouse in order to draw fire. A shore battery did open fire on the *Lind*, judged to be 76-mm (3-inch) guns. She returned fire, silenced the guns with direct hits, then retired from the area, leaving trees and camouflage on fire.

---

**Ship's Log: Sunday 18 March 1951**   1215 Arrived Keelung, Formosa.

---

A soft, warm rain was falling. The temperature was in the low seventies. The air felt cold and clammy.

Keelung is a sprawling port city located on the northern tip of Formosa, about thirty miles from the capital of Taipei. It was hard to know exactly how many people really lived there because of the recent influx of Chinese exiled from the mainland. Most of the refugees lived in densely packed shanties hastily thrown up around the city's outskirts. Very few streets were paved.

At 4:30 P.M. liberty was announced for 1st section, starboard watch. That meant only one-fourth of the men could be ashore at one time, thereby keeping enough crew on board to get underway and fight a war in case we had to leave in a hurry. Chief Fred Pierce and I went ashore together to hoist a few.

---

**Ship's Log: Monday–Friday 19–23 March 1951**   Moored at Keelung, Formosa.

---

Rain, rain, and more rain. Condition III gun watches were maintained throughout the night from 6 P.M. til 8 A.M. The gun crews bitched like hell. No rest even in port!

Now in its thirty-third day, the siege of Wonsan erupted in another gunfire duel. Shell splashes were observed near the HMNS *Evertsen*. The *English*, now a veteran at this sort of thing, closed the firing range and proceeded to destroy several previously unreported gun emplacements on Kalma Gak. All enemy batteries were silenced.

Every afternoon, it seemed, the bombardment group could expect some enemy action, especially around sunset. The setting sun favored the shore batteries due west of the anchorage areas. The situation was never dull. All hands kept themselves ready to come to general quarters on a moment's notice.

---

**Ship's Log: Saturday 24 March 1951**   1842 Underway for Sasebo, Japan.

---

The day started out as a routine in-port Saturday. Captain's inspection was held at ten in the morning. Liberty was announced for the 3d section, starboard watch to commence at 1:30 P.M. The weath-

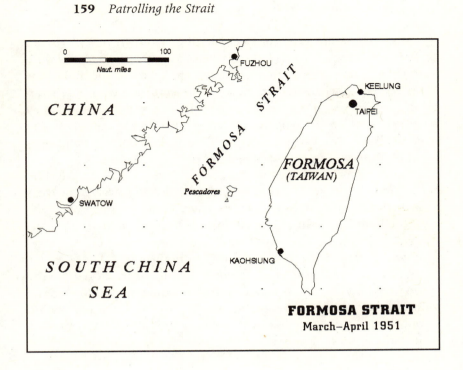

er, as it had been almost every day, was misty with on-again-off-again rain.

Our tranquility was interrupted at 2:45 when an urgent message blared over the loudspeakers: "Attention all hands. Attention all hands. Liberty for the crew has been canceled. Repeat, all liberty has been canceled!"

That announcement was immediately followed by another: "The following personnel report to Ensign White on the quarterdeck: Chief Watson, and petty officers Gamble, Hoisington, Hook, and Garwood. Repeat, Chief Watson, petty officers Gamble, Hoisington, Hook, and Garwood report to the quarterdeck immediately!"

White and Watson were already on the quarterdeck when I got there. The other three arrived shortly. White handed each of us a shore patrol armband and belt. "We're getting underway in two hours," he said tersely. "We've got to go round up the crewmen who have already gone ashore and get them back to the ship." He didn't elaborate.

The six of us were joined at Fleet Landing by Ensign Jack Davis and three petty officers who had already been assigned shore patrol duty for the day. That gave us a total of ten men to fan out through the city. We scoured every bar, restaurant, souvenir shop, and cat-house in an effort to round up our buddies. Some of them were not too happy about the deal. In the end, we managed to round up all but seven: Arend Folkens, Bob Cooper, Eugene Hinson, John Sorcek, Dan Cochran, Bob Rummel, and Jesse Aragon.

Another surprise lay in store for us when we got back to the ship. Up on top of mount 52, Claude Gray and his gunnery gang were busily painting an American flag. This creation measured 13 by 7 feet, with the blue field being 62 by 45 inches. Each red-and-white stripe was 6.5 inches wide. The guys hadn't had time to paint on the forty-eight white stars by the time we cast off from the buoy.

As soon as we cleared the harbor, Captain Buaas kicked up the speed to twenty-five knots on a course that would take us toward the west coast of Japan. No explanation was offered as to our destination or purpose. Nor were we told why we were sporting a freshly painted American flag atop mount 52.

---

**Ship's Log: Sunday 25 March 1951**   Steaming independently en route Keelung, Formosa, to Sasebo, Japan. Speed is 25 knots. Armament condition 3 and material condition BAKER are set. Ship is darkened.

---

It was unusual for us to steam at a sustained speed of twenty-five knots. It was rough on men and equipment to slam-bang through the waves in such a hell-bent-for-leather fashion. It also burned up a helluva lot of fuel—about forty gallons per mile. Nevertheless, the *Borland* held this speed for thirty-six hours, carving a swath through the waters of the East China Sea straight as an arrow toward the west coast of Japan, never deviating from our base course of 044 degrees.

"Does anybody know what's going on?" I asked Ensign Charles Hampton, our air defense officer.

"Damned if I know. Your guess is as good as mine," was his reply.

Clearly, though, something was afoot.

**Ship's Log: Monday 26 March 1951**  0915 Moored starboard
side to USS HAMUL (AD-20).

The mystery deepened when we reached Sasebo. Without ex-
planation, we tied up alongside the destroyer tender *Hamul* (AD-20).
Then a cargo ship, USS *Deal* (AKL-2), snuggled up on our other side.
We were neatly sandwiched between two larger ships. Highly unusual.

Lieutenant (j.g.) Melesky, the communications officer, took me
aside. "Gamble, I need your cooperation."

"Sure," I replied, though perplexed.

"You recall when we made that special trip into Sasebo last Christmas to get our SPS-6 radar antenna fixed?"

"Yes," I nodded.

"Well, it's just happened again. We had to make a flying trip into
Sasebo to get our SPS-6 radar antenna repaired."

"But I don't understand," I protested. "There's nothing wrong with
our SPS-6."

"You and I know that. But that's the word the captain wants to put
out among the crew. So if anyone asks, just tell them that we had to
get our radar antenna fixed. Okay?"

My curiosity was piqued. I watched for signs of unusual activity.
The only thing out of place was a flurry of activity around our coding
room. From that, I figured they were either, (1) installing some new
and highly secret coding equipment or (2) rigging explosive charges
with which to blow up the highly secret equipment in case the ship
should fall into enemy hands. Or both.

**Ship's Log: Thursday 29 March 1951**  0601 Entered Keelung,
Formosa. 1031 Underway to relieve the USS CUNNINGHAM
(DD-752) on patrol.

We had a four-hour layover in Keelung. We remained at battle stations the whole time in port as if expecting an imminent attack
from air or sea. "Goddamn, Mr. White, what's going on?" I asked.

He shrugged.

"Well, you see more of the captain than I do. Hasn't he said anything to the officers? Any clues?"

"The only thing I've heard is that there have been reconnaissance reports of the Chinese amassing troops along the coast—a couple hundred thousand or more—and invasion craft. We can only assume from that they intend to invade Formosa. That's about all I can say."

"It's that imminent, huh?"

"We don't know. Today. Tomorrow. Next week. Next month. Who knows?"

"Do you think maybe they're just bluffing?"

"Well, all I can say is MacArthur thought they were bluffing last November when the Chinese were massing troops at the same time he was promising we'd be home by Christmas. He sure found out different, didn't he?"

"What's to keep them from coming across the strait?"

"You're looking at it!" he said.

"You mean, *we're* it?"

"You've got it, Ace. We're the first line of defense against the invasion of Formosa. Two lonely destroyers, the *Borland* and *Lofberg,* are all that stand between mainland China and Nationalist Formosa."

"Holy shit!" I exclaimed. "What do we do if the Chinese *do* attack?"

"We try to survive long enough for help to arrive."

Our "Keelung Seven"—as those left behind on the twenty-fourth came to be called—returned to the ship. They had spent the time under technical arrest aboard the USS *Mispillion.* Apart from being a bit grungy from lack of toilet gear and change of clothing, they seemed to have weathered their sojourn in good spirits.

Mostly, they were worried that this might result in a black mark on their records. Lieutenant Commander Roddy assured them he didn't consider it their fault, nor would he file charges.

---

**Ship's Log: Friday 30 March 1951**   At 0001 relieved the USS CUNNINGHAM (DD-752) on station. Began single ship patrol on line running 030T, distance 24 miles, and 230T, distance 24 miles. 1405 Exercised crew at general quarters. 1410 Held damage control drill. 1421 Held fire drill.

---

We remained at a higher than normal state of readiness. We had been warned that Formosa could be the next "likely" target for the Chinese. Conversely, Chiang Kai-shek might take advantage of our exigency in Korea to stage a "return to the mainland," further exacerbating the military crisis in the Far East.

Moreover, there wasn't any doubt that MacArthur wanted to go to war, full war, with Communist China. He believed it was asinine for Washington to decline Chiang's repeated offers of assistance.

We were sitting like ducks in a pond while a titanic struggle was raging around us. Washington, on the one hand, wanted to contain the war. MacArthur, on the other, wanted to expand it.

---

**Ship's Log: Saturday 31 March 1951**  Maintaining single ship patrol in Formosa Strait. 0935 Made inspection of all magazines and smokeless powder samples.

---

History was being made. The siege at Wonsan, which had begun on February 16, had set a new record. Fifty days of continuous naval bombardment passed the previous record established at Vicksburg almost a century earlier.[2]

We also learned that enemy response to this continuous bombardment involved a buildup of artillery and garrison forces, plus a persistent effort to remine the harbor. Of the twenty-eight mines swept during the month of March, twenty of them were shiny and new.

---

**Ship's Log: Sunday 1 April 1951**  Steaming as before. Maintaining single ship patrol in Formosa Strait. 1107 Rendezvoused with USS CUNNINGHAM (DD-752), received on board McCLELLAND, George S., CT3, for temporary additional duty.

---

An unusual, almost eerie, chain of events seemed to point in the direction of a major activity in which we were destined to play a central role. For one, there was the sudden departure from Keelung and the high-speed run to Sasebo. For another, there was our remaining at battle stations while at Keelung. Another link was now forged in the chain of mystery.

At midmorning the *Cunningham* pulled alongside us to transfer aboard a telecommunications specialist. These guys work mostly in cryptography centers, not aboard ships. This guy arrived with just a ditty bag and tool kit. Obviously he did not intend to stay long.

The specialist spent most of the day in the crypto room. His activity was cloaked in secrecy. Lieutenant Melesky, the communications officer, wasn't talking. Neither were any of the other officers—if indeed they knew.

---

**Ship's Log: Monday 2 April 1951** 1127 Rendezvoused with USS CUNNINGHAM (DD-752) to transfer passenger by motor whale boat.

---

Our mystery guest left in late morning. His departure was shrouded in as much secrecy as his arrival.

Apparently, the *Cunningham* hung around our area throughout the night. She waited just over the horizon to pick him up as soon as his work was completed.

---

**Ship's Log: Tuesday–Wednesday 3–4 April 1951** Steaming independently in Formosa Strait as single ship patrol.

---

Dear Anna: At midmorning, word was passed over the ship's PA system: "All hands not on duty, report topside. The sun is shining!" A scramble ensued up ladders and companionways. For the first time since we'd been in Formosan waters, the sun broke through the heavy, gray overcast. Unfortunately for the slowpokes, the sun stayed out only a few short minutes and the slowpokes didn't get to see it. Love, Rusty

---

**Ship's Log: Thursday–Saturday 5–7 April 1951** Moored at Keelung, Formosa.

---

Captains's inspection on Saturday, following which I went ashore. I tried to call my honey from the international telephone exchange in Keelung, but the operator could not get through to the States. Big disappointment. I did have a letter waiting for me back at the ship though.

My sweet love. I shall be very close to you this night, for I am feeling your love at this very moment—I sense your presence in a way that only you and I can understand. I look forward to the day when we can be face-to-face and continue in our sharing, and until then I will keep you close in my heart and my love will be with you wherever you go.   Anna

## 17   ACTING AS DECOY

*April 8–13, 1951*

**Ship's Log: Sunday 8 April 1951**   1552 Underway to join the USS THOMASON (DD-760) in Formosa Strait.

General MacArthur chafed under the restrictions placed on him by Washington. That was no secret. Indeed, he made his frustrations plainly known in several public pronouncements and private talks with visiting congressmen.

What was not as well known was the extreme lengths he was willing to go in order to get around or subvert those restrictions.

First, he was forbidden to bomb or strafe any military installations north of the Yalu River, the border between North Korea and the Chinese province of Manchuria. Further, U.S. planes were not allowed to cross the Yalu even if engaged in hot pursuit of enemy fighter aircraft. MacArthur felt that the "safe haven" north of the Yalu gave the Communists an unfair advantage. He told his aide, Gen. Courtney Whitney, that "Red Chinese aggression in Asia could not be stopped by killing Chinese in Korea, no matter how many."

Second, MacArthur clearly did not agree with the political strategy of establishing and holding a defensible line at the 38th parallel as the first step to negotiating a peaceful settlement. He seemed not to understand the American public's growing distaste for war and its antipathy toward the prospects of being drawn into an even greater war. He criticized stopping at the 38th parallel as falling short of "accomplishing our mission in the unification of Korea." In response, Secretary of State Dean Acheson advised him pointedly, "That is not your mission."

By mid-March 1951, a strong line had been established along the 38th parallel. The prewar status had been virtually restored, and the two armies were of approximately equal strength. To Washington, this seemed like an auspicious time to try to negotiate a peace. President Truman told his cabinet, "It would now be in their interest at least as much as ours to halt the fighting."

MacArthur viewed the peace move as a "sellout," a political move that would end the war without victory. He told a correspondent for the *London Daily Telegraph* that his troops "were circumscribed by a web of artificial conditions," and for the first time in his career he "found himself in a war without a definite objective." He hinted darkly that the decisions coming out of Washington were the result of a sinister element at work, a plot that had reached the top echelons of the administration.

When Gen. Matthew Ridgway, commander of the U.S. Eighth Army, arrived from Washington, MacArthur asked him if he had observed anything unusual about President Truman's behavior. Ridgway opined that the president appeared perfectly normal to him. MacArthur confided, "I have confidential information from an eminent physician who examined Truman that he has a long history of malignant hypertension. This condition causes him to experience great mood swings and do irrational things." In other words, MacArthur was questioning Truman's mental stability.

MacArthur's public statements in March 1951 indicated that he felt the war should be carried to the Chinese mainland. He was firmly convinced that war with China—and possibly the Soviet Union—was inevitable, and in his opinion it would be better to expand the war now rather than later. He released a statement to the press without any prior review by, or notification to, the Joint Chiefs of Staff in which he characterized China as a vastly overrated military power. "Even under conditions which now restrict the activity of the United Nations forces and the corresponding military advantages which accrue to Red China," he said, "it has shown its complete inability to accomplish by force of arms its conquest of Korea."

Unbeknownst to MacArthur, the National Security Agency monitoring station at Atsugi Air Force Base near Tokyo had intercepted some very damning messages. They were from the Spanish and Portuguese embassies in Tokyo, in which the envoys reported to their superiors on confidential briefings given them by General MacArthur. Both countries were run by right-wing dictators with whom MacArthur had long had an affinity. The message intercepts were substantially the same: MacArthur had informed them that he was confident he could transform the Korean War into a major conflict in which he could dispose of the Chinese Communist question once and for all, and he did not want Spain or Portugal to be alarmed if this happened. He said the Soviet Union could either stay out of the war or face destruction itself.

In short, MacArthur was undertaking to carry out his own foreign policy program independent of, and in direct contravention to, the administration in Washington, D.C., which he felt was controlled by subversives. He declared to these—and possibly other—foreign governments that he had no intention of abiding by political restrictions on the military, and it was his intention to force the United States into what he considered a necessary war.

On March 19 the State Department sent a communiqué to MacArthur indicating that the United Nations was now preparing to discuss conditions of settlement in Korea. For the next several days, State and Defense Department officials worked quietly to refine the proposed presidential announcement and clear its wording with the UN allies. On March 24, however, MacArthur sabotaged the president's peace initiative by issuing his own "peace overture" that was a thinly disguised slap in the face to the Chinese and a calculated incitement for them to continue the war, not end it. Later, MacArthur boasted that he had torpedoed one of the most "disgraceful plots" in American history.

Obviously, Washington had a renegade military commander on its hands. To Truman, the issue of who ran U.S. foreign policy was more important than the diplomatic furor caused by MacArthur's immoderate statements. MacArthur was openly defying the policy of his commander in chief, the President of the United States, and the orders of the Joint Chiefs of Staff. Yet it was much more than a question of "who's in charge here"; the bigger threat was MacArthur's machinations to draw the United States into a larger war.

At the very same time the Joint Chiefs of Staff were debating how to curb MacArthur's future as a military commander, they were also considering another directive that would expand his authority to wage military warfare. On April 4 the general proposed a possible action against mainland China. In turning down the request, Gen. Omar Bradley, chairman of the JCS, said they feared that MacArthur might make a premature decision to carry it out.[1]

**Ship's Log: Monday 9 April 1951**   Patrolling independently in Formosa Strait. 0930 Completed inspection of magazines and smokeless powder samples.

We departed Keelung under a cloud of mystery. No one seemed to know where we were going or why, nor did Captain Buaas have anything to say about the matter. If, indeed, he knew.

Dear Anna:  This evening we were treated to one of the most beautiful sunsets I had ever seen in my life. The seas were relatively calm, like a great looking glass. As the sun dipped over the western horizon and disappeared from view, the snowy underbellies of the cumulus clouds lit up in a brilliant red. The red of the clouds, in turn, reflected off the glassy waters, and for a few glorious moments the ocean seemed like a sea of blood. For me it was like a religious experience.

**Ship's Log: Tuesday 10 April 1951**   0410 Maneuvered alongside USS RUSH (DD-714) to receive officer messenger. 1515 Exercised the crew at general quarters. 1709 maneuvered alongside USS LOFBERG (DD-759) to exchange officer messenger. 1735 Set armament condition III on gunnery stations.

The predawn arrival of an officer messenger added to the mystery of our mission. The USS *Rush* (DD-714) made a direct speed run from Tokyo specifically for this purpose. We could only speculate what this meant.

"Officer messenger" is a mode of delivery used only for messages of the highest secrecy, typically sealed orders. The contents are considered too sensitive to be entrusted to radio encryption or guard mail.

By 5:00 P.M., he was gone—transferred to the squadron commander's ship, the *Lofberg*. That led to further speculation that we were involved in some kind of secret—perhaps dangerous—mission.

**Ship's Log: Wednesday 11 April 1951**   Proceeding independently to area off Swatow, China. 1030 Exercised crew at general quarters. 1100 On birddog station off Swatow, China. Commenced maintaining station. 1600 Departed birddog station. 1615 Secured from general quarters.

---

At reveille, with a tropical dawn just breaking in the east, the crew of the *Borland* was treated to an eyeball view of the land mass of mainland China. Shrouded in a luminous morning mist, the low-lying coast appeared ephemeral and mysterious. It gave us a spooky feeling somewhat like looking into the barrel of a gun with a shell in its chamber and the hammer cocked.

The *Borland* edged closer in to shore and by 11:00 A.M. had taken a position three miles off Swatow (Shantou), a major port city located on the Han River estuary. Our engines were brought to a full stop, and then we just sat there dead in the water. We were already at general quarters, but lest there be any mistake about the danger we were in, word was passed that we should be prepared to defend ourselves "vigorously against possible hostile action."

Over the horizon in back of us, being careful to stay outside the twelve-mile limit in international waters, were the carriers *Boxer* and *Philippine Sea* and other elements of Task Force 77. As yet, the carriers' planes were unarmed, although my friend Jack Powers, a technician aboard the *Boxer*, told me that bombs and ammunition were stacked on deck ready to arm the aircraft at a moment's notice.

Within minutes of our coming on station, armed motorized junks began to converge around us. Almost before we knew it we were surrounded by a dozen or more of the damn things. Somehow, this situation seemed more ominous than anything we had encountered before. More armed junks streamed out of the Han River estuary, and eventually the count got to forty-seven—with probably more out of sight around the headland.

These junks were far from the picturesque sailing boats so often pictured in tourist literature. These were warships ranging from 70 to 110 feet in length and displacing four hundred to six hundred tons. Such a fleet presented numerous small targets, hard to hit, even harder to sink.

Moreover, every one of them was armed, many of them mounting what appeared to be 76-mm artillery pieces. Some of them may also have been carrying torpedoes—it was hard to tell. They took positions ranging from five hundred to fifteen hundred yards away, completely encircling our lone destroyer, each side eying the other warily. No one on the *Borland* had to be told that we were going to find ourselves in a very ticklish situation if either side opened fire. One armed junk, or even a few, would have been little match for a U.S. destroyer, but forty-seven of the critters would have spelled almost certain doom for our thinly armored vessel.

Someone asked, "Couldn't we just ram them?" "Sure," I said, "but what would such a collision do to our own ship?" After all, those things were not constructed of boxwood; that was six hundred tons of heavy wooden planking. Damage to the *Borland* would have been extensive, if not disabling.

What made our situation even scarier was the knowledge that earlier in the year the navy had inaugurated a series of experiments to determine the optimum choice of weapons against a junk fleet. Those tests found them almost impossible to sink.

It wasn't hard to comprehend the precarious predicament we were in. We were cut off from any clear route of escape; no matter which direction the ship might head, we would have to run a gauntlet of enemy warcraft, some of which undoubtedly would try to ram the ship in order to slow her down or disable her. We stared at them, and they stared at us.

Captain Buaas said his greatest fear was not a running gun duel but a boarding attempt. Shades of days of yore! He feared that somehow they might manage to disable the ship by shooting at or fouling the screws and then try to board us. Their numbers would have been overwhelming. So he devised a scheme: in the event something like this happened, we would spray oil on the boats attempting to board and set them ablaze.

After two hours of this stand-off, planes from Task Force 77 began overflying the area at 1:00 P.M. Officially, these flights were billed as reconnaissance runs, but never before had I seen "reconnaissance" planes make repeated passes of mock dive-bombing and simulated strafing runs over a large military airfield such as the one situated just on the other side of Swatow. From time to time, planes would peel off and buzz the junks. For an incredibly tense and nerve-wracking two hours, high-speed military jets continued to scream over at low altitude, acting as though they were going to shoot up everything in sight.

Why would they do this? The "official" explanation was that this exercise was to scare the Chinese and keep them from invading Formosa. Poppycock! The fact is that if the Chinese had fired on any of the ships or planes, then the *Boxer* and *Philippine Sea* would have immediately armed and launched their aircraft to strike coastal installations in retaliation. Moreover, the battleship and cruiser force was positioned to bombard the China coast and establish a beachhead; and there were enough destroyers on hand to cover a landing.

It was also the case that the Nationalist Chinese Army on Formosa was poised just a few miles away, highly trained, fully equipped, and prepared to launch their boats and landing equipment for just such a mainland incursion. They had been begging to get into the war; MacArthur wanted them in the war; but Washington had steadfastly refused.

Happily for everyone concerned, the Chinese showed great restraint. No shots were fired that day, and we didn't have to shoot our way out of there.

Finally, the planes went away. A sense of relief swept over the crew when they did not return. At 4:15 P.M. we were released from our battle stations and the ship was directed to return to patrol. Very gingerly we threaded our way through the encircled junks, lest we accidentally bump into one and unwittingly create an unpleasant incident. These had been a hairy, scary seven hours. I was emotionally and physically drained.

---

**Ship's Log: Thursday 12 April 1951**   Steaming singly en route Formosa Straits patrol area from birddog station. 1715 Alongside USS MISPILLION (AO-105) for fuel and mail.

---

Bright and early, we got word that General MacArthur had been fired. It was April 12 our time (April 11 in the United States). I made a special note of that date because it was my sister Shirley's birthday—in my family it seemed as if things always happened on Shirley's birthday.

Among the officers and enlisted men of the *Borland*, there didn't seem much doubt but that we were put out there to be "sitting ducks" while MacArthur tried to provoke the Chinese Communists into some kind of retaliatory action. If the Chinese had risen to the bait, such a retaliatory action would undoubtedly have been characterized as an "attack" on American warships. This in turn could be just the trigger MacArthur needed to expand the war to the mainland of China as he had been advocating. "I'm glad they got rid of that crazy bastard," one of the officers was heard to remark.

That may explain the botched job of informing MacArthur of his dismissal. Under ordinary circumstances, a military commander of MacArthur's stature would be entitled to depart with proper honors and dignity. But things didn't happen that way. A decision had already been made several days earlier by the president and Joint Chiefs of Staff that MacArthur must be relieved; however, the timing and the circumstances had not yet been worked out. About three in the afternoon of April 10 (April 11 in Tokyo), Truman decided to act. MacArthur was entertaining Sen. Warren Magnuson and an executive of Northwest Airlines at the embassy when Col. Sid Huff, his personal pilot, delivered the brown envelope that informed him he had been relieved of command. No pomp and circumstance, no ceremony, no formal change of command, no nothing. He was out!

As to the question of why carry on the activity near Swatow rather than some city farther north such as Shanghai, the reasoning seemed to be that Swatow was situated on the Formosa Strait, which the U.S. patrolled regularly. Hence, a claim could be made to Congress and the UN that the ships were there on regular business, whereas had the ships and planes moved in on Shanghai where they had no business being, it would have been harder to convince world authorities that the United States was not the instigator. It all boiled down to a question of legitimacy: the U.S. could plausibly claim a legitimate reason for its warships being near Swatow, whereas no such legitimacy could be claimed for them to be at Shanghai.

---

**Ship's Log: Friday 13 April 1951**  Steaming independently en route to birddog station off Swatow, China. 0630 Exercised crew at general quarters. 0950 Secured from general quarters. Changed course to 090T, speed 23 knots, proceeding to join Task Force 77.

---

One more brief foray into the "lion's den" was planned. However, the exercise was terminated early, and no U.S. planes flew over. Thankfully, the Chinese sent no junks out to meet us. The *Borland* was then released from patrol duty and ordered to rejoin Task Force 77, now on its way north. Our mission in the Formosa Strait was over.

Task Force 77 was proceeding at flank speed back to its operating area off North Korea. The eight-day absence of air support from its planes over the combat zone had been costly to the troops fighting on the ground. This hiatus in fast carrier operations had let the interdiction program get almost out of hand.

\*   \*   \*

The "public" story was that President Truman dismissed the recalcitrant general over his statements challenging administration policy. The underlying story was far more ominous. And while the Swatow adventure may not have been the single event that triggered MacArthur's firing, the incident apparently sent a clear signal to Washington about what lengths MacArthur was willing to go to circumvent his superiors and force a wider war—a signal the president dared no longer ignore.

## 18   BABY-SITTING THE BIG BOYS

*April 16–May 13, 1951*

---

**Ship's Log: Monday 16 April 1951**   Steaming with Task Force 77 in operating area off east coast of Korea. 1913 PHILIPPINE SEA reported man overboard; this vessel diverted to commence search. 2001 Ceased search.

---

Searchlights pierced the night sky as all hands lined the rail to search the water for a seaman reported to have fallen over the side of the USS *Philippine Sea*. A warship is always a dangerous place to be, but nothing is more feared by seamen than being lost overboard. Sometimes we found them, sometimes we didn't. This search ended happily when, after an hour, the *Philippine Sea* reported she had conducted a careful muster of the crew and no one was missing.

For two weeks, the planes of Task Force 77 had been absent from the skies of Korea because of the adventure in Formosa. The Communists took advantage of the lull to repair damage wreaked upon their rail network in February and March. This, in turn, enabled them to move thousands of vehicles and fresh combat divisions to the south.

Although an aircraft carrier could probably fend off attacks from aircraft, the submarine presented the major hazard. No submarine attacks had yet developed, but it was common knowledge that Soviet submarines were monitoring our every move. After all, we were fighting Soviet guns, Soviet radar, Soviet planes, and Soviet mines, so why not Soviet subs?

The standard battle group was a "screen" of destroyers that formed concentric circles around the "big tops." The number of destroyers might range from five to twenty or more. An attacking submarine would have to penetrate the destroyer screen before it could get a shot off at one of the carriers. The spacing of the destroyers around the screen was carefully designed to prevent that from happening.

---

**Ship's Log: Tuesday–Thursday 17–19 April 1951**   Steaming in company with Task Force 77; carriers conducting flight operations throughout day.

---

Dear Rusty:  As I am thinking about you at the close of this day, I am holding an image of you in my mind and I feel very close to you. I know in my heart and my mind that I must have been created especially for you—to love you and share my life with you. You feel so right as a part of me—that element of completeness never experienced until knowing you. I am so grateful that I have come to know that I shall go on loving you through all eternity. You are like no other person that I have ever known and I am committed to you in a way that brings a deep sense of satisfaction.   Love, Anna

Realizing how close MacArthur had come to provoking a third world war, General Ridgway sent a telex to all air, naval, and ground chiefs under his command in which he advised:

> The grave and ever present danger of an extension of current hostilities in Korea places a heavy responsibility upon all echelons of this command, but particularly upon those capable of offensive action.
>
> International tensions within and bearing upon this theater have created acute danger of World War III. It is the intense determination of our people, and of all the free peoples of the world, to prevent this catastrophe, if that can be done without appeasement or sacrifice of principle.[1]

---

**Ship's Log: Friday–Saturday 20–21 April 1951**   Steaming in company with Task Force 77. Aircraft carriers conducting flight operations throughout day.

---

Dear Anna: Do you remember the song, "I saw a rainbow at midnight"? Well, I never thought I would see one, but believe it or not, tonight I actually did see a rainbow at midnight . . . and as in the words of the song, it reminded me of you. One of my buddies called me out on deck to witness the rare phenomenon, and at first I thought he was kidding. But I went, and I'm glad I did. The moon was full and bright, and the sky was slightly misty with a light overcast. And sure enough, there was a faint but distinct rainbow visibly hanging there in the eastern sky.   Love, Rusty

Commodore Lang acquired a reputation of being a martinet, a strict military disciplinarian. No detail was too small to escape his attention. For example, Lang decided that the destroyers in his squadron had to carry the full amount of supplies that navy regs said all ships should carry. He had found an obscure regulation that decreed a ship should have on board at all times a minimum thirty-day supply of flour. He sought to enforce it.

When the word went out among the skippers in our division to lay in a thirty-day supply of flour, one of the other captains called Commander Buaas and asked, "Is this for real?" Buaas, who knew Lang's idiosyncrasies as well as anyone, advised, "Yes, you'd better get it."

We ended up carrying so much flour that it wouldn't all fit in the storerooms. We had to lash some topside underneath the ladders. That laughingly became known as "the commodore's flour." It got hard as a rock and became unusable, but by golly, we had the flour!

A new division of destroyers joined the force. One of the skippers was a Naval Academy classmate of Buaas's. When word got to him about the commodore's flour, he sent Buaas a message asking about it. Buaas told him, "Yeah, Johnny, you'd better comply."

Not wanting to be cited for noncompliance, this recently arrived skipper made a deal with one of the aircraft carriers. The next time he came alongside for refueling, the carrier supplied him with the needed flour. Well, the laborious process of transferring flour by highline so delayed his departure from the carrier that it threw the task force off schedule. Commodore Lang was raising hell—why was this ship alongside so long?

Word got back to Lang that they were getting flour. He got so mad that he ordered the entire division into Sasebo and reported them as being unready for sea.

That, in turn, made ComDesFlot One very unhappy.[2] It was a blot on the admiral's record that one of his destroyer divisions had been ordered into port as being "unfit."

---

**Ship's Log: Sunday 22 April 1951**  0915 Made sonar contact and left formation to develop and evaluate. 0954 Sonar contact evaluated non-submarine.

---

The long-anticipated Chinese spring offensive began with a thrust down the center. As had happened so many times before, the ROK troops were the first to collapse. U.S. Army and Marine forces were left unprotected on their flanks. General Van Fleet, Ridgway's successor as commander of the Eighth Army, ordered a withdrawal.

Once again, U.S. naval forces at sea responded with alacrity. Intensified close support from carrier-based aircraft inflicted heavy casualties, causing the enemy to pay dearly for every mile of ground gained. Also, the amphibious force hurriedly drew up plans for another series of feints that would be carried out over the next few days.

The *Borland* boasted a number of talented musicians. Among them were Seaman Joe D. Smith, a first-rate steel guitar player, Solon Gray, who played the clarinet and could dance the old soft shoe, an accordionist, and several guitarists. In fact, about the only instruments we lacked were the drums and a bass—mainly because these were too big to store in a footlocker.

Nearly every evening a bunch of guys would congregate in the machine shop for an informal jam session. Sometimes it lasted far into the night. Mostly, they played country and western.

One day when we pulled alongside a carrier to return a rescued pilot, the flattop paraded its ship's band to welcome the returning aviator. That gave our guys an idea: If an aircraft carrier could have a band, why not a destroyer?

The next time we went alongside a carrier, our musicians brought their instruments up on the boat deck and proceeded to serenade the "airdales." Unfortunately, the wind, sea, and machinery noises drowned out their music. What they needed was an amplifier.

I couldn't play an instrument. But I could hook up a loudspeaker. That helped. I went one step further. I built an audio mixer that could "mike" each instrument separately.

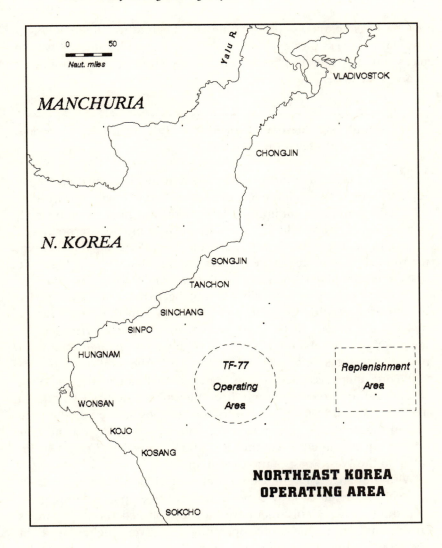

They named themselves the Ramboles. Thenceforth, whenever we went alongside another ship—be it carrier, battleship, cruiser, or sister destroyer—we would "parade" our little band. Before we knew it, the sheer novelty of a tin can having its own band gained us quite a bit of recognition.

On this particular Sunday we had the audacity to serenade Rear Adm. R. A. Oftsie, Commander Task Force 77, when we came alongside his flagship, the *Princeton*. Airmen by the hundreds lined the flight and hangar decks and applauded every number. The admiral was so pleased that he had his photographer take pictures that later appeared in *Stars and Stripes*.

---

**Ship's Log: Tuesday 24 April 1951**   1952 Maneuvered alongside USS ASHTABULA (AO-51) for fuel.

---

The task force instituted a new and much-needed system of replenishment. To avoid the loss of one day out of every four in refueling and rearming, Admiral Oftsie developed a plan whereby each day the task force would join the logistic ships in late afternoon and load until midnight. While this made a long working day for the men, it also made it possible for the carriers to keep pace with the high rate of expenditure of aviation gasoline and ordnance.

Until now, such a schedule had not been practical. The Service Force of the Pacific Fleet, like every other unit in the armed forces, had felt the impact of fiscal cutbacks in the postwar defense meltdown. Of the four main types of fleet supply ships, namely, ammunition, oilers, stores, and refrigerator ("reefers"), the total roster of Service Force ships assigned to the Western Pacific on June 25, 1950, consisted of one reefer and one fleet oiler, plus a destroyer tender, a fleet tug, and an LST on loan for training purposes. The only hospital ship in the Pacific Fleet had been decommissioned. Only one ammunition ship remained in commission, the *Mount Katmai* (AE-18), located on the West Coast of the United States.

With the arrival of a sufficient number of support ships in Far Eastern waters, the decision was made to shift the emphasis to night replenishment. A replenishment area was established about fifty miles farther out from the task force operating area. Every night after flight operations ceased, the entire Task Force 77 would set a course for the replenishment area, top off all eighteen to twenty ships with fuel, ammunition, and stores, and be back on station in time to resume morning flight operations. Naturally, night replenishment carried a much higher risk of collision or a man being washed overboard. But it minimized downtime away from combat operations.

**Ship's Log: Thursday 26 April 1951**  1903 Gained sonar contact bearing 197T, distance 1350 yards. Evaluated possible submarine. Manned ASW battery and general quarters stations. 1912 Contact evaluated non-submarine. 2014 USS PHILIPPINE SEA reported man overboard, commenced search. 2130 USS DUNCAN (DDR-874) recovered man.

Sea conditions were too rough for flight operations on our side of the peninsula.

Over on the west coast, carrier aircraft off the Yellow Sea fended off a two-pronged Communist attack to recapture Seoul. One prong pushed down the Pukhan valley, while the other attempted to ferry troops across the Han River. Both moves failed. Carrier aircraft kept all but a few Chinese from crossing the Han, and these were easily handled by the ROK Marines. The Pukhan thrust was stalled by the army's 24th and 25th Divisions.

We were treated to another example of Kenny Beggs's offbeat humor. About eight in the evening, we got a call that the loran (*long range navigation*) was malfunctioning. Beggs had the ET watch. He went up to take a look at it.

When he returned, I asked for a report on what was wrong.

"I think it had a queer electron in there," he said.

"Queer electron?" I asked, puzzled.

With a completely straight face he replied, "Yeah. It's been going around blowing fuses."

**Ship's Log: Monday 30 April 1951**  Screening for Task Force 77. 1455 USS BUCK (DD-761) joined formation.

The Communist spring offensive had largely petered out. In the end, their advance reached a maximum of about thirty miles and no decisive advantage was gained. UN estimates of casualties inflicted on the enemy claimed seventy thousand for the April push.

My buddy Claude Gray got put on report. The gun boss reported him for allowing his crew to sit down while on watch. Gray said the captain ordered it because he was the one who caught them sitting down.

At captain's mast Gray received loss of four liberties for "improper performance of duties."

Also, the USS *Buck* returned to service following replacement of her bow lost in a collision the previous November.

---

**Ship's Log: Tuesday 1 May 1951**   Steaming in company with Task Force 77 in operating area off east coast of Korea.

---

May 1, 1951, was the only time torpedoes were used by the U.S. in the Korean War. They were used to destroy the 250-foot high dam of the Hwachon Reservoir.

Intelligence sources indicated the enemy was planning to launch a major advance. They would have to cross the Pukhan and Han Rivers. They planned to close the sluice gates of the dam in order to lower the water level of the Pukhan and Han Rivers to fordable depths. To forestall this possibility, the U.S. Eighth Army requested the sluice gates be destroyed.

Earlier high-level bombing attacks by B-29s proved ineffective. The dam-busting task was given to the pilots on the USS *Princeton*. They determined that torpedoes were the only ordnance capable of blowing out the 20-foot high, 40-foot wide, and 2.5-foot thick gates.

The low-level attack would be difficult and hazardous, owing to the terrain. The reservoir was surrounded by high hills, and the straightaway was very short. Only two planes could go in at a time, and the torpedo drop had to be very accurate. On top of this, the area surrounding the dam was heavily fortified with enemy antiaircraft batteries.

Eight AD Skyraiders made the run. They were accompanied by twelve F4U Corsair fighters for flak-suppression. Weaving their way through the flak, the pilots of the *Princeton* did their job: the center flood gate was completely knocked out and a ten-foot hole blasted in the second gate. The impounded waters were released upon the plain below.

---

**Ship's Log: Saturday 5 May 1951**   Screening for Task Force 77 while conducting flight operations. 1419 Sighted floating mine, proceeded to destroy mine.

---

The minesweeper JML 306 was struck by a mine and sunk off Sokto. This was the first such loss since February.

Mines continued to be a problem. A new and more serious threat emerged—drifting mines. Not only were the Russian moored mines fused to remain armed after breaking loose, many more had apparently been launched as "drifters" to take advantage of the prevailing southerly currents.

We suspected Soviet mine-laying submarines were laying mines in the path of the task force. Some were new and shiny.

---

**Ship's Log: Sunday–Saturday 6–12 May 1951** Yokosuka, Japan, moored starboard side USS BRYCE CANYON (AD-36).

---

Commander Buaas felt sure we were going to be "under the gun" when we tied up alongside the *Bryce Canyon*. All because of the "commodore's flour" incident. ComDesFlot One was not happy that Commodore Lang had declared one of his destroyer divisions as "not ready for sea." Accordingly, we assumed we'd be watched very carefully for any rules infractions.

We didn't have to wait long. It was a warm, sunshiny day. Dean Beeler, signalmen third, stripped down to the waist and went up to the bridge to chip paint. The admiral spotted him. He dressed down Commodore Lang for the people in his division not being in uniform. Lang, in turn, called upon Buaas to put the man on report.

Beeler got off with only a warning.

Dear Anna: This afternoon I journeyed to nearby Kamakura to visit the shrine of the *Diabutsu* (Great Buddha). This awesome statue of the compassionate Buddha stands 37 feet tall, is cast in bronze, and becomes all the more impressive when we consider it was cast in 1292, three centuries before the first Europeans reached Japan.

Our guide said it's the number one tourist attraction among the Japanese, and I have no reason to doubt that because of the vast numbers of schoolchildren there with teachers and families—and all with cameras. In fact, the guide bragged that Japan was a nation of photographers. He took great delight in reciting a little joke: "When the Lord Jesus left, he instructed his disciples, 'Go ye into the world and instruct all nations,' but when Jesus got to Japan, he said, 'Go ye into the world and *take pictures*'!"

On Wednesday I finally got my phone call through to my darling. Talked for six minutes. Cost twenty-five dollars. It was 1:00 A.M. May 9, 1951, but 11:00 P.M. May 8 there.

---

**Ship's Log: Sunday 13 May 1951** Moored as before, Yokosuka, Japan.

---

Mother's Day. I sent Mom a card, but had no way to call or to know if she got it.

Our DBM radio direction finder had been giving erratic readings, so I decided to clean the antenna slip rings. The DBM platform—nothing more than a steel-mesh grid about a foot wide—was on the forward rim of No. 2 stack. It afforded a nice view of the harbor.

It was a pleasant Sunday afternoon. There were a fair number of sailing craft in the bay—more than I would have imagined for such an impoverished nation.

Down below me, I observed men moving around our deck and also on the *Lofberg*, tied up on our starboard side. These were new recruits fresh from the States. They were being conducted on an indoctrination tour of the ships.

Over on the *Lofberg*, the recruits, wearing crisp, new dungarees, were clustered around the hedgehog battery (antisubmarine rockets). They were getting a demonstration of their operation and firing mechanism. I paid scant attention.

All of a sudden I heard a muffled "Whump!" It was such an unusual sound that intuitively I sensed something terrible had happened.

I looked around. A man was soaring off into space. He looked like a dummy shot out of a circus cannon. Another man was lying on the *Lofberg*'s deck, his head blown away. The other six or eight were standing immobile, transfixed in their spots, seemingly unable to move.

Down on our main deck, Jerry Jerome, bos'n's mate third class, was conducting a similar tour for the *Borland*'s new recruits. I cupped my hands and yelled down to them, "Trouble on the *Lofberg!*"

"What kind of trouble?" someone yelled back.

"Explosion," I yelled. "Port side, 01 deck. With injury. Get over there!"

Four or five guys started running the direction I pointed. I slid, more than climbed, down the ladder and headed after them. Even with a late start, I managed to be among the first to arrive.

A man lay on the deck, flat on his back, arms akimbo, his entire skull missing. Yet the skin of his face remained grotesquely intact, flopped out there like a rubber Halloween mask, still attached at the lower jaw. Spurts of blood were pumping out from the base of the skull. Apart from that flow of blood, his body showed no twitching or movement of any kind. The poor soul had died instantly.

The *Lofberg's* doctor arrived within a couple of minutes and took charge. Immediately he announced that no one should touch or move the body until a preliminary investigation could be conducted. Our doc, Hugh Combest, crossed over to render assistance, bringing with him a cloth to cover the body. The man's blood continued to form into a thin, red rivulet that flowed aft across the 01 deck and dripped down over the edge onto the main deck below.

The kid's shattered skull splatted against the side of our No. 1 5-inch gun mount and came to rest on the rain-guard above the entry hatch. Jerome had the mettle to climb up there to retrieve the gruesome object and return it to the *Lofberg*. He said it was like carrying a bloody football helmet.

There was a lot of oohing and aahing as curious onlookers gathered to ogle the death scene. Later, as the rubberneckers began to break up and drift away, one smart-ass tried a little sick humor: "All that gore, and me without a spoon." He laughed.

Blind fury welled up inside me. Without thinking I wheeled around and hit that guy as hard as I could, smashing his nose and breaking his front teeth. "You keep your goddamn mouth shut!"

Frogmen from the nearby *Diachenko* came over with scuba gear to search for the man who had been blown out into the harbor. It took about two and a half hours to locate the body in the murky water. They found him about 150 feet away. He was dead before he ever hit the water. A large hole was blown in his back, right between the shoulder blades.

These were new men, fresh out of boot camp, and only seventeen years of age. One hell of a Mother's Day message to send their parents.

The cause of the accident was never known. Investigators were not able to determine why the safety mechanism failed.

That scene plagued my sleep for many nights. Frequently, I would dream of a face lying in front of me like a rubber mask, blood spurting out from a decapitated brain stem. I would force myself to wake up from the bad dream. Sometimes it was hard to get back to sleep.

# 19  SCREENING AGAINST SUBMARINES

*May 15–June 14, 1951*

---

**Ship's Log: Tuesday 15 May 1951**  USS REDFISH (SS-395) conducted simulated attack on task force. Attack successful. Submarine passed through screen without detection.

---

That day brought an embarrassment bred by overconfidence. We were caught with our pants down when the submarine *Redfish* successfully slipped through the destroyer screen to make a simulated attack on the "heavies." Had this attack been for real, we could have lost a carrier, a cruiser, and possibly a battlewagon.

If the Soviets had unleashed their submarines in force, they would have changed the entire nature of the Korean War. There were never enough U.S. destroyers to provide more than minimal coverage for the carrier task force and also enforce a blockade. Given the length of the seaborne supply lines, a serious submarine offensive could have forced the United States to choose between forming huge convoys like those of World War II or pulling out and relinquishing its presence in the Far East altogether.

What of the estimated fourscore Soviet submarines based in Vladivostok? Whereas the carriers could operate from beyond MiG range and fight off attacks from longer-range aircraft, they could not operate beyond the range of the Soviet submarine. There was considerable danger the Soviets might support the North Koreans with underseas warfare if the situation there became critical.

A submarine can detect a surface ship long before the surface ship can detect a submarine. The undersea craft can usually avoid detection if its skipper has a mind to. Conversely, a submarine that wished to attack would have to come within range of our sonar detection devices. We therefore operated under the assumption that any submarine within range of our sonar was, per se, in an attack mode and his intentions were hostile. Accordingly, submarine contacts were invariably attacked at once.

The first five months of the war brought eighty reports of possible submarine contacts. Most were evaluated doubtful and some as definitely nonsubmarine. January through March brought very few contacts, but in April and May the frequency of contacts picked up.

The increased possibility of Soviet submarine intervention prompted a step-up in antisubmarine training.

---

**Ship's Log: Wednesday–Friday 16–18 May 1951**   Steaming with Task Force 77 off east coast of Korea while conducting aircraft operations. This vessel detached from formation to station 10 miles east on radar picket duty.

---

A renewed Communist attack began under a blanket of fog and rain that hampered UN defensive action. After being weathered in for two days, the planes of Task Force 77 resumed close air support at the battle line. Following an appeal from Eighth Army for all possible support, the *Princeton* delayed her departure for Yokosuka to permit another period of three-carrier operations.

The increasing strength of enemy antiaircraft fire was being felt. Combat losses from April 1 through May 15 totaled three F9Fs, eight ADs, and nineteen Corsairs. Task Force 77 had its worst day on the eighteenth when six planes failed to return.

---

**Ship's Log: Saturday–Sunday 19–20 May 1951**   Screening carriers PRINCETON, BOXER, and PHILIPPINE SEA for aircraft operations.

---

The destroyer *Brinkley Bass* was on a solo assignment in Wonsan Harbor to provide harassment fire. Enemy shore batteries were relatively inactive. Everything seemed deceptively quiet. The skipper took the ship in close to shore where the crew could spray the beaches with 40-mm fire.

Suddenly, she found herself on the receiving end of heavy shelling from hidden 120-mm enemy shore batteries. Only by rapid, evasive maneuvering was the ship able to escape without taking any direct hits. One near miss to starboard, however, sprayed the ship with shrapnel, which caused minor structural damage and wounded ten men in the 40-mm gun mounts. One wounded gunner later died from his injuries.

**Ship's Log: Monday–Friday 21–25 May 1951** Sighted floating mine; USS JOHN W. THOMASON left formation to destroy floating mine by gunfire.

The battleship *New Jersey* returned to war action. The Big Jay's baptism was memorable for her crew. After bombarding at Kansong on the twentieth, the *New Jersey* moved to Wonsan to participate in the siege. Here, on the twenty-second, she took one hit and one near miss. The striking shell hit number one turret, causing little damage. But a near miss killed one man and wounded three who were exposed topside.

Rocket ships were sent in for two night bombardments of known gun emplacements. Plunging fire of seventy-seven hundred rockets delivered by *LSMR-409* and *LSMR-412* produced impressive results. Intelligence reports indicated the enemy was clearing the harbor of personnel.

In fact, the second Communist spring offensive ended in a rout. The Chinese were retreating as fast as possible. As the weather cleared, UN forces were out in strength, bombing and strafing the roads. Chinese troops were even trying to flee in daylight hours with great loss of life. There was also a perceptible effect on morale. Prisoners began to surrender in unprecedented numbers—seventeen thousand in the last two weeks of May.

A cruiser and two destroyers were nearly caught in a friendly fire incident. An air force B-29 bomber was returning from a raid at Rashin only seventeen miles from the Soviet frontier when it jettisoned a string of bombs into the ocean. The pilot didn't bother to look below. He damn near hit the *Helena* (CA-75), *Hubbard* (DD-748), and *Rogers* (DDR-870). These ships had earlier bombarded Rashin and were standing by to provide lifeguard duty if needed.

**Ship's Log: Saturday 26 May 1951** 0020 Developed engineering casualty, dropped out of formation with orders to remain within voice radio range.

It was a balmy Saturday afternoon. We were at GQ. Mr. White had his hatch open but wasn't scanning the horizon. Instead, he was carrying on a conversation with Stan Houk, the trainer. Houk had shifted over to the pointer's position. Manders now occupied the trainer's slot—nose buried in an ever-present paperback novel.

Momentarily tiring of his reading, Manders peeked out at the ocean through the optics. Unexpectedly, he spotted what he thought to be a submarine periscope. He let out a yell that scared the hell out of all of us: "There's a submarine out there!"

Manders lost control of himself. He bounced up and down in his seat and slewed the controls wildly back and forth, all the while continuing to shout, "There's a submarine out there, bigger'n shit, bigger'n shit, bigger'n shit."

White had to reach down and kick the slew switch out of automatic so that he could take control himself.

We got permission to leave the screen to investigate the sighting. But like so many previous sightings, this one proved to be negative and we were never able to establish sonar contact.

What did Manders see, a submarine or floating log? We never found out. This fright nevertheless reminded us that we could not afford to relax our vigil even for a few moments. All ship movements were being monitored constantly by Soviet submarines.

---

**Ship's Log: Sunday–Wednesday 27–30 May 1951**  Steaming in company with Task Force 77 conducting aircraft flight operations off east coast of Korea. Heavies include USS BON HOMME RICHARD (CV-31), USS BOXER (CV-21), USS PHILIPPINE SEA (CV-47), and USS PRINCETON (CV-37).

---

The boredom was oppressive. Every day was like the one before—constant steaming, carrier landings and launches, frequent GQs, nighttime replenishments, and chasing down spurious sonar contacts. Temporary relief came when we received mail from a passing ship.

My Precious Darling: Tonight you are uppermost in my thoughts. Your image looms strikingly clear in my mind—you are consuming my deepest feelings and most precious thoughts.

As I walked outdoors tonight the brilliance of the moon had a startling effect on me and thoughts suddenly began to flow as never before. It was as though my life was opened before me.

From this time forward I am what I shall become because of our relationship—never will I be without a part of you joined to my heart and mind and soul. No honor, no distinguished award, no recognition, and no achievement even resembles the greatness I now experience. And, finally, I believe that what we share in our loving, in all that we are as one, brings me closer to holding hands with the Creator and at one with the universe. Love forever, Anna

---

**Ship's Log: Thursday 31 May 1951** 1503 F9F crashed about 4,000 yards bearing 060T, commenced maneuvering to pick up pilot. 1531 Heard and sighted air bursts off port bow, source undetermined. 1651 Left formation at speed 27 knots to investigate possible plane crash, reported 4 miles southeast of formation center. 1655 Searched area, no evidence of down aircraft observed.

---

Cigarette moochers were always a pain. One of the worst offenders was Grady Breed, radarman third. It seemed like he was always without a cigarette.

Each person had his own defenses for coping with moochers. Some used ridicule. Shorty Hall, for example, routinely asked, "Do you also want me to hold my finger up your ass until you build up suction." Others tucked their pack in their socks and pretended they were fresh out. I took to using Bull Durham and rolling my own because few guys knew how to roll a cigarette.

Not even that put a damper on Breed's mooching. So one day I took a near-empty Bull Durham bag, mixed in some shavings from the pencil sharpener and scrapings from a rubber eraser, and laid in wait. The next time Breed asked me for a smoke I handed him this special blend. I thought surely it would asphyxiate him.

No such luck. I watched his face as he lit up, hoping to see some change in expression. Nothing. So I asked, "How's the tobacco?"

"Good. Good. Tastes great!"

Disgusted, I tossed him the sack and said, "Here, keep it. You may want another one."

**Ship's Log: Friday 1 June 1951**   Alongside USS WALKE
(DD-723) to transfer radar spare parts.

I got my butt chewed out royally by Mr. MaCamont over what I thought was a trivial matter. Initially, I attributed it to his merely flexing his muscle, having just made j.g. Later I decided he was right.

The USS *Walke* had radioed over to ask if we had a certain part for the SG surface radar. I sent one of the junior technicians down to the storeroom. He reported back that we didn't have any, so I radioed a "negative" back to the *Walke*.

Thanks to MaCamont's diligence, the spare parts and inventory control system we established back in the States had served us well for these many months. Not only the *Borland* but other ships as well. When we first got over there, a ship needing a spare part would call, "Does anyone have such-and-such a spare part?" We always answered quickly and usually affirmatively. That happened so often that eventually instead of putting out an open call to the task force, these guys would call us specifically, "Paddycake, do you have the spare part we need?"

Anyway, MaCamont didn't believe it when I said we didn't have the requested part. He asked if I had checked on it personally. I replied, "No, I have confidence in my men, and if Pearch says we don't have it, we don't have it."

Unconvinced, MaCamont went down to the spare parts locker to find out for himself. Sure enough, he came back fifteen or twenty minutes later toting the offending part. That's when he chewed me out.

**Ship's Log: Saturday 2 June 1951**   Steaming as before.

The sea was calm and the skies partly overcast. A line of rain squalls rolled directly over us. Afterward, the air was crisp and clear, scrubbed of the light haze that usually hung over the east coast of Korea.

Sam Stock stuck his head in the ET shack. "Hey, Gamble, you gotta come outside. There's something I want you to see."

I followed him out to the 01 deck, starboard side.

"Look over there," he said, gesturing. "Tell me what you see."

"Why, it's an island. It looks to me like Ullung Do. What's so unusual about that?" I asked, somewhat perplexed.

"How far away would you say it is?"

"Oh, about fifteen or twenty miles."

"Wrong! It's over seventy miles away."

"Impossible!" I exclaimed. "If that island were seventy miles away, it would be over the horizon and out of sight."

"Let's go into CIC and check it out," he said, grinning like the cat that just ate the canary.

Still thinking this was some kind of a trick, I checked the radar. Sure enough, there was Ullung Do on the screen, and it was fully seventy miles away.

I dashed back out on deck to observe what, to me, was a once-in-a-lifetime phenomenon. Already the image was beginning to fade. In another ten minutes it had broken up and disappeared completely. Visibility returned to normal.

Apparently, what happened was this: a cold downdraft followed behind the rainstorm and brought a lot of relatively cold, dry air from the upper atmosphere down close to the surface of the ocean. That cold, dry air acted like a prism to refract the light rays so that we were able to see much farther than we ordinarily would. Then a few minutes later, as the air filled up again with dust particles and atmospheric pollution, the image began to fade away.

The effect was surreal, spooky, otherworldly. I didn't write home about it because I didn't think anyone would believe me.

---

**Ship's Log: Tuesday 5 June 1951**   1845 Took lifeguard station astern USS PRINCETON (CV-37) for night air operations.

---

The entire task group went to GQ around 7:30 P.M. A plane crashed on the starboard side of the flight deck of *Princeton*. It burst into flames, which spread to the after end of the hanger deck. Sixteen were killed on the catwalk around flight deck. The pilot was thrown clear of a fiery hell and was picked up by the whirlybird. Miraculously, he survived.

---

**Ship's Log: Wednesday 6 June 1951**   1248 Proceeding on course 000T, speed 20 knots, on search and rescue mission, aircraft in emergency landing, distance 40 miles. USS PRINCETON helicopter proceeding ahead. 1410 Pilot rescued by helicopter.

---

The cruiser *Los Angeles*, joined by the battleship *New Jersey* and screening destroyers, bombarded enemy positions in the vicinity of Kosong. Inland, the marines launched an attack on the Hwachon Reservoir, just north of the 38th parallel.

My friend Sgt. James Cotton, who survived being shot between the eyes at Yudam-ni, picked up his second battle wound here. Cotton's platoon was bringing up the rear of a column of 250 riflemen and three tanks when a mortar round went off almost between his feet. It picked him up and tossed him nearly ten feet. He felt like his skin was on fire. His uniform, though sopping wet from rain, was smoking, yet he couldn't find any place where he had been hit. Still dazed from the concussion, he started up the road again with his troops.

One of the men noted, "Look, there's blood on your leg." Cotton pulled up his pants leg to inspect but didn't find any wound. Then his friend noted, "Your hand looks all bloody." Cotton took off his jacket. It was only then he realized that a piece of shrapnel had hit him in the elbow and come out by his wrist.

The intrepid marine then walked a mile back down the road to the aid station. When he got there, the medics announced, "Congratulations! You've got the honor of being the first casualty in the battle of Hwachon Reservoir." He got to go home.

Although neither Anna nor I spoke of marriage, we seemed to have mutually and quietly moved to an understanding that we would live the rest of our lives together.

My beloved: As we steam along at night we leave a broad trail of glowing lights where the propellers disturbed the water. Small sea creatures cause this trail of light behind the ship. I'm holding your letters in my hand . . . gazing at this phosphorescent wonder . . . and feeling almost as if I could reach out and touch you.

I marvel at how much and how well we "fit" together in attitude, interests, aspirations, personalities, and attributes. Surely God created us for each other and for a great purpose. You are very precious in my sight, and I want to live out my life loving you.

---

**Ship's Log: Sunday 10 June 1951**   1424 Casualty port engine. 2207 Engineering casualty repaired, port engine back in use.

---

It was a lazy Sunday afternoon. The weather was calm. The sun was out. Tony Frio had the sonar watch.

We spent the latter part of the morning and early afternoon with the replenishment group. About 2:30 P.M. the port engine pooped out and we had to drop out of formation to effect repairs. Lieutenant (j.g.) Melesky was officer of the deck (OOD). The captain was off the bridge.

This day, Frio took it upon himself to provide a little comic relief to brighten up an otherwise dull and inconsequential Sunday afternoon. Anthony D. "Tony" Frio, a second-generation Italian from Hoboken, New Jersey, had the build of a prize fighter but the gentleness of a dove. Melesky was his hapless victim.

Frio called up on his sound-powered phones, "Hey, Bridge, it looks like I've got an Italian submarine on the sonar screen."

Melesky took the bait. "How can you tell it's an Italian submarine?" he wanted to know.

"Well, it has to be Italian," Frio said. "The sonar is going, 'Ping . . . . wop! Ping . . . .wop!'"

---

**Ship's Log: Monday 11 June 1951**   0655 Maneuvering to investigate mine sighted astern of formation. 0728 Sunk mine by .30 caliber gunfire. 0943 Left screen to investigate sonar contact.

---

"Mr. White, can I ask you a question?" asked Stan Houk as he sat at general quarters. We were running down another of our many sonar contacts.

"Sure, go ahead." White's head poked out of the observation hatch, scanned the horizon. Strong winds had come up; the seas were heavy, but the sun was shining and it was warm.

"Can submarines lay mines?"

The gun control officer looked startled. "Sure they can. Why do you ask?"

"Well, that mine we sank this morning . . . it was shiny and new . . .

yet we're a hundred miles out at sea. It doesn't seem possible it could drift that far and still look so new, does it?"

White bit his lip pensively. It was obvious this question had been discussed in the wardroom. "Keep this under your hats," he said, "and if you say I told you, I'll deny saying it. But there is a strong possibility that these mines we've been seeing lately have been released by submarines. We've known all along Soviet submarines have been monitoring our movements. They've probably also figured out that 'Point Oboe' is where the fast carrier task force conducts its launch and recovery operations. So, what better location to sow their mines?"

He paused, then added, "I think every one of those Soviet sub skippers would give his eyeteeth to bag one of our big carriers. That's our biggest worry—not orders from Moscow but a renegade skipper who wants to be a hero."

---

**Ship's Log: Tuesday 12 June 1951**  0619 Engineering casualty, port engine. Dropped out of formation to effect repair. 0740 USS WALKE (DD-723) damaged by underwater explosion port quarter, 26 men killed, 41 wounded. This vessel maneuvering to render assistance. 1049 Commenced assisting USS HUBBARD while she investigated a sonar contact. Exercised crew at general quarters, manned ASW battery. 1226 Secured from general quarters. 1234 New sonar contact, sounded general quarters. 1256 Contact evaluated non-submarine, secured from general quarters. 1307 Proceeding to investigate possible periscope sighting by ASW aircraft. Search negative. 1514 Joined USS WALKE, base course 190T, speed 3 knots. 1622 USS RECLAIMER (ARS-82) arrived to assist WALKE into port. This vessel proceeding to rejoin screen.

---

The sea was calm, glassy, visibility good. We had dropped out of formation because of problems with our after main condenser. This meant we could not get up to aircraft launch speed. The USS *Walke* (DD-723) moved up to take our station in the screen.

At 7:03 A.M. the task force turned into the wind on course 030 degrees true and commenced air operations, speed twenty-five knots. Seventeen minutes later at 7:20, air operations ceased, the formation turned left to 000'T, and dropped speed to twenty knots. On the *Borland,* we mirrored the formation's course and speed changes as well as we could while effecting repairs. Comdr. Marshall Thompson, skipper of the *Walke* was in his sea cabin, scratching his chin, wondering whether to shave now or wait until after breakfast. The clock on the wall read 7:40.

An urgent call crackled over the radio from the *Walke:* "Ganymede, Ganymede, Jointweed has been mined!"

"Say again?" asked the task force commander. He needed to be sure.

"Repeat, this is Jointweed in station four. We have struck a mine!" (Jointweed was the *Walke*'s voice call.)

"Roger, what is your condition?"

"Explosion port quarter, listing badly to port, settling rapidly at the stern, speed reduced to five knots. Over."

"Roger. Stand by." There was about a ten-second pause, then Ganymede issued instructions, "Sharkfin, Paddycake, proceed immediately to render assistance as needed to Jointweed. Keep us advised." (Sharkfin was the *Hubbard.*)

The *Hubbard* and *Borland* were the two ships most logically to be given this assignment. The *Hubbard* (DD-748) was the *Walke*'s division flagship. Our ship was out of formation due to its inability to make speed.

We were presented with a ghastly sight. The *Walke* had a horrendous hole twenty-six feet long and fifteen feet high gaping from her port rear quarter. Her main deck was buckled upward. She listed ten degrees to port and was down at the stern until the freeboard on the port quarter was one foot.

Our guys were extremely wrought up emotionally by the *Walke*'s catastrophe. But for the grace of God, that might have been us lying out there so horribly maimed and twisted.

The explosion occurred in the aft crew's quarters. Some of the off-duty men were enjoying a last cigarette or cup of coffee before going on watch. Many were still in their bunks, having stood the midnight-to-four watch. A few elected to seek the luxury of an extra hour's sleep in lieu of breakfast. Those guys didn't stand a chance. The sudden explosion and inrush of seawater transformed the tranquil scene into one of darkness, confusion, and pain. Death came instantly to twenty-four men. Injury to forty-three more—nine of them seriously. Two of the seriously injured later died. The death toll climbed to twenty-six.

One of those who died was a fellow Iowan Harold Meyers, electrician's mate third. Meyers and I enlisted only a few days apart at Des Moines. He left behind a wife and two sons, aged four and nine.

Another dead man was Radarman First Class Bob Bertain. Only six weeks before, he had been recommended for a medal for outstanding performance while the ship was under fire in Wonsan. He had expressed pride in a newborn son whom he had never seen, and now never would.

Robert Dawson, RDSN was lucky. Resting in the top bunk, port side, he never heard the explosion. His bunk was slammed up against the overhead by the blast. When he came to, the sleeping compartment was filled to the overhead with water. It was impossible to breathe. Thinking the ship was going down, he thought of his mother. What would she think when family friend "Kingie" Waugh, the postman, handed her *the* letter. Miraculously, Dawson freed himself from the wreckage and, with shipmate Bill Johnson, dragged himself to safety.

As soon as flooding was under control, the *Hubbard* came alongside. She transferred the division's medical officer to *Walke* and began receiving the dead. At 8:27 *Walke* commenced pumping fuel from port tanks to correct the list. At 8:50 the cruiser *Helena* hove to and began receiving the more seriously wounded as well as providing additional medical personnel. Equipped with doctors, operating rooms, and every needed facility, the *Helena* gave help to the wounded.

A total of eleven bodies were recovered and identified that morning. Five were removed and identified later in Sasebo. Ten men were never recovered.

At 10:38 the *Walke* reported sonar contact, bearing 280, range 1,700 yards, target width 10 degrees, metallic echo, low Doppler. Identified as submarine. The *Hubbard* began an immediate depth charge attack. The *Borland* assisted. Following the *Hubbard*'s initial run, we regained contact—again classified as sub—and laid down a pattern of hedgehogs. Contact was lost as we passed over the target due to short range and "mushiness" of the echo.

At 10:51 we regained contact and proceeded to fire a pattern of contact charges. The *Hubbard* assisted. This time, we heard two underwater explosions and observed a slight oil slick on the surface of the water. Comdr. B. D. Wood, skipper of the *Hubbard*, confirmed the explosions and oil slick. There was never any doubt in our minds we were chasing a submarine and had killed one—probably Russian. However, not enough physical evidence floated to the surface to confirm the kill. The Russians reported no losses. It went into the books as "possible submarine."

With what happened to the *Walke*, we tended to overreact to even the slightest threat. Additional sonar contacts were made at 11:36, 12:03, and 12:34. All were identified as nonsubmarine. Again, at 1:07 a patrol plane thought it spotted a periscope. We investigated but could not locate anything. The *Bradford* (DDE-545) reported a large, dark object forty feet long surfaced in her wake. It rose to a height of five feet, then settled rapidly. No conning tower was visible. After an attack by the *O'Brien* at 11:00, a series of underwater explosions were heard. Several oil slicks and light debris floated to the surface. None of these was an amount consistent with the much larger quantities that typically followed the sinking of German and Japanese submarines during World War II.

Something exploded against the *Walke*. Was it a mine? A torpedo?

Commander Thompson, the *Walke*'s skipper, remained firmly convinced it was a torpedo. Commander Wood of the *Hubbard* also reported it as a possible torpedo.

Why the *Walke*? Perhaps it was indeed a torpedo that was not meant for the *Walke* but one of the aircraft carriers. The *Walke* just happened to get in the way.

In answering this question, there were five pieces of evidence to consider: (1) The *Walke* was just completing a left turn from course 030 to 000 when the explosion hit. The stern should have been sliding *away from*, not toward, a mine. Therefore, it was doubtful the ship could have taken a mine on her port rear quarter. (2) It was considered "gospel" that at speeds over ten knots a mine would have been washed away by the bow wave. Yet at the time of the explosion *Walke* was doing twenty knots. (3) Immediately prior to the explosion, two engineering petty officers felt something strike the ship. They described it as feeling "like a heavy log." It's difficult to imagine a motionless mine striking the rear quarter with that much force. (4) The explosion occurred six feet below the waterline. It required some convoluted reasoning by the naval investigator to attribute this to a mine that floats on the surface. He had to fantasize a new kind of mine that "hovered" just beneath the surface. (5) Just before the explosion a fireman standing on the boat deck reported seeing three groups of bubbles in the water extending in a line a short distance from the ship. In my mind, a bubble pattern seemed more consistent with an electric torpedo than with a mine.

In the end, investigators waffled on the issue, saying: "The available evidence does not indicate conclusively what type of agent damaged the *Walke*. The choice seems to be narrowed down to either a torpedo or a mine." Their equivocation seemed to hinge on the inability of the *Hubbard* and the *Borland* to offer incontrovertible proof of a submarine kill. To wit: "An electric torpedo is possible, but the presence of a submarine near the *Walke* at the time of the damage has not been proven, although alleged submarine contacts were made."[1]

Shorty Hall, when he heard the results of the investigation, exploded in disbelief. "That's the first goddamn mine that ever left a wake!"

"But why would they want to cover it up?" I asked naively.

Shorty proffered a cynical observation: "They do not want to admit we are fighting Russians. Nor will they indicate that any of our men are being killed by the Russkies. They want to avoid an incident that might screw up negotiations for a peace conference. There are special rules to keep people back in America from knowing what's really going on out here."

---

**Ship's Log: Wednesday 13 June 1951**    1700 Stopped dead in water to lock port shaft. 2215 Increased speed to test port engine main condenser.

---

In what could only be considered the worst case of bad timing imaginable, we were within twenty-four hours of leaving for home when George Whapham, radioman third class, came down with a severe appendicitis attack. He had to be transferred to the USS *Princeton* for emergency surgery. We sailed off without him.

---

**Ship's Log: Thursday 14 June 1951**    1029 Exercised crew at general quarters for antiaircraft firing practice. Expended 60 rounds of 5" AAC, 139 rounds 40MM projectiles.

---

The USS *Thompson* (DMS-38) ran into trouble at Songjin. She had closed to within 40-mm range of the shore and slowed to investigate several boxcars on a railroad siding when suddenly the enemy wheeled out four twin-mount 3-inch mobile guns from a concealed position behind a rocky hill and started firing.

The control officer reported from the main battery director that he saw two splashes, one off the port bow, the other off the port quarter.

The third shot was a direct hit, striking the ship at frame 27 to port, piercing a watertight bulkhead, and lodging in the lower sonar room. In an effort to present the smallest target possible while steaming out of range, the captain ordered hard right rudder, engines full ahead. Meanwhile, the ship was returning counterbattery fire from mounts 52 and 53. (Mount 51 would not bear on the target.)

Mount 52, which had been firing as the ship turned, took a hit that instantly killed the trainer when an enemy shell passed through his upper shoulder and neck. The gun captain, Herbert Gilmore, GM2, calmly told the bridge he would have to go off the line while he removed the remains of the trainer. Gilmore quickly got the gun back into operation and managed to fire three more rounds before training into the stops.

A third hit passed through the captain's sea cabin, struck the IC tube supporting the main battery director and severed its electrical supply, and finally lodged in the pilothouse bulkhead. This round resulted in the decapitation of the chief quartermaster and severely wounded both the executive officer and the OOD. According to the captain's report, "The appearance of the bridge at this time was not very pleasant; it took determination and courage to face the skull of the quartermaster which was literally splattered over every square inch of the pilothouse, and the blood and flesh of LT. Lynn which covered the pilothouse deck."[2]

Lieutenant Lynn (the executive officer) was bleeding profusely. Lieutenant (j.g.) Pittman, despite his own severe chest wound, crawled over to Lynn and jammed his fist into the largest wound to keep him from bleeding to death until a pressure bandage could be applied.

A fourth shell passed through the after fireroom where it removed the top of the skull of a boiler technician and tore off the arm of a nearby fireman before coming to rest in the battery charging panel. Still another hit was sustained on the underside of the 40-mm gun tub, but despite this damage the gun captain had the presence of mind and leadership ability for his crew to fire the remainder of their ready service ammunition, estimated to be 306 rounds.

One of the most heroic individuals was the helmsman, a mere seaman apprentice. John Lain remained steadfastly at the wheel, zigzagging the ship violently in an effort to throw off the enemy gunners, even as shells were passing through the sea cabin and the mast abaft the bridge. "I couldn't duck while I was at the wheel," he remarked, even though he was advised to do so.[3]

Another person who reacted with coolness under fire was the ship's damage control officer. When he arrived at the scene of a holed forward compartment, the water was already waist deep and rushing in at an ever-increasing rate. He issued a single order to his men, "Let's get to it." Then he led the way down the ladder.

In all, the *Thompson* took thirteen direct hits before she pulled out of enemy range. It was estimated that the enemy fired from eighty to one hundred rounds.

## 20   HEADING FOR HOME

*June 15–July 2, 1951*

---

**Ship's Log: Friday 15 June 1951**   0035 This vessel, with USS LOFBERG, USS THOMASON, and USS BUCK detached from Task Force 77 to proceed to port at Yokosuka, Japan. 0947 Commenced passage through Shimonoseki Straits.

---

I had a terrible time trying to fall asleep. Every time I started to doze off, images flashed before my mind of ships blown up by mines. I saw mangled and tangled bodies. Wraithlike faces drifted past—death-masks of those two kids killed on the *Lofberg*, faces on the bloated bodies floating off Mokpu, faces of other men I'd seen killed or maimed during the last eleven months.

This was our last night in mine- and submarine-infested waters. I kept thinking what a cruel twist of fate it would be to have made it this long, only to be blown up on our last night before going home.

At length, I carried my blanket up to the fire control radar room. It was an out-of-the-way location well above the waterline where I felt safe from a mine explosion. Stretching out on the hard steel deck, I tried to get some sleep. The sleep god's magic potion worked. I slept right through breakfast and morning muster.

I awoke to find myself in a whole lot of trouble. It hadn't occurred to me to inform anyone where I sacked out. Lieutenant Commander Roddy read me the riot act. He said that when I didn't show up for muster, they were about to report me as missing and presumed overboard. I mumbled an explanation and an apology.

"Well, you need to be more considerate next time," he warned sternly. "This will not go on your record, but I want you to realize how serious a problem you almost created for us. The commodore actually considered turning the squadron around to run a man-overboard search for you."

At 9:45 A.M. we started through the passage into the inland sea. We were happy to be taking this route because it cut a full day off our homeward journey.

The four destroyers traveled single file. The land on either side seemed so close we could almost reach out and touch it. Someone said a destroyer was the largest warship that could safely transit this passage. I knew better. The largest battleship in the world, the *Yamamoto*, had sortied through this narrow strait in 1945 on her final fatal cruise to strike the American fleet off Okinawa.

---

**Ship's Log: Saturday 16 June 1951**   1349 Arrived Yokosuka, moored Berth 12.

---

The wind was blowing so strong when we pulled into Yokosuka that Captain Buaas couldn't bring the ship alongside the pier. We kept getting blown away. After the third try, he took us back out into deeper water and dropped anchor while we waited for a harbor tug to come to our assistance. It took an hour-and-a-half. How embarrassing!

Liberty was granted to the crew.

I had one last stop to make. That was the Mikimoto Pearl Store, one of the "must" shops on everybody's list. I planned to formally ask Anna to marry me. The pearls would be her engagement gift.

Kokichi Mikimoto was a Japanese businessman who developed a process for growing what he called "cultured" pearls. Prior to his pearl cultivation, women dove for pearls off the outlying islands of Japan in what could best be described as a hit-or-miss operation—even after bringing up a thousand oysters they might not find even one with a valuable pearl. Mikimoto's research turned up a substance called muscarine, which he imported from my home state of Iowa. He ground the muscarine into small beads and placed these inside the mantle of an oyster. In three years a pearl would be formed that was virtually indistinguishable from the real thing. However, because the process was new and as yet controversial, Mikimoto pearls sold for about half the price of the natural variety.

It took me nearly an hour to make a selection. One would have thought this was the most important decision of my life. In some respects, it was. The clerk, sensing this was a very personal matter, exhibited infinite patience. She showed me strand after strand, carefully explaining the subtleties of coloration and texture.

At length, I settled on a sixteen-inch strand of perfectly matched white pearls with a pink glow. They were smooth and round and felt warm to the touch. "The more you wear them, the prettier they are," she said as she wrapped the gift.

---

**Ship's Log: Tuesday 19 June 1951**   0806 Underway from Yokosuka, Japan, to Midway Island en route continental United States.

---

The morning sky was overcast. It was cold and spitting rain. Yet half the crew lined the fantail as we departed Yokosuka. Most carried cameras. My last shot was of the receding coastline highlighted by the frothing wake of the ship. We were really hauling ass out of there.

One guy who didn't make the return trip with us was Clyde Wheeler. He "went Asiatic," a term applied to servicemen who became so attracted to the Orient—its women or culture—that they elected to stay and make it their home. Most of these were social misfits who found an acceptance and respect here that they never experienced back home.

In Wheeler's case, though technically not married according to U.S. law, he got himself transferred to Sasebo where he had a Japanese "wife." He learned to speak Japanese and was accepted into the girl's family.

That night, for the first time in eleven months, we did not darken ship at sunset. Nor did we have sunset GQ.

---

**Ship's Log: Saturday 23 June 1951**   Arrived Midway Island, moored port side to Pier 2. 1146 Commenced pumping fuel. 1545 Underway en route to Pearl Harbor.

---

It was a case of New York Yankee catcher Yogi Berra's famed malapropism, "It's deja vu all over again." This was our second time to experience Saturday, June 23.

We crossed the international dateline. Clocks had to be set back by twenty-four hours. A day that started out to be Sunday, June 24, was, by a flick of the watch stem, transformed back to Saturday. As Snuffy Smith would say, "Confoosin' but not amoosin'."

Midway Island was a lonely outpost in the middle of the great expanse of the Pacific, barely more than a dot on the map. There was hardly anything there but sand, coconut trees, gooney birds, and a fueling station.

Midway is probably best remembered for the World War II Battle of Midway. The battle took place almost exactly nine years earlier, June 3–6, 1942. In that action the U.S. Navy turned back the mighty Japanese fleet and altered the tide of the war.

We tied up to the fueling dock about 11:45 A.M. Word was passed that we could leave the ship and go over to the recreational swimming beach, a short distance away. Most took advantage of the opportunity.

Jerry Jerome intercepted me and said, "Hey, Gamble, just the man I'm looking for. Got ten dollars on you?"

"Sure, but what do you need ten dollars for around here?"

"Cornwell and I've got a deal. I've got a buddy who works over at the PX, and he'll bootleg a case of beer for us for thirty bucks. We need another guy to throw in with us. Okay?"

"Sure," I said. A cold beer would taste mighty good about then.

The three of us headed for the PX. Jerome's buddy was waiting. The place was closed, but he had a key. We picked up a case of Blatz beer from the cold storage locker. At thirty bucks a case, I figure he probably cleared twenty-five on the deal. But what the hell, who was to complain?

About halfway to the beach, we couldn't wait any longer. We cracked open the case and each of us popped a can. Mine foamed all over me in the hot, tropical sun. But I didn't care. Never had beer tasted so good!

To hell with swimming! We plopped ourselves down on the beach in the shade of a big palm tree and savored our treasure. It wasn't long before we attracted a crowd—all hoping to share in our good fortune. We only handed out beer to our special friends. It was amazing to see how many people who hardly spoke to us before now began acting like bosom buddies.

This was our "day in the sun." Three pictures of our little beach party made it into the ship's cruise book.

---

**Ship's Log: Monday 25 June 1951**  1607 Arrived Pearl Harbor, moored port side to USS BUCK.

---

My Dearest Anna: You have no idea how I look forward to seeing you. I had planned to save this until I got home. But I am so anxious I cannot wait.

You are everything I have ever dreamed of, my hope and my inspiration. Your entry into my life is the most precious of gifts. Without hesitation or reservation I can say that I want to live out my life loving you.

Will you marry me?

Enclosed is a strand of pearls. I intend them to be an engagement gift.

I hope you will be at the dock when the ship arrives. If your answer is yes, please be wearing the pearls.

If you are not wearing the pearls, I will know your answer is no; and I will not say any more about it. But I'll keep on loving you.  Rusty

---

**Ship's Log: Tuesday 26 June 1951**  Moored Pearl Harbor.

---

Solon Gray, Roy Pippin, and Cecil Schubert came back from liberty about 10:30 P.M., happy as larks and drunk as skunks. Their once-white uniforms were now a disgrace. Lieutenant (j.g.) Selby was OOD. I was petty officer of the watch.

These three radiomen had spent the evening at a Hawaiian luau where they learned to do one of the native folk dance routines. Having imbibed too many mai-tais, they insisted on performing the dance for us on the quarterdeck.

Three drunken sailors lined up in a chorus line on the deck of a U.S. warship and went through all the hip motions, hand movements, and words of a Hawaiian song:

We're going to a hukilau.
We throw our nets out into the sea,
And all the *ami, amis* come swimming to me.
Oh, we're going to a hukilau,
A huki, huki, huki, huki, huki, huki, huki, huki-lau.

---

**Ship's Log: Wednesday–Sunday 27 June–1 July 1951**    En route from Pearl Harbor en route to San Diego, California.

---

Lassitude set in. We were feeling the emotional aftershock of having spent eleven months in the combat zone. Some suffered from sleeplessness. Others found an impairment of their ability to function in their duty stations. A few expressed disillusionment and anger at the war. Almost none wanted to talk about their experience. It was as if a numbing process had set in, and it would be a long time before the emotional scars healed.

---

**Ship's Log: Monday 2 July 1951**    1101 Arrived San Diego, California, moored port side to Navy Pier.

---

By 4:00 A.M. everyone was out of his bunk. Guys were keyed up and there was so much frivolity that further sleep was out of the question.

We shaved, showered, and put on our dress whites in preparation for entering port. The minutes and hours ticked by damnably slow.

At long last, we were rounding Point Loma and turning into San Diego Bay. As we glided slowly up alongside Navy Pier at the foot of Broadway, the stirring strains of a military band welcomed us home. One year, almost to the day, after we left.

Anxiously I scanned the yelling, waving crowd. Wives, mothers, fathers, girlfriends, children, well-wishers—all jumped up and down on the dock striving to see and be seen.

I was trying to get a glimpse of my Texas beauty. Would she be there? Would she be wearing my pearls?

Everywhere I looked I saw faces. But not hers. I became frantic. Had I presumed too much? Tears welled up, blurring my vision. A cold clamminess encircled my heart. Never had I felt so alone, so forlorn.

Surely she got my letter. It went airmail. Maybe her plane was late. Maybe she went to the wrong pier.

Then I spotted Anna. She was standing quietly at the very back of the crowd, away from the other people, neither jumping nor waving. She was wearing a pale green tailored jacket over a white skirt. Her hands were in her jacket pockets. A hesitant smile graced her lips. When she was sure I saw her, she gave me a shy little wave with her right hand. I felt on top of the world.

I looked to see if she was wearing the pearls. I didn't see them. Thud! My heart dropped. I was disappointed but not dismayed. She was here, and that's what ultimately mattered.

The crowd began to thin. Anna walked slowly and deliberately toward me, hands still in her jacket pockets. When she reached a point directly opposite me about twenty feet away, she stopped.

Slowly, ever so slowly, she opened the front of her jacket. There, lying softly around her neck were the pearls. I thought my heart would burst. Anna would be my bride!

# EPILOGUE: TWO MORE YEARS

Peace talks began on July 15, 1951, amid high hopes and overt optimism. Adm. Turner Joy was the UN's chief negotiator. But there was no joy at Panmunjom. While the negotiators negotiated and the hagglers haggled, the bloody war dragged on for two more agonizing and demoralizing years.[1]

The war now entered a second phase, dubbed the *sitzkrieg*. This was a "sitting war" in which the two sides fought mainly to control a battle line that more or less followed the 38th parallel, sometimes moving a few miles either way. The same hills were captured, lost, and recaptured over and over again. From this feckless activity came such colorfully named sites as Heartbreak Ridge, Bloody Ridge, the Punchbowl, and Iron Triangle.

On the afternoon of July 17, shore batteries at Wonsan opened up on the destroyers *O'Brien, Blue,* and *Cunningham* from three sides of the harbor. The ships immediately went into an evasive maneuver known as the War Dance. They steamed an elliptical pattern at twenty-two knots, firing batteries in each sector as their guns came to bear. Amazingly, despite more than five hundred shell splashes being counted, none of the ships received a direct hit.

Optimism over a possible speedy end to the war was dashed on August 23 when the Communists abruptly walked out of the meeting. Their stated reason was that a U.S. aircraft had bombed the neutral zone at Kaesong and killed a Chinese platoon leader. UN investigators could find no evidence of the attack and concluded that the incident was staged as an excuse to end the negotiations. The talks remained suspended for two full months.

While the investigators haggled over the Kaesong incident, General Ridgway pursued his strategy of keeping an unrelenting military pressure on the enemy. He ordered stepped-up ground and air attacks on Communist positions.

On September 8, the destroyer escort *William Sieverling* (DDE-441) took a direct hit in her fireroom, which caused some flooding but no casualties.

A serious accident occurred on the USS *Essex* (CV-9) on September 16. A damaged F2H Banshee jet floated over the barriers and crashed into parked aircraft. It caused a gasoline fire that destroyed four planes, killed seven men, and injured twenty-seven more.

Barely two weeks later, the *Small* got smaller, so to speak. On October 7, the USS *Ernest G. Small* (DDR-838) went in close to shore at Hungnam to draw shore battery fire so that the cruiser *Helena's* gunners could spot enemy gun emplacements. She hit a mine. The explosion occurred at the crew's mess hall. Nine men were killed and eighteen injured. The bow of the ship was torn loose by the blast and began to shake violently, endangering the ship. The skipper reinforced the watertight bulkhead aft of the break, then backed the ship off to dislodge the stricken portion. His maneuver was successful. Eighty-five feet of the ship's forward section drifted off, later to be sunk by gunfire from another destroyer. They proceeded to Kure, Japan, at four knots, going backward all the way. It took them four days to go the four hundred miles, during which time they went to abandon-ship stations twice when they thought the ship was about to sink in rough seas.

On the eleventh of October, the USS *Renshaw* (DDE-499) was hit at Songjin with slight damage and one casualty. Six days later the *Samuel N. Moore* drew shore battery fire at Hungnam, with moderate damage and three casualties.

The *Helena's* turn came on October 17, when enemy shore battery fire caused moderate damage and four casualties.

Armistice negotiations resumed again on October 25 at Panmunjom. The atmosphere was cold and mistrustful. Three major issues were up for consideration: the truce line, exchange of prisoners, and mechanisms to guarantee enforcement of the armistice.

Some people wondered if Ridgway and Washington had needlessly prolonged the war. The five months of talks had resulted in another sixty thousand UN casualties, of which twenty thousand were Americans.

The battle over the truce line was settled on November 27, more or less along the existing battle line. Delegates then turned to the two remaining issues, exchange of POWs and enforcement of the armistice.

The question of POW exchange probably could have been settled in a few days if Washington had agreed to an all-for-all exchange, as required by the rules of the Geneva Convention. However, for humanitarian—and possibly public relations—reasons, Washington insisted that repatriation be on a *voluntary* basis. Of the 132,474 names on the

UN list, preliminary polling indicated that approximately 40,000 of these would refuse repatriation to Communist control. The Communist reaction was complete shock and dismay. On April 28, 1952, they walked out again, recessing the talks indefinitely.

Throughout the on-again-off-again talks, the navy continued to patrol both coasts by surface and air, seeking to interdict the enemy's efforts to strengthen its positions with armament and supplies.

The USS *Gloucester* (PF-22) suffered twelve casualties on November 11 from shore battery fire at Hongwon. The USS *Hyman* (DD-732) received moderate damage from a single hit at Wonsan on November 23 but, fortunately, no casualties.

On January 11, 1952, the USS *Dextrous* (AM-341) took a single hit at Wonsan, resulting in three casualties. The USS *Porterfield* (DD-682) received minor damage from a hit at Sokto on February 3. The following day the *Endicott* (DMS-35) was hit twice at Songjin. On February 22, also at Songjin, the *Shelton* (DD-790) suffered fifteen casualties from three hits. The *Rowan* (DD-782) took a hit at Wonsan. The *Henderson* (DD-785) was hit at Hungnam on the twenty-third.

Action during March 1952 resulted in the battleship *Wisconsin* (BB-64) taking three casualties from a hit at Songjin on the sixteenth, followed by the *Brinkley Bass* (DD-887) suffering three casualties and moderate damage from a hit at Wonsan on the twenty-fourth.

Six times during April Communist guns found the range on U.S. warships: the *Endicott* got hit on April 7 at Chongjin and again at Songjin on April 19. The *Osprey* (AMS-28) was hit at Songjin on April 24. The *Cabaldo* (LSD-16) suffered two casualties at Wonsan on April 26. And on the last day of April two ships were hit in the same action at Wonsan—the USS *Maddox* (DD-731) and USS *Laffey* (DD-724).

Also in April, a major tragedy occurred when an explosion in the forward eight-inch turret of the heavy cruiser *Saint Paul* (CA-73) took thirty lives.

After the Communists broke off armistice talks on April 28, a stalemate existed. But the stalemate brought no rest. The Communists infiltrated the POW compounds. Once inside, they fomented uprisings and riots. The most spectacular riot occurred at Koje on May 12. The Communists seized the camp commander, Brig. Gen. Francis T. Dodd. To save his own life, Dodd signed a "confession" of UN atrocities. The Communists exploited Dodd's confession to generate worldwide publicity questioning the UN's role in Korea.

All through the summer of 1952, the talks at Panmunjom remained stalemated.

At sea, the dreary war went on, day after day, watch after watch. Naval aircraft ranged over North Korea; gunnery ships continued their interdiction of coastal targets; and the minesweepers were kept busy clearing fresh mines. By the end of May 1952, navy and marine pilots had dropped as much tonnage on Korea as was their total for the entire war against Japan.[2]

The USS *Leonard Mason* (DD-852) was damaged by shore battery fire at Wonsan on May 2. Steaming in to Songjin on May 7, the *James C. Owens* (DD-776) took six hits and ten casualties. The *Herbert J. Thomas* (DDR-833) took a hit at Wonsan on May 12. While providing gunfire support at Hungnam on May 14, the *D. H. Fox* (DD-778) suffered two casualties from shore batteries. For a second time, the LSD *Cabaldo* was hit at Wonsan on May 23. Minesweepers *Muralet* (AM-372) and *Swallow* (AMS-36) received hits on May 25 while sweeping Songjin Harbor, and on 30 May the minesweeper *Firecrest* (AMS-10) was strafed by machine-gun fire when she ventured too close to the beach at Songjin.

The siege at Wonsan was now well into its second year. Initially begun as a way of taking some pressure off the Eighth Army, that need had long since passed and the siege was now institutionalized. Two or three destroyers were maintained continually on station, generally for two weeks at a stretch.

The routine had become familiar. Every afternoon they could expect some enemy action. Gunnery officers spent long hours in the main battery director watching for muzzle flashes on the beach and tell-tale shell splashes in the water.

One of the favored techniques was to "head for the splash." When enemy spotters saw their shot had landed too short or long, left or right, they cranked in a correction. Since it was unlikely that the next shell would come down in the same place, the skipper headed for the last splash.

There was a certain wry humor about the whole enterprise. For example, the officer in tactical command—generally the senior destroyer skipper—enjoyed the honorific title of Mayor of Wonsan.

Daylight patrol of ships was somewhat restricted during June and July. Only one ship was hit during the month of June; that was the

USS *Buck* (DD-761). She suffered two casualties and the loss of her motor launch on June 13 from a direct hit at Kojo.

In a vain hope to drive the Communists back to the bargaining table, Gen. Mark Clark, Ridgway's successor, authorized massive bombing attacks on North Korea.[3] On June 23 a joint effort by navy, marine, and air force pilots pummeled eleven North Korean hydroelectric plants and related facilities south of the Yalu River, destroying some 90 percent of North Korean power generation and causing a two-week electrical blackout over all of enemy country. The attacks flattened what was left of the North Korean capital of Pyongyang and destroyed an oil refinery only eight miles from the Soviet border.

The attack precipitated a major public relations gaffe. We had not notified our UN allies of the contemplated attacks. This ignited widespread protests in cities around the world, including Paris and London.

The destroyer *Orleck* (DD-866) was on patrol at Songjin on July 19 when she found herself on the receiving end of approximately fifty rounds of enemy 75-mm. She dodged all but one and suffered four men wounded.

August 1952 turned out to be a bad month for the siege vessels. It began with the USS *John A. Pierce* (DD-753) off Tanchon on August 6 when she took seven direct hits that caused the loss of ten men. The *Barton* (DD-722) lost two men at Wonsan on the tenth as a result of shore battery fire. Two days later, the USS *Grapple* (ARS-7) suffered major damage and flooding at Wonsan from a hit below the waterline—fortunately, no casualties. On the twentieth, the *Thompson* (DMS-38) was patrolling off Songjin when an air burst over her bridge caused thirteen casualties from shrapnel. Two ships came within range of shore batteries at Wonsan on August 27—the destroyer *McDermut* (DD-677) and minesweeper *Competent* (AM-316); neither suffered extensive damage.

Also on August 27, a ship was lost to mines for the first time since February 1951. The fleet tug USS *Sarsi* (ATF-111) hit a mine and sank in the waters off Hungnam. Following this loss, a decision was made to discontinue bombardment of this marginal port.

Critics were beginning to question the wisdom of continuing the siege at Wonsan. A sizable force and expenditure of ammunition were required to maintain the siege, defend the harbor islands, and prevent remining of the harbor. On the other hand, reliable intelligence indicated that the enemy had committed eighty thousand troops and the extensive installation of shore batteries and antiaircraft weaponry to its defense, which justified the argument that the siege continued to hold down large enemy forces.[4] Besides, to abandon the siege now would be an apparent admission of defeat.

On September 1, the navy launched its biggest air strike yet. All morning and afternoon, deck loads from the *Essex, Princeton,* and *Boxer* delivered tons of ordnance to North Korea's remaining industrial facilities along the Manchurian and Soviet borders. Planes worked over oil storage and an iron mine at Musan and targets at Hoeamdong, synthetic oil production facilities at Aoji, bridges across the Yalu at Hyesanjin, and a munitions factory near Najin.

That same day saw the destroyer *Agerholm* (DD-826) take a direct hit while patrolling the bombline at Kansong, resulting in one casualty. Shore batteries opened fire on the *Frank E. Evans* (DD-734) at Tanchon on September 8; sixty-nine splashes were counted as she adopted evasive maneuvers and returned fire. Near misses caused only superficial damage and no casualties.

History was made on September 10 when a marine Corsair flyer became the first pilot of a propeller-driven aircraft to shoot down a MiG-15 jet.

At sea, floating mines continued to preoccupy destroyer commanders. Their apprehension was warranted. During the month of August, for example, the Seventh Fleet sighted and sank more than forty of these drifters.[5] On September 16, the destroyer *Barton* (DD-722), while steaming screen in Task Force 77 some ninety miles east of Wonsan, hit a mine that blew a five-foot hole in her side, killing five and wounding seven.

The *Alfred A. Cunningham* (DD-752) came under intense fire while patrolling off Songjin on September 19. Three 105-mm batteries opened up on her at the relatively close range of thirty-five hundred yards. The first round was a direct hit. Zigzagging out of there at twenty-five knots, she became the target of 130 rounds, of which 4 were direct hits and 7 were air bursts. Miraculously, she got off with only eight casualties.

Washington unveiled a new "peace package" to the Communists on September 28, 1952. It tried to make the voluntary repatriation more palatable by increasing the number of guaranteed returnees to 83,000 rather than the original estimate of 70,000. The Communists weren't buying. They rejected the package on October 8. It would be six months before there was another meeting.

Immediately thereafter, the Communists stepped up their ground operations along the truce line in the Iron Triangle, and the UN launched a limited counterattack. Bitter and costly fighting for a few inconsequential hills finally petered out; neither side had the force or the will to overcome the other. The two sides resumed their limited patrols and massive artillery duels, and dug in for the long, cold winter ahead.

The *Perkins* (DDR-887) had eighteen casualties on October 13 when she was straddled with two near misses at Kojo that sprayed the decks with shrapnel. The *Osprey* (AMS-28) had four casualties the following day when she ventured within range of the same guns. Eight casualties resulted when the USS *Lewis* (DE-535) was targeted by four to six guns at Wonsan on October 21. A week later, the *Mansfield* (DD-728) was straddled by forty rounds from four guns at a range of six thousand to eight thousand yards at Wonsan, thought to be radar controlled; despite several frightening near misses, she experienced only minor shrapnel damage.

Initially relatively few heavy-duty guns defended the harbor at Wonsan, but as the war wore on the shore defense system around Wonsan strengthened steadily. The harbor's main defense guns were cleverly camouflaged 122-mm and 155-mm artillery pieces hidden inside caves or tunnels. The guns were wheeled out for firing, then rolled back inside for protection before they could be destroyed by American counterbattery fire. These shore batteries were positioned so as to cover the ship operating area in the swept channel. Spotting the exact caves in which the guns were located was difficult. Hitting them was even more difficult.

On November 3 the destroyer *Uhlmann* (DD-687) was taken under fire by shore batteries; of the 160 rounds lobbed at her, 3 were direct hits causing thirteen casualties. The minesweeper *Kite* (AMS-22) had five casualties on November 19. The next day, the *Thompson* (DMS-38) was hit by enemy fire for the third time in eighteen months. *Hanna* (DE-449) had one casualty on November 24 from a direct hit while patrolling at Songjin.

Nineteen-fifty-two was a presidential election year. Republican candidate Dwight Eisenhower vowed to voters that he would go to Korea in a personal effort to end the war. He fulfilled that promise on December 2 when he arrived for a three-day visit.

Much to the chagrin of Generals Clark and Van Fleet, Eisenhower showed little inclination to win the war militarily. Until now, it had been known as "Truman's War." But Eisenhower foresaw that the longer the fighting continued into his own presidency, the more likely that he would be saddled with the onus of the war's unpopularity. Accordingly, he sought to end it quickly by diplomatic means.

Immediately after taking office in early 1953, Eisenhower turned to power diplomacy. First, he rescinded Truman's order that had neutralized Formosa, thereby raising the possibility Chinese Nationalists might invade the mainland. Second, he dropped strong hints that if the deadlock were not broken, he might not confine the war to Korea. Shades of MacArthur! He even hinted he might employ nuclear weapons as well. Thereafter, the prospects for an armistice seemed markedly to improve.

No U.S. warships were damaged by enemy shellfire in the months of December and January. February 1953 was also a light month with only the destroyer *Halsey Powell* (DD-686) receiving a hit at Hwa-do, which destroyed her motor whaleboat and caused two casualties.

March 16, 1953, marked the second anniversary of the start of the Wonsan siege. Minesweeper *Gull* (AMS-16) suffered two casualties resulting from a direct hit in that harbor. The following day, the destroyer *Taussig* (DD-746) was on the receiving end of forty-five rounds, suffering one hit and one casualty. The cruiser *Los Angeles* (CA-135) was hit at Wonsan on March 28, with only minor damage.

Abruptly, on March 28, the Communists came back to the bargaining table, seemingly in a more conciliatory mood. They expressed agreement with an earlier UN proposal for an exchange of sick and wounded POWs, and would allow a neutral state to supervise the exchange and interview POWs who refused repatriation.

The *Los Angeles* (CA-135) came within range of the heavy guns at Wonsan on April 2. This exchange cost her thirteen casualties. Wonsan guns also got the *Maddox* (DD-731) nearly a year to the day from her earlier set-to, causing three casualties. Three days later the *James E. Kyes* (DD-787) had nine casualties from a 155-mm hit.

Six times in the month of May, Wonsan batteries succeeded in hitting American ships: the *Maddox* (DD-731) on May 2, the *Owen* (DD-536) on May 2, the *Bremerton* (CA-130) on May 5, the *Samuel N. Moore* (DD-747) on May 8, the *Brush* (DD-745) on May 15, and the *Swift* (AM-122) on May 29. These actions resulted in eleven casualties.

The Communist negotiators seemed to be pursuing a delaying strategy in hopes of outlasting the American resolve. Time was on their side. They knew the war was extremely unpopular in the United States: it was costing American lives at an alarming rate, and people were clamoring to end the fighting at almost any price. The longer the Communists held out, the more concessions they might gain.

General Clark decided that heavy military pressure was needed to force the Communists into an armistice. Accordingly, he conceived the idea of destroying the North Korean rice crop in order to starve them into submission. Day after day, from May 13 to May 27, massive air strikes blasted away with great success at the intricate web of earthen irrigation dams, thereby destroying the interlocking rice paddies with flooding.

Although the overall effects of this bombing on the rice crop was debatable, it was nonetheless a fact that on June 4 the Communist delegates agreed to the mechanics of the main POW exchange. This cleared the last stumbling block for a final armistice agreement.

The saga of the USS *John A. Bole* (DD-755) typified the siege at this stage of the war. She entered Wonsan Harbor on June 11 for a two-week stint on the firing line, relieving the USS *Wiltsie* (DD-716), which suffered minor damage from a single hit and several air bursts from enemy shore batteries.

By this time, all skippers knew they had to keep moving. They couldn't just sit at anchor and lob shots at the enemy. That was a prescription for disaster. Moreover, they had a comparatively small area to navigate in because of the minefields. Accordingly, Comdr. H. G. Leahy, the *Bole*'s skipper, kept his ship in motion the whole time he was there so the enemy's computers couldn't get a good course-and-speed track on her. He steamed a circular pattern with left standard rudder, making such course adjustments as dictated by wind and currents so as to keep the vessel within the operating area.

On June 15 the *Bole* found herself on the receiving end of more than one hundred rounds of large caliber fire, but none of these was a direct hit.

Because the steady steaming consumed large quantities of fuel, the *Bole* had to go out to sea on June 17 to refuel. She was relieved temporarily by USS *Henderson* (DD-785). During the *Bole*'s absence, the *Henderson* took a hit.

The eighteenth was a bad day for siege ships. The USS *Irwin* (DD-794) took a main deck hit that caused five casualties. Harder hit was the USS *Rowan* (DD-782) with five hits, one punching a two-foot hole in her starboard side near the waterline. Nine people were injured, two seriously.

The *Bole* was relieved on June 25 by the USS *Gurke* (DD-783). The *Bole* had not yet cleared the harbor when her replacement came under enemy fire. *Gurke* took three hits, shrapnel from five near misses, and suffered three casualties.

Commander Leahy was glad to put Wonsan behind him. His ship had been the target of enemy shore batteries four times during their fourteen days on the bombline. The ships that preceded *Bole,* relieved her, and succeeded her had all been damaged by enemy shellfire. As .he exited the harbor, Leahy commented, "I felt like turning my radio off because I didn't want to hear someone say, 'Go back there.'"

The USS *John W. Thomason* (DD-760) drew fire on July 7 from more than 150 rounds, receiving shrapnel damage from several near misses but no casualties. The same day, the *Lofberg* (DD-759) and *Hamner* (DD-718) received 300 rounds, but no hits. The *Irwin* (DD-794) got hit again on July 8, in which action five men were wounded.

The last ship to be hit by Communist shore fire was the cruiser *Saint Paul* (CA-73). On July 11 she received severe underwater damage from a single 90-mm shell.

Peace seemed at hand. On July 27 the delegates met at Panmunjom to sign the armistice agreement. As set forth in its terms, firing was to cease all along the front at ten o'clock that night.

The destroyers *Wiltsie* and *Porter* and the cruiser *Bremerton* fired salvos at Wonsan targets until one minute before the 10:00 P.M. deadline.

The cost of the last two years while "peace negotiations" were going on was ghastly—63,200 American casualties, 12,300 killed on the field of battle. The Communists returned a total of 3,597 American prisoners of war. The mortality rate of those Americans taken captive in Korea was especially high—approximately 40 percent did not survive their harsh treatment.

# Notes

### Chapter 3. Enforcing a Blockade

1. James A. Field, Jr., *History of United States Naval Operations Korea* (Washington, D.C.: U.S. Navy, 1962), 138.

2. Bruce Jacobs, *Korea's Heroes* (New York: Berkley Publishing, 1953), 21–35.

### Chapter 6. In to Inchon

1. Malcolm W. Cagle and Frank A. Manson, *The Sea War in Korea* (Annapolis, Md.: Naval Institute Press, 1957), 298.

### Chapter 7. Mangled by Mines

1. Joseph C. Goulden, *Korea: The Untold Story of the War* (New York: Times Books, 1982), 228.

2. The description of a burial at sea was adapted from E. J. Jernigan, *Tin Can Man* (Arlington, Va.: Vandamere Press, 1993), 141.

### Chapter 9. North to the Border

1. The one-star flag rank of commodore was abolished in 1948 and replaced by a new, lower grade of admiral, designated Rear Admiral (lower half).

2. Captain Lang did not step aboard the *Borland* again until July 1951 at Commander Buaas's change-of-command ceremony, on which occasion Buaas had the satisfaction of reading special commendations for men who had performed so well in Korea—commendations that Lang had tried to block.

3. Edwin P. Hoyt, *The Bloody Road to Panmunjom* (New York: Military Heritage Press, 1985), 54.

### Chapter 10. Covering a Retreat

1. Hoyt, *Bloody Road to Panmunjom*, 78.

2. President Truman presented the Medal of Honor to LTJG Thomas Hudner on April 13, 1952. Jesse Brown's widow attended the ceremony. The ac-

count of Brown's crash and the attempted rescue was taken from Edward F. Murphy, *Korean War Heroes* (Novato, Calif.: Presidio Press, 1992), 122–24.

3. Sgt. James Cotton returned to Dog Company in Korea on February 1, 1951, at which time there was not a single man left with whom he had previously served. He was wounded again on June 6, 1951, at Hwachon Reservoir, following which he returned home.

### Chapter 11. Evacuating Hungnam

1. Field, *History,* 284.

### Chapter 12. Escorting the Escorts

1. Hoyt, *Bloody Road to Panmunjom,* 150.

2. The *Gearing*-class destroyers were merely enlarged editions of the *Allen B. Sumner* type, with an additional fourteen-foot length spliced in amidships.

3. Goulden, *Korea,* 431.

4. Ibid., 434.

5. Under similar night air operations in April 1952, the DMS *Hobson* got in front of the carrier *Wasp* and was run down and sunk with a loss of 176 lives.

6. During normal steaming, the firerooms were cross-connected so that one fireroom could service both enginerooms, port and starboard screws. But during battle stations or any hazardous situation, the firerooms were split for independent operations.

7. Field, *History,* 312–14.

### Chapter 13. Feigning an Invasion

1. Seoul was not reoccupied until a month later, March 15, 1951.

### Chapter 14. Setting the Siege at Wonsan

1. Ralph M. Tvede, *Fireball,* Newsletter of USS *Ozbourn* DD-846, vol 2, no. 3, July 1993. By a remarkable coincidence, although ENS Tvede and LTJG Moriarty had never met before, Tvede's mother, Helen Tvede, worked within a few feet of Moriarty's mother-in-law, Ann Doherty, at the Board of Public Works in San Francisco.

### Chapter 15. Tangling with Typhoons

1. My imagery of the typhoon's fury draws heavily on C. Raymond Calhoun, *Typhoon: The Other Enemy* (Annapolis, Md.: Naval Institute Press, 1981).

2. *Action Report,* Serial 006, USS *Wallace A. Linn* (DD-703), March 15, 1951.

3. Many people felt the "Battle of Carlson's Canyon" was later fictionalized in James Michener's powerful novel *The Bridges at Toko-ri* (New York: Random House, 1953).

### Chapter 16. Patrolling the Strait

1. Clay Blair, *The Forgotten War* (New York: Time Books, 1987), 755.

2. The Wonsan bombardment would go on for another two years until June 1953, thereby establishing a record that may never be broken.

### Chapter 17. Acting as Decoy

1. The account of MacArthur and the Joint Chiefs of Staff was based on Goulden, *Korea.*

### Chapter 18. Baby-sitting the Big Boys

1. Blair, *The Forgotten War,* 815.

2. ComDesFlot One (Commander Destroyer Flotilla One) was the admiral in command of all destroyers in far eastern waters.

### Chapter 19. Screening against Submarines

1. *Action Report,* Serial 387, USS *Walke* (DD-723), June 19, 1951, second endorsement from Commander Seventh Fleet. (Author's note: In an unusual move, this action report was classified as top secret and not released until the time of this writing.)

2. *Action Report,* Serial 0001, USS *Thompson* (DMS-38), June 17, 1951.

3. Ibid.

### Epilogue: Two More Years

1. Truce talks began at Kaesong, ancient capital of Korea. On October 8, 1951, they moved to a deserted mud hut village called Panmunjom and continued there throughout the next two years.

2. Field, *History,* 428.

3. On May 12, 1952, Gen. Mark Clark replaced General Ridgway in Tokyo, who, in turn, relieved General Eisenhower as Supreme Commander of NATO—a prestigious and sought-after post. Eisenhower entered the race for president of the United States.

4. Captured records revealed that the North Koreans were concerned with defending against a four-divisional assault at Wonsan, accompanied by subsidiary landings at Kojo and Hungnam, and by a northward thrust of Eighth Army through the Iron Triangle and the eastern mountains. (Field, *History,* 434.)

5. The supposition that floaters were no accident was borne out by the signing of the armistice in July 1953. In contrast to frequent sightings of loose mines while fighting was in progress, only one was sighted in the five months following the armistice. (Field, *History,* 444.)

# Glossary

**ASROC**  Antisubmarine Rocket.

**ASW**  Antisubmarine Warfare.

**Binnacle**  The stand or support for the ship's magnetic compass.

**Binnacle list**  A list of personnel excused from duty because of illness or injury, traditionally placed in the binnacle by the officer of the watch. Though the custom has vanished, the name remains.

**Bulkhead**  Walls or partitions within a ship.

**CIC**  Combat Information Center.

**CincFE**  Commander in Chief Far East (Gen. Douglas MacArthur until April 12, 1951, then Gen. Matthew Ridgway).

**ComDesRon**  Commander Destroyer Squadron.

**ComNavFE**  Commander Naval Forces Far East.

**Companionway**  Stairs, set of steps leading from one deck to another. Also called a "ladder."

**Conn**  Control of the ship's movements. The officer in control has the conn.

**Counterbattery fire**  Fire directed against active enemy weapons.

**CruDiv**  Cruiser Division.

**CTE**  Commander Task Element.

**CTG**  Commander Task Group.

**DesDiv**  Destroyer Division, normally consists of four destroyers.

**DesRon**  Destroyer Squadron, normally consists of two destroyer divisions.

*Do*  Korean word meaning "island."

**Galley**  Kitchen.

**GQ**  General quarters, all hands at their battle stations.

**Head**  Toilet and washroom.

**Hedgehog**   An antisubmarine, mortar-type projectile, contact-fused.

**Interdiction**   Destruction of roads, bridges, railroads, tunnels, supply routes, etc., to prevent the support of enemy front lines.

**JOC**   Joint Operations Control.

**LCT**   Landing craft, tank.

**Loran**   *Lo*ng *Ra*nge *N*avigation; a system of electronic navigation.

**LSD**   Landing ship, dock.

**LSM**   Landing ship, medium.

**LSMR**   Landing ship, medium, rocket.

**LST**   Landing ship, tank.

**LSU**   Landing ship, utility.

**Master-at-arms**   Ship's police. The term originated in olden days when the master-at-arms had control of the ship's hand weapons and trained the crew in their use.

**Oil king**   Petty officer aboard ship who keeps fuel oil records.

**Overhead**   Same as civilian word "ceiling."

**Picket**   Ship or aircraft stationed away from a formation or in a geographic location for a specific purpose, such as air-warning.

**Radar**   *Ra*dio *d*irection *a*nd *r*anging; an instrument for determining the presence of objects by radio echoes.

**SAR**   Search and rescue.

**Scullery**   Compartment in a ship where dishwashing is done.

**Scuttlebutt**   Gossip, rumor.

**SFCP**   Shore fire control party; a unit sent ashore to provide "spotting" or control of naval gunfire against shore targets.

**Shack**   Nickname for any compartment designated for a particular work or activity, for example, radio shack.

**Shore Patrol**   Naval personnel ashore on police duty.

**Shot line**   Light nylon line used in line-throwing gun.

**Skivvies**   Underwear.

**Sonar**   *So*und *n*avigation *a*nd *r*anging.

**SOPA**   Senior officer present afloat.

**Sortie**   To depart, the act of departing.

**TE**   Task Element, a subunit of a Task Group.

**TF**   Task Force.

**TG**   Task Group, a subunit of a Task Force.

**UDT**   Underwater demolition team; specially trained men who do reconnaissance and demolition work along beaches prior to an amphibious assault.

# Index

## About the Author

James Edwin Alexander, Ph.D., is former dean of the Meinders School of Business at Oklahoma City University and an investment adviser. He received his education from the University of the Pacific, Boston University, Claremont Graduate School, and Vanderbilt University, earning Ph.D.'s at the latter two institutions. He is listed in *Who's Who in the World* and *Who's Who in Finance and Industry,* and is the author of thirteen previous books. During the Korean War he served aboard the USS *John A. Bole* (DD-755) and USS *Hanson* (DDR-832). He retired from the U.S. Naval Reserve with the permanent rank of chief warrant officer.

**The Naval Institute Press** is the book-publishing arm of the U.S. Naval Institute, a private, nonprofit society for sea service professionals and others who share an interest in naval and maritime affairs. Established in 1873 at the U.S. Naval Academy in Annapolis, Maryland, where its offices remain today, the Naval Institute has almost 85,000 members worldwide.

Members of the Naval Institute receive the influential monthly magazine *Proceedings* and discounts on fine nautical prints and on ship and aircraft photos. They also have access to the transcripts of the Institute's Oral History Program and get discounted admission to any of the Institute-sponsored seminars offered around the country.

The Naval Institute also publishes *Naval History* magazine. This colorful bimonthly is filled with entertaining and thought-provoking articles, first-person reminiscences, and dramatic art and photography. Members receive a discount on *Naval History* subscriptions.

The Naval Institute's book-publishing program, begun in 1898 with basic guides to naval practices, has broadened its scope in recent years to include books of more general interest. Now the Naval Institute Press publishes about 100 titles each year, ranging from how-to books on boating and navigation to battle histories, biographies, ship and aircraft guides, and novels. Institute members receive discounts of 20 to 50 percent on the Press's nearly 600 books in print.

Full-time students are eligible for special half-price membership rates. Life memberships are also available.

For a free catalog describing Naval Institute Press books currently available, and for further information about subscribing to *Naval History* magazine or about joining the U.S. Naval Institute, please write to:

Membership Department
U.S. Naval Institute
118 Maryland Avenue
Annapolis, Maryland 21402-5035

Telephone: (800) 233-8764
Fax: (410) 269-7940